Securitizing Islam

WITHDRAWN

Securitizing Islam examines the impact of 9/11 on the lives and perceptions of individuals, focusing on the ways in which identities in Britain have been affected in relation to Islam. 'Securitization' describes the processes by which a particular group or issue comes to be seen as a threat, and thus subject to the perceptions and actions which go with national security. Croft applies this idea to the way in which the attitudes of individuals to their security and to Islam and Muslims have been transformed, affecting the everyday lives of both Muslims and non-Muslims. He argues that Muslims have come to be seen as the 'Other', outside the contemporary conception of Britishness. Reworking securitization theory and drawing in the sociology of ontological security studies, *Securitizing Islam* produces a theoretically innovative framework for understanding a contemporary phenomenon that affects the everyday lives of millions.

STUART CROFT is Professor of International Security at the University of Warwick. His work is in the field of security studies and his latest book is *Culture, Crisis and America's War on Terror* (2006).

Securitizing Islam

Identity and the Search for Security

STUART CROFT

CAMBRIDGE
UNIVERSITY PRESS

CAMBRIDGE UNIVERSITY PRESS
Cambridge, New York, Melbourne, Madrid, Cape Town,
Singapore, São Paulo, Delhi, Tokyo, Mexico City

Cambridge University Press
The Edinburgh Building, Cambridge CB2 8RU, UK

Published in the United States of America by Cambridge University Press,
New York

www.cambridge.org
Information on this title: www.cambridge.org/9781107632868

First published 2012

Printed in the United Kingdom at the University Press, Cambridge

A catalogue record for this publication is available from the British Library

Library of Congress Cataloguing in Publication data
Croft, Stuart.
    Securitizing Islam : identity and the search for security / Stuart Croft.
        pages cm
    Includes bibliographical references and index.
    ISBN 978-1-107-02046-7 (hardback) – ISBN 978-1-107-63286-8 (paperback)
    1. Terrorism–Prevention–Government policy–Great Britain.   2. Terrorism–
    Social aspects–Great Britain.   3. Terrorism–Religious aspects–Islam.
    4. Islam–Great Britain.   5. Muslims–Great Britain.   6. Islamic
    fundamentalism–Great Britain.   7. Internal security–Great Britain.
    8. National security–Social aspects–Great Britain.
    9. Great Britain–Public opinion.   10. September 11 Terrorist Attacks,
    2001–Influence.   I. Title.
    HV6433.G7C76 2012
    363.325′160941–dc23
    2011044363

ISBN 978-1-107-02046-7 Hardback
ISBN 978-1-107-63286-8 Paperback

Contents

Figures

Tables

Acknowledgements

I have benefited from many colleagues' comments and from their willingness to commit time and energy to helping me hone my ideas more precisely. Thanks in particular to Paul Williams at George Washington University, Jonathan Githens-Mazer and Tony King at Exeter, Theo Farrell at Kings, Friedrich Kratochwil at the EUI, Matt McDonald at the University of Queensland, and to Chris Browning, George Christou, Rita Floyd and Oz Hassan in Warwick. A number of others have also made really helpful contributions to elements of the work in progress, through discussion and through sharing their own work, and I would like to thank Tahir Abbas, Trine Flockhart, Richard Jackson, Catarina Kinnvall, Keith Mander, Rens van Munster, Nick Vaughan-Williams and Mike Williams. I am also grateful to detailed and thoughtful comments by two referees on the manuscript. This book was written while I had the privilege of an ESRC Director's Award; and many of the ideas and inspirations came from working with colleagues on the *New Security Challenges* Programme, funded by the ESRC, and latterly also the AHRC and Foreign and Commonwealth Office, of which I was Director for eight years. Particularly important influences here were Conor Gearty, Marie Gillespie, James Gow, Paddy Hillyard, Andrew Hoskins and Ben O'Loughlin. I would like to thank those who were supportive on various field trips, at the British Library and across Scotland and Northern Ireland. I also benefited from feedback on presentations of elements of this analysis at the universities of Birmingham, East Anglia, Edinburgh, Exeter and Warwick, and also at presentations at the British International Studies Association, and at the International Studies Association. But above all, thanks to Jane and Sam for tolerating my absence and absent-mindedness while working on this project.

Introduction

In February 2011, British Prime Minister David Cameron gave a high-profile speech to the Munich International Security Conference. Despite war in Afghanistan and unrest in the Middle East, he said that 'the biggest threat that we face comes from terrorist attacks, some of which are, sadly, carried out by our own citizens ... we should acknowledge that this threat comes in Europe overwhelmingly from young men who follow a completely perverse, warped interpretation of Islam.'[1] For Cameron, 'We need to be clear: Islamist extremism and Islam are not the same thing.'[2] However, British Muslim 'young men also find it hard to identify with Britain too, because we have allowed the weakening of our collective identity.'[3] Terrorism from 'Islamist extremism' was the fundamental challenge: 'At stake are not just lives, it is our way of life.'[4] And the solution was 'a clear sense of shared national identity that is open to everyone'.[5] The problem stemmed from (warped) Islam; the solution was to be more Britishness. It is that calculation, and that relationship, that this book seeks to interrogate.

In the period since the attacks of 11 September 2001 in the United States, conflict with violent radicalized Muslims has for many in the United Kingdom apparently impacted on their lives only tangentially. Of course, this is not true for the people who died in the London bombings, or for British citizens killed in and affected by attacks abroad, such as those in Bali or Istanbul; nor for soldiers and their relations who have fought in Iraq and Afghanistan. But for the vast majority, Britain may have been involved in conflict, but Britons have not been at war. Most citizens have seemingly been spectators: watching events in the media, occasionally affected in passing, such as by

---

[1] PM's speech, at Munich Security Conference, 5 February 2011, at www.number10.gov.uk [accessed February 2011].
[2] *Ibid.*   [3] *Ibid.*   [4] *Ibid.*   [5] *Ibid.*

1

additional airport security. However, this apparent spectator status is actually not so; the securitization of particular identities impacts upon the lives of all who are involved in these securitization processes – those whose identity is part of the securitizing agents, as well as those who are securitized. Securitization, 'in which egotistical collective political actors (often but not always states) mainly construct their securitizations against (or in the case of security communities with) each other' is thus often seen as a matter of high politics but, as I will argue, it is also a process that deeply affects social interaction, and everyday life.[6]

This book is concerned with just such processes – the ways in which 'Britishness' has come to be constructed in contradistinction to a new Islamist terrorist Other; and how, in the process, everyday lives are reconstructed.

Everyday lives have been deeply and profoundly affected by this conflict. It has produced a sense of 'new times', or 'new realities', which affects our expectations and our behaviours, our sense of identity. In order to gain insight into these processes, I develop the concept of ontological security: to understand the ontological security – the security of the self – not at the level of the state, as in contemporary international relations writing, but rather at the level of individuals. Ontological security is that sense of order and continuity in the life of an individual that is produced intersubjectively. In Britain, as in other countries, nationality provides one resource for the ontological security of individuals. And that sense of nationality, that Britishness, has been redefined in direct relation with the terrorist other.

As a direct result of the 'new times', everyday lives have been transformed profoundly, and in some cases tragically. Three examples will illustrate the range of those transformations: the highly contrasting cases of Yasir Abdelmouttalib, Robert Cottage, and Paul Chambers. For each, their experiences and their treatment by wider society has been framed by the new securitization.

In 2004, while on his way to Friday prayer at London Central Mosque, and dressed distinctively, Yasir Abdelmouttalib was identified from a bus as a Muslim and subsequently attacked by a group

---

[6] Barry Buzan and Ole Waever, 'Macrosecuritisation and Security Constellations: Reconsidering Scale in Securitisation Theory', *Review of International Studies* 35:2, 2009: 254.

of youths.[7] He was abused, spat upon, and then beaten so hard that he was in a coma for three months, and although he survived, he was disabled permanently by the attacks. The one assailant convicted for the assault was thirteen years old at the time of the attack. The Judge, Nicholas Madge, told him, 'Witnesses described it as a ferocious attack. One referred to the anger in your eyes, another said you were using powerful and really hard swings.'[8] Such hatred of a man that the boy had never met, but who was the symbol of that which he despised with such violent passion. Abdelmouttalib was clear in his own mind as to why he was attacked: 'All the time television talks about Osama bin Laden and I think they thought, "Let's take revenge." They are not human beings. No human would attack someone like this.'[9] And yet the court case did not find that this was a religiously motivated attack; as the Judge told the convicted perpetrator, 'Had there been evidence of racial or religious aggravation the sentence would have been longer.'[10]

When he was lying in hospital, Yasir Abdelmouttalib's mother believed that he was treated as a terrorist suspect by the police: she said 'He was lying in a coma in hospital and we thought he might not live and the police were asking questions about which mosque did he go to.'[11] In contrast, Robert Cottage's crimes were not seen through the frame of terrorism. Cottage was convicted in 2007 for stockpiling chemical explosives.[12] He also had BB guns, a cross bow, gas masks, two 56-kilogram bags of sugar, a box of mini flares, half a ton of rice, 34 gas canisters, a selection of pellets and an air pistol, and printed bomb 'recipes' from *The Anarchist's Handbook*. He was 'radical' in his views, according to his wife – who had reported him to the police.

[7] For a detailed account see Jonathan Githens-Mazer and Robert Lambert, 'Islamophobia and Anti-Muslim Hate Crime: A London Case Study', European Muslim Research Centre, January 2010, at http://centres.exeter. ac.uk [accessed February 2010].
[8] Quoted in Nicole Martin, 'Five and a Half Years for Boy who Blinded Muslim', *Daily Telegraph*, 21 December 2004, at www.telegraph.co.uk [accessed February 2010].
[9] Hugh Muir, 'Boy, 14, Beat Muslim Student in Racist Attack', *The Guardian*, 30 November 2004, at www.guardian.co.uk/uk [accessed February 2010].
[10] Quoted in Martin, 'Five and a Half Years for Boy who Blinded Muslim'.
[11] Quoted in Githens-Mazer and Lambert, 'Islamophobia and Anti-Muslim Hate Crime', p. 34.
[12] See 'Ex-BNP man jailed over chemicals', *BBC News*, 31 July 2007, at www. news.bbc.co.uk [accessed December 2009].

The prosecutor in Court, Louise Blackwell, reported: 'He became more religious and controlling of her [his wife]. He removed the aerial from the television so she couldn't watch what he described as the brain-washing material being put out by the government.'[13] Cottage's case was: 'I believe it is everyone's God-given right to defend themselves and their families if they are attacked … The breakdown of the financial system will inevitably put an unbearable strain on the social structures of this country.'[14] His claim to a defensive strategy was accepted by the Judge, Mrs Justice Swift, who said: 'It is important to understand that Cottage's intention was that if he ever had to use the thunder flashes, it was only for the purpose of deterrence.'[15] Cottage's far-right sympathies were not seen in terms of terrorism; as the police officer at his arrest, Superintendent Neil Smith, explained: 'He's not a terrorist and it's not a bomb factory.'[16] When, also in 2006, police received intelligence about bombs in Forest Gate in a house occupied by Muslims, there was a raid of 250 police officers, many in protective clothing, and one of the occupants was shot.[17] The frame of reference defined the nature of the police responses in these two analogous circumstances.

The third case is very different. Paul Chambers was and is an avid 'tweeter'. Like many others around the world, he would fill his day with thoughts to be shared with others via the social networking site Twitter. In January 2010, he planned to fly to Northern Ireland, but those plans were jeopardized by bad weather affecting the airport in Doncaster. He 'tweeted' his 'followers' as follows: 'Crap! Robin Hood airport is closed. You've got a week and a bit to get your shit together,

---

[13] Louise Blackwell, quoted in 'BNP candidate was "stockpiling chemicals for civil war"', *The Citizen* (Burnley), 2 July 2007, at www.burnleycitizen.co.uk [accessed September 2009].

[14] Quoted in Duncan Campbell, 'Ex-BNP Candidate Jailed for Stockpiling Explosives', *The Guardian*, 31 July 2007, at www.guardian.co.uk [accessed September 2009].

[15] *Ibid.*

[16] Quoted in Charlotte Bradshaw, 'Ex-BNP Man Held in "Bomb" Swoop', *The Citizen*, 2 October 2006, at www.burnleycitizen.co.uk [accessed September 2009].

[17] See for example Nigel Morris, 'Police Forced to Apologise for Forest Gate Terror Raid', 9 June 2006, at www.independent.co.uk [accessed September 2009]; for analysis see Katherine E. Brown, 'Contesting the Securitisation of British Muslims: Citizenship and Resistance', *Interventions* 12:2, July 2010: 171–82.

otherwise I'm blowing the airport sky high!!'[18] Five days later, this message was identified by a manager at the airport, reported to airport security, and onwards to the police, who arrested Chambers, and after a seven-hour interrogation and the seizure of his computer, he was charged under the 2003 Communications Act, which makes it an offence to send 'indecent, obscene or menacing messages over a public electronic communications network'.[19] A Senior District Crown Prosecutor wrote to one of Chambers's supporters: 'The starting point under the public interest test is that it is always in the public interest to prosecute unless there are significant circumstances not to do so. In this case, given the times in which we live and the concern caused to the airport security staff, it was decided that no such circumstances exist.'[20] Chambers was found guilty, had to pay fines and fees of £1,000, and lost his job because he had a criminal record. After the trial District Judge Jonathan Bennett set out his judgement in *R v. Paul Chambers*, including the assessment that

I have to consider the final part of the 'tweet' – *'otherwise I'm blowing the airport sky high'*. The context is we live in a society where there are huge security concerns particularly in relation to airports and air travel. I do not need to repeat the very real incidents there have been in the UK in recent years let alone worldwide. With that background I can have no doubt that the remark posted by the defendant is menacing.[21]

That is, Chambers's comments had a different legal force because of the 'context'.

In such ways, everyday life is transformed by processes of securitization. The securitized Muslim identity was a reason for Abdelmouttalib's near fatal beating, for Cottage's actions to be seen as that of a non-terrorist and for Chambers to gain a criminal record. In this book,

[18] Chambers, quoted in Paul Brooke, 'Frustrated Air Passenger Arrested under Terrorism Act after Twitter Joke about Bombing Airport', *Daily Mail*, 19 January 2010, at www.dailymail.co.uk [accessed May 2010].
[19] Tim Bradshaw, 'Fine over Twitter Message on Blowing up Airport', *Financial Times*, 11 May 2010, at www.ft.com [accessed June 2010].
[20] Name withheld, Senior District Crown Prosecutor in a letter to M. Flaherty, dated 17 March 2010, reproduced at www.facebook.com [accessed May 2010].
[21] Jonathan Bennett's judgement of 10 May 2010 is at http://jackofkent.blogspot.com [accessed July 2010]; italics in the original.

I seek to identify the ways in which Britishness – like all identities, one in motion and constantly being reframed and regrounded – has been constructed in contradistinction to a newly securitized identity: that of the Radical Other, the 'jihadi' British Muslim. The trope of Otherness ascribed to (British) Muslims and the developing trope of Britishness that will be shown to exist in a variety of social spaces, from jokes to the way people express reactions to moments of drama, impacted not only on defence policy and policing, but throughout official practices.

The societal 'context' referred to by District Judge Jonathan Bennett in *R. v. Paul Chambers* is a product of securitization. And that process of securitization has had impact upon the way in which official practice operates. In July 2004 – a year before '7/7' – £8 million was invested in the launch of 'Preparing for Emergencies – What You Need to Know'. This 22-page leaflet was printed and sent to 25 million households, and was designed, through subsequent updates, to alert citizens to what they needed to do at home, at work and when travelling to minimize the risks of emergencies taking place, and to mitigate their effects should they take place. Inevitably, terrorism is seen to be one of those risks. And the danger to the transport system was particularly emphasized.[22]

Keep alert

Terrorist bomb attacks mostly happen in public places, especially where people gather or travel.
Remember to:
- be vigilant
- look out for suspicious behaviour, vehicles or packages
- do not hesitate to tell the police

Establishing new routines in everyday behaviour was a key part of the ongoing exercise. These should be seen as a part of everyday activity, and should not overwhelm other routines; they should simply be added as a normal part of 'our' routines, as below.[23]

---

[22] 'Helping to Prevent a Terrorist Attack', at www.direct.gov.uk [accessed October 2009].
[23] 'Current threat level', at www.homeoffice.gov.uk [accessed October 2009].

> **What should you do?**
>
> You should always remain alert to the danger of terrorism, look out for suspicious bags on public transport or any other potential signs of terrorist activity you may encounter.
>
> But you should not let the fear of terrorism stop you from going about your day-to-day life as normal. Your risk of being caught up in a terrorist attack is very low.

As part of the general work connected with preparing for emergencies, local authorities have been developing risk registers, focusing on *risk* rather than on *threats*. Yet of course, terrorism issues have to be considered – and 'new' forms of terrorism at that. Staffordshire, for example, explains:

This does not mean that we are not considering threats within our risk assessment work, but given the sensitivity of the information supporting these risk assessments and the potential for use by adversaries, specific details will not be made available via this web-site. Threat scenarios that are being considered include, for example, Chemical, Biological, Radiological attacks and Electronic attacks, e.g. affecting utilities and communications, attacks on crowded places and attacks on transport systems.[24]

Communicating the sense of threat has been particularly significant in London since the events of '7/7' the Metropolitan Police have run a variety of campaigns to alert members of the public 'with concerns about suspicious behaviour to report them to the confidential Anti-Terrorist Hotline'.[25] Police campaigns have focused on the everyday nature of the threat all around – the threat from within, as it were. This is not to say that the more fearful elements of the 'new terrorism' were ignored. The Home Office's Office for Security and Counter Terrorism has focused in particular on the dangers of terrorists developing chemical, biological, radiological, nuclear and explosives threats, one of the key markers of the concern with the 'new

[24] 'Staffordshire Community Risk Register', *Staffordshire Prepared*, at www.staffordshireprepared.gov.uk [accessed October 2009].
[25] The quote, and the following documents, are reproduced at *Metropolitan Police*, 'Latest News', February 2007, at http://cms.met.police.uk [accessed October 2009].

terrorism'. The website explains that 'Our aim is to become a centre
for excellence in countering CBRNE terrorism. This includes identifying and driving the improvements needed to counter the CBRNE
threat, from prevention to preparation for an attack, and investing in
scientific research to enable greater understanding of the threat and
ways to improve our response.'[26] In February 2007, the Metropolitan
Police launched new posters under the heading 'Terrorism If you suspect it Report it'. In the first, the everyday nature of the terrorist
threat was stressed; everyone, in their everyday working and home
life, needed to be alert. Worrying signs were everyday, with images
surrounded by text: the camera ('Have you seen anyone taking pictures of security arrangements?'); the white van ('If you work in
commercial vehicle hire or sales, has a sale or rental made you suspicious?' and 'Do you know someone who travels but is vague about
where they are going?'); the personal computer ('Do you know someone who visits terrorist-related websites?'); and the mobile phone
('Anonymous, pay-as-you-go and stolen mobiles are typical. Have
you seen someone with large quantities of mobiles? Has it made you
suspicious?').[27] A second poster followed the same theme. There was
a picture of a padlock ('Are you suspicious of anyone renting commercial property?'); an everyday bottle of chemicals, presumably for
cleaning ('Do you know someone buying large or unusual quantities
of chemicals for no obvious reason?'); facial protection ('Handling
chemicals is dangerous. Maybe you've seen goggles or masks dumped
somewhere?'); a passport ('Do you know someone with documents in
different names for no obvious reason?'); and a credit card ('Cheque
and credit card fraud are ways terrorists generate cash. Have you seen
any suspicious transactions?').[28] The threat was all around us, and
in our everyday lives, communicated powerfully with the imagery of
everyday items. In the latter poster, the passport was a British one,
reinscribing the local, British nature of those threatening 'our' security. To add to this, a postcard was produced, one side of which read
as follows:[29]

[26] 'Chemical, Biological, Radiological, Nuclear, and Explosives', *Office for Security and Counter Terrorism, Home Office*, at http://security.homeoffice.gov.uk [accessed October 2009].
[27] 'Van Poster 1', note 25.
[28] 'Lock Poster', *ibid.*   [29] 'Postcard', reverse, *ibid.*

COMMUNITIES CAN
DEFEAT TERRORISM.
YOU CAN HELP MAKE
LONDON A HOSTILE
PLACE FOR TERRORISTS.
TERRORISTS NEED RECRUITS.
Do you know someone whose behaviour has
changed suddenly?

TERRORISTS NEED PLACES TO LIVE.
Are you suspicious of your tenants or neighbours?

TERRORISTS NEED TRANSPORT.
Has a vehicle sale or rental made you suspicious?

TERRORISTS NEED STORAGE.
Are you suspicious of someone renting
commercial property?
Let the police decide if the information you have
is important.

The main message was also reproduced as a window sticker, to be widely distributed and shown. And, to further the campaign by the Metropolitan Police, a radio advert was produced, with the following statement:[30]

Female voice-over:

How d'you tell the difference between someone just video-ing a crowded place and someone who's checking it out for a terrorist attack?

How can you tell if someone's buying unusual quantities of stuff for a good reason or if they're planning to make a bomb?

What's the difference between someone just hanging around and someone behaving suspiciously?

How can you tell if they're a normal everyday person, or a terrorist?

[30] 'Radio Script', *ibid.*

Male voice-over:

The answer is, you don't have to.

   If you call the confidential Anti-Terrorist Hotline on 0800 789 321, the specialist officers you speak to will analyse the information. They'll decide if and how to follow it up.

   You don't have to be sure. If you suspect it, report it.

THOUSANDS OF PEOPLE TAKE PHOTOS EVERY DAY.

WHAT IF ONE OF THEM SEEMS ODD?

Terrorists use surveillance to help plan attacks, taking photos and making notes about security measures like the location of CCTV cameras. If you see someone doing that, we need to know. Let experienced officers decide what action to take.

Using classic advertising techniques – female voice to draw the listener in (trustworthy, caring, everyday), and the male voice to impose authority – the short radio advert was yet another way of making the threat to 'us' real, local and immediate.

   The 2008 anti-terrorism campaign was extended beyond the Metropolitan Police area, to include those other parts of the United Kingdom with direct experience of the new terrorist threat – West Yorkshire, Greater Manchester and the West Midlands. The imagery was simpler; perhaps the 2007 campaign had produced posters that were too cluttered and somewhat off-putting to the eye. So for 2008, instead of a range of everyday items and tools, each poster focused on just one. The first image was of a camera, with the instruction:[31]

THOUSANDS OF PEOPLE HAVE MOBILES.
WHAT IF SOMEONE WITH SEVERAL SEEMS SUSPICIOUS?

YOU SEE HUNDREDS OF HOUSES EVERY DAY.
WHAT IF ONE HAS UNUSAL ACTIVITY AND SEEMS SUSPICIOUS?

---

[31] 'Camera', at www.met.police.uk [accessed October 2009].

If cameras should be a focal point – even in cities with high proportions of tourists – the second poster showed a front door; making the
threat appear real from your street, maybe even from next door.[32]

And the third image was that of the mobile phone; the danger from
the person next to you on the bus or train, or from the workmate.[33]
As with the 2007 campaign, the Metropolitan Police also commis-
sioned a radio advert, following the same approach as before.[34]

The 2009 campaign brought the visual image of the threat home
with photographs of London streets. In 'Chemicals', a woman walks
down a residential street with a child in a pushchair, walking towards
a wheelie bin with (presumably empty) bottles of chemicals protrud-
ing from the top. The caption reports: 'These chemicals won't be used
in a bomb because a neighbour reported the dumped containers.'[35]
In 'CCTV', a high street scene – seven women, two small children,
a teenager and two elderly men – go about their business with the
caption 'A bomb won't go off here because weeks before a shopper
reported someone studying the CCTV cameras.'[36] Again, the message
was taken to the airwaves as well as the newspapers: 'In London, this
includes the *Evening Standard*, Magic, Heart, Total LBC, Smooth
and Capital FM.'[37]

As well as the lives of individuals being affected by the need to
change routines around the neighbourhood and when travelling and
shopping, change has also been sought in business behaviour. The
Centre for the Protection of National Infrastructure explains:[38]

> The bomb attacks in London in July 2005 were a graphic reminder
> that the threat from terrorism is real and serious. People need to
> be prepared to deal with the rare circumstances when terrorism
> touches their lives and businesses.

[32] 'Door', at www.met.police.uk [accessed October 2009].
[33] 'Phone', at www.met.police.uk [accessed October 2009].
[34] For the transcript, see www.met.police.uk [accessed October 2009].
[35] Poster 'Chemicals', at www.met.police.uk [accessed October 2009].
[36] Poster 'CCTV', at www.met.police.uk [accessed October 2009].
[37] 'New Campaign to Urge Londoners to Report Suspicious Activity',
Metropolitan Police, 4 January 2009, at www.met.police.uk [accessed
October 2009].
[38] 'Why Security Planning is Important', *Centre for the Protection of National
Infrastructure*, at www.cpni.gov.uk [accessed October 2009].

Terrorism is not just about physical attack. It might take the form of attacks on vital information or communication systems, causing disruption and economic damage. Some attacks are easier to carry out if the terrorist is assisted either directly or indirectly by an 'insider' or by someone with specialist knowledge or access. Terrorism may include threats or hoaxes designed to frighten and intimidate.

Incidents might include having to deal with a bomb threat or with suspect items sent through the post or left on the premises. In the worst case, your staff could be directly affected by a terrorist bombing.

Businesses have been exhorted to develop a security plan, with elements focusing on how to deal with bomb threats, how to search premises, and how to evacuate buildings safely. But it is not just the routines of city businesses that are affected. Farmers are told to protect their fertilizers: 'Since the early 70s inorganic nitrogenous fertilisers (sometimes spelt fertilizers) have been misused by terrorists as an ingredient in home-made explosive (HME).' Later, the advice makes it clear that farms and agricultural companies are targets: 'There is no doubt that terrorists will target those things that are easy to obtain. Please report ANY suspicious activity at or near your premises, it may prove to be a missing part of a bigger picture.'[39] Indeed, it is not just farmers that are affected; those instructed to change their behaviour are 'Farmers and growers, Buying groups, Agricultural Contractors, Hauliers, Storage services, Merchants, Blenders, Importers, Manufacturers'.[40]

The counter-terrorism narrative then seeks to change routines and behaviours among the public in the neighbourhood, when travelling, and at work. And it is also changing behaviour in schools. Preventing Violent Extremism is an initiative to provide resources for those in schools – teachers, management, governors – to review and reassess how the school works. For example, the advice is as follows:[41]

---

[39] 'Secure Your Fertiliser', *National Counter Terrorism Security Office*, at www.secureyourfertiliser.gov.uk [accessed October 2009].

[40] 'Who Should Secure Their Fertiliser?', *National Counter Terrorism Security Office*, at www.secureyourfertiliser.gov.uk [accessed October 2009].

[41] 'Summary of Practical Advice for Schools', *Teachernet*, 8 October 2008, at www.teachernet.gov.uk [accessed October 2008].

Teaching, Learning and the Curriculum

Aim: a curriculum and pedagogy which promote knowledge, skills and understanding to build the resilience of pupils and explore controversial issues.

Through:

- a curriculum adapted to recognise local needs, challenge extremist narratives and promote universal rights
- teaching and learning strategies which explore controversial issues in a way which promotes critical analysis and pro social values
- use of external programmes or groups to support learning while ensuring that the input supports the school goals and values.

Action by: *curriculum managers, staff who lead on links with external groups.*

The Department for Children, Schools and Families offered specific curriculum advice. Perhaps most significantly in this context, schools are encouraged to debate scenarios, to consider how they would respond to challenges, and how normal routines might be affected by radicalization. One such challenge is:[42]

Scenario 3

A supply teacher leaves a book in the school library which has a lengthy passage about martyrdom including a phrase 'this indicates that seeking to be killed and pursuing martyrdom are legitimate and praiseworthy acts'.

Concern with the dangers of violent extremism impact upon the way in which schools teach, through Personal, Social, Health and Citizenship Education. Discussing community cohesion and preventing violent extremism is a duty placed upon schools, and is often

---

[42] 'Pupil Support and Challenge Case Studies: What Would Your School Do?', Department for Children, Schools and Families, 8, *Teachernet*, at www.teachernet.gov.uk [accessed October 2009].

taught in these PSHE/PSCHE classes. There are a variety of resources to help teachers impact upon the views of children. Some lie outside official structures. The Geographical Association, for example, is 'an independent charity with a core objective of furthering the learning and teaching of geography. The GA promotes and supports geography teaching by producing acclaimed resources for teachers, holding quality CPD events and lobbying government.'[43] It explains why teachers should engage enthusiastically with this work:

We teach children and young people about CC [community cohesion] and PVE [preventing violent extremism] because we want to make a difference to learners. In and out of school life, children and young people live, interact and work in communities that are diverse in terms of cultures, religions or beliefs, ethnicities and social backgrounds. We use the school community as a platform to provide meaningful interactions ... This positive teaching and learning environment also helps pupils learn to understand and value diversity, challenge assumptions and build resilience to the messages of violent extremists.[44]

Then there are other resources, such as the Watch Over Me series of films designed for secondary school children from the Kids Task Force. *Watch Over Me III* examines 'Road safety, weapons, internet safety, diverting children away from crime through sport, extremism and community cohesion, self-image'.[45] And finally, those in education need to act as barometers of mood:

Schools can also help local authorities and police understand tensions affecting their pupils. Schools will observe or hear how communities are feeling, may witness an event that has happened, or be aware that something might happen. In all these three types of situation information from schools is important to help the local authority or police gain a whole community view and so protect young people from harm or causing harm.[46]

---

[43] Geographical Association, 'About Us', at www.geography.org.uk/ [accessed April 2010].
[44] Geographical Association, 'Why Teach Children and Young People about Community Cohesion and the Prevention of Violent Extremism?', at www. geography.org.uk [accessed April 2010].
[45] Kids Taskforce, 'Watch Over Me III', at www.thekidstaskforce.com [accessed February 2010].
[46] 'Understanding the Threat Nationally and Locally', *Teachernet*, 8 October 2008, at www.teachernet.gov.uk [accessed October 2009].

In all these different areas of life – interaction with the police, with business, in schools – the work has been to impact upon everyday life. This is the work that a process of securitization does, and Chapter 2 of this book examines the nature of securitization theory, offering a new take by relaxing four of the principal pillars of the work of the Copenhagen School. Chapter 1, though, begins by looking at how we theorize about the ways in which security policy impacts upon the lives of people in liberal democracies, and in doing so it draws upon ontological security theory. By understanding ontological security – the security of the self, rather than physical security – at the level of individuals (rather than the state, the tendency in much contemporary international relations scholarship) we are able to understand how securitization processes impact upon the everyday. For securitization is about shaping relations between identities in particular, and confrontational, ways. That is, securitization shapes the identity of the securitized and the securitizer. In the contemporary United Kingdom, this means that securitization has reshaped what we understand by 'Britishness', and Chapter 1 illustrates how the content and form of Britishness has altered by looking at cultural manifestations in three distinct historical periods. With an understanding of ontological security and the new take on securitization theory developed in Chapter 2, Chapter 3 then looks at the nature of Britishness, and argues that the foundational moment of contemporary British identity has been constructed through the experiences of the 1940s; Britons' sense of when their current story began dates from the Second World War. As Prime Minister David Cameron explained in an interview with John Humphrys on the *Today* programme:

DC: 1940 to me is the proudest year of British history bar none. We stood on our own ...
JH: Quite so.
DC: ... against the Nazi tyranny ... It is the proudest year in all of British history.[47]

Chapter 3 argues that this foundational moment is constantly remade – as above – for contemporary purposes, and the chapter looks – through cultural artefacts – at the construction of the key values of

[47] David Cameron interviewed by John Humphrys on the *Today* programme, BBC Radio 4, 28 July 2010, at http://news.bbc.co.uk [accessed July 2010], from 3.21 minutes to 3.28.

contemporary Britishness in evidence at the millennium. Chapter 4 then takes that baseline and examines how Britishness has changed and been called upon by high-profile authoritative figures during the 'war on terror'; Chapter 5 examines the range of securitizing agents in more detail. The Conclusion sets out what we have learned about securitization and the everyday through ontological security theory, and what this says about contemporary Britishness.

Through this book, I want to argue that ontological security at the level of the individual – routines and narratives that are themselves constructed intersubjectively – is crucial in understanding collective processes of securitization. Securitization theory needs to be restated in this light, but when that is achieved it becomes a much more valuable analytical tool for understanding how, through particular practices, identities securitize others. And thereby I want to show how, in the specific case of the United Kingdom, discourses and practices of 'Britishness' have led to the securitization of Islam.

1 | *Ontological security and Britishness*

Introduction

'Security' has a variety of connotations, depending upon one's perspective; security as survival; security as power; security as well-being. Ontological security, however, focuses on the relationship between identity, narrative and security. The concept of ontological security has permeated through a variety of disciplines in the social sciences, particularly since the publication of Giddens's *Modernity and Self-Identity* in 1991.[1] Drawing originally from work in psychiatry, ontological security focuses on the nature of the security of the self. Ontological security is achieved through the creation of a series of relationships performed through everyday routines and practices. This helps individuals avoid being paralysed by deeply disturbing questions: what is life about? What happens when I die? These routines and everyday practices may involve work, the home, religion – and, for many, also relate to national identity. That is, for many who live in the United Kingdom, a firm sense of Britishness is part of the fabric of life upon which they can rely for predictability, and therefore this identity structure contributes to the ontological security of many individual British citizens.

For some authors in international relations, such as Jennifer Mitzen and Brent Steele, it is possible to scale up the theoretical insights concerning ontological security from the individual to the level of the state. These are valuable and insightful approaches, which allow a number of key propositions to be made and tested. However, this is not the route followed here. I am not arguing that Mitzen and Steele are wrong – merely that their work is a rather different branch. The focus here is on how Britishness connects with the sense of security that pervades everyday life for particular sets of individuals.

[1] Anthony Giddens, *Modernity and Self-Identity*, Cambridge: Polity, 1991.

This chapter sets out the concept of ontological security, and then examines how in different periods of time particular images came to symbolize that which Britishness represented. But those images – caricature, documentary films, an exhibition – not only reflected that which the creators understood intersubjectively to be the nature and values of the national identity; they also communicated those ideas and reaffirmed them widely in society. And in so doing, they sought to fix the nature of identity in a way that would provide structures to support the ontological security of individuals.

Ontological security

Joyce Davidson discussed the difficulties that Susan faced in living her life. Susan was agoraphobic, the sufferer of panic attacks in social contexts where no obvious route of 'escape' is apparent. Travelling to the shops can seem threatening if by public transport; and indeed, undertaking the shopping itself can be a huge problem. For some women whose identity is structured through performing tasks they relate to 'wife' or 'mother', such as shopping, there is a need to per-form the act balanced by a fear of being trapped while enacting it. If the balance is such that the act – here, shopping – can't be carried out, the sense of self-worth is deeply undermined. As Susan said herself, 'It destroys your confidence. It takes your confidence ... it knocks it right out of you.'[2] Failure to perform the 'normal' – the 'routine' – was deeply damaging to Susan: 'You feel like, you know, a bad parent, because you couldn't do all the things that the other parents were doing ... I just felt that I wasn't doing my so-called-job properly.'[3] But Susan did not simply give up; she was self-reflexive, and developed strategies: 'if I was going to the shops I would wait for my husband so that he would come with me, you know, I found all these different ways. Or I would get someone else to go to the shops for me.'[4] The bus was the particular focus of her fear: 'I was on the bus ... and I got these weird feelings and I genuinely believed that I was going to die.'[5] And so she retreated, incorporating home as her defined space of safety, of security. The social spaces had become, in Davidson's

<hr>

[2] Susan quoted in Joyce Davidson, *Phobic Geographies: The Phenomenology and Spatiality of Identity*, Aldershot: Ashgate, 2003, p. 63.
[3] *Ibid.*   [4] *Ibid.*, p. 64.   [5] *Ibid.*, p. 69.

words, 'threatening to the sufferer's feeling of "ontological security" '
in which she had followed a well-worn strategy whereby her own four
walls became 'an essential element in her "ontological security".'[6] As
for other sufferers, the agoraphobia was undermining 'her self-confi-
dence and ontological security, in a deep rooted and enduring way'.[7]
'Anxiety becomes all consuming':[8] Susan suffered from an ontological
insecurity, and needed support in her psychological struggle.

The key themes that Susan was able to articulate so clearly from
the perspective of the ontologically insecure – the 'failure' to perform normal routines, deep anxiety, reflexivity to produce coping
mechanisms, deep impact upon the sense of worth and integrity – are
many of the components of theorizing about ontological security,
and much contemporary work on the subject is framed by Anthony
Giddens's investigation in *Modernity and Self-Identity*, in which he
focused on the relationship between high modernity and the human
condition. Before Giddens, however, R. D. Laing wrote about ontological security – and, indeed, he coined the term – in *The Divided
Self* (1960).[9] Laing's interest as a psychiatrist was perhaps more in
ontological *in*security than in its opposite; his work in part sought
to challenge conventional, medically based psychiatry, to argue that
mental health was not simply a biological condition, but had to be
understood, in addition, socially. That is, Laing wanted to understand the conditions of mental illness through means other than a
purely biological analysis, in the vein that Susan's comments on her
own suffering allowed Joyce Davidson to understand the nature of
individual insecurity.

In order to be able to specify the nature of illness, Laing set out his
focus on ontological insecurity by introducing the ideal type of the
ontologically secure individual.

A man may have a sense of his presence in the world as a real, alive, whole,
and, in a temporal sense, a continuous person. As such, he can live out into
the world, and meet others: a world and others experienced as equally real,
alive, whole and continuous.

---

[6] *Ibid.*, pp. 69 and 24 respectively.
[7] *Ibid.*, p. 117.   [8] *Ibid.*, p. 58.
[9] R. D. Laing, *The Divided Self*, London: Penguin, 1990; originally published
   by Tavistock Publications, 1960.

Such a basically *ontologically* secure person will encounter all the hazards of life, social, ethical, spiritual, biological from a centrally firm sense of his own and other people's reality and identity.[10]

Susan, as we have briefly seen, did not enjoy such a comfortable position. From this, Laing was able to set out those conditions that described the ontologically insecure in psychological terms:

The individual in the ordinary circumstances of living may feel more unreal than real; in a literal sense, more dead than alive; precariously differentiated from the rest of the world, so that his identity and autonomy are always in question. He may lack the experience of his own temporal continuity. He may not possess an over-riding sense of personal consistency or cohesiveness. He may feel more insubstantial than substantial, and unable to assume that the stuff he is made of is genuine, good, valuable. And he may feel his self as partially divorced from his body.[11]

Such a lack of what Laing defined as 'primary ontological security' would mean that the individual would be constantly threatened by the everyday experiences of any life. The individual would lack a sense of self and agency, and would be subject to fears, anxiety and dread, in different forms, and at different times – experiences, and sense, so well articulated by Susan about her own life.

Laing's focus on the social impacts on the individual is mirrored in Giddens's sociological account. Giddens, of course, accepts the psychological foundation of ontological security, but focused in particular on the relational aspect. That is, what is of particular interest to him, and what he adds to the concept that is at the core of the analysis in this book, is what he describes as the 'mutuality of experience'.[12] That is expressed through the intersubjective nature of existence. As Giddens puts it, individuals need to be able to communicate comprehensibly when 'asked by another to supply "a reason" or "reason"

---

[10] *Ibid.*, p. 39; italics in the original to denote 'Despite the philosophical use of "ontology"' ... I have used the term in its present empirical sense because it appears to be the best adverbial or adjectival derivative of "being",' footnote, *ibid*.

[11] *Ibid.*, p. 42.

[12] Anthony Giddens, *The Consequences of Modernity*, Palo Alto, CA: Stanford University Press, 1990, p. 92.

for, or otherwise explicate, certain features of his or her activity'.[13] For Giddens, ontological security is brought about when humans are able to trust that they can bracket off all sorts of possibilities; that they can therefore rely on a social normality, a predictability, which then structures their practical everyday interactions as natural, normal and commonsensical. As Giddens puts it, 'The natural attitude brackets out questions about ourselves, others and the object-world which have to be taken for granted in order to keep on with everyday activity.'[14] The ontologically secure individual does not worry about the meaning of life, or of his or her life, or of its purpose; does not worry about the social world collapsing. Everyday interactions are therefore largely unproblematic (except in times of crisis, which Giddens discusses separately), and are based upon an intersubjective understanding that creates the boundaries of the normal: 'What makes a given response "appropriate" or "acceptable" necessitates a shared – but unproven and unproveable – framework of reality.'[15] Of course, this framework can be culturally specific; what may be appropriate and acceptable in one time and place may not be in another. This allows humans to create and develop their own personal narratives, their own situational accounts of who they are and why they behave as they do. These biographies give a sense of direction, and of worth. And it is the quality of the reliability of those narratives for the individual that creates the sense of ontological security. It is an ability to make sense of oneself and one's behaviour in conditions in which there are no possible foundational roots. To quote Giddens at some length:

To live our lives, we normally take for granted issues which, as centuries of philosophical enquiry have found, wither away under the sceptical gaze. Such issues include those quite properly called existential, whether posed on the level of philosophical analysis, or on a more practical level by individuals passing through a period of psychological crisis. They are questions of time, space, continuity, and identity. In the natural attitude, actors take for granted existential parameters of their activity that are sustained, but in no way 'grounded' by the interactional conventions they observe.

---

[13] Anthony Giddens, *The Constitution of Society: Outline of the Theory of Structuration*, Cambridge: Polity, 1984, p. 73.
[14] Giddens, *Modernity and Self-Identity*, p. 37.
[15] *Ibid.*, p. 36.

Existentially, these presume a tacit acceptance of the categories of duration and exception, together with the identity of objects, other persons and ... the self.[16]

These existential concerns are those that are held in place by a firm sense of ontological security.

In an interview reflecting on his work and the reaction to it, J. G. Ballard gave voice to the sense of vacuum that can underpin modern life:

I think that people perceive that life is probably meaningless, that we're an accident of fate biologically, and that societies that we inhabit, far from being social structures that reflect deep, enduring needs, are in fact gim-crack, almost extemporized sets of rules that someone in charge of a lifeboat might impose on survivors sitting around him; so many biscuits per day, you know, and half a pint of water. And that society's just a set of opportunistic conventions that we accept in order to facilitate ordinary life, just as we accept that we drive in this country on the left side of the road; and we all know that that doesn't reflect some deep pre-existing meaning within our lives ... I mean, given the hollowness of existence, I think people are beginning to wonder, sort of, what does life really offer us in terms of it's possibilities.[17]

Perhaps once, for many in the West, that firm sense of ontological security was provided by Christianity, of whichever hue: that there were answers to the meaning of life, and to our future beyond life, and that there were practices to be performed to continue underlining that faith. In high modernity, without such all-encompassing belief systems, individuals seek other routes. For Ballard, 'Some people reach out to bizarre cults, others move into drugs, but these are all rather desperate remedies.'[18] But for others, it is the family, the home, work, and identification with a cause – national, cultural, local, and yes, for some still, religious – that constructs the foundation around which life can be lived.

That which is held back by a sense of ontological security is 'the fear of being overwhelmed by anxieties that reach to the very roots

---

[16] *Ibid.*, p. 37.
[17] J. G. Ballard, 'Grave New World', interview by David Gale, BBC Radio 3, 10 November 1998, at www.jgballard.com [accessed September 2009].
[18] *Ibid.*

of our coherent sense of "being in the world" '.[19] This is not 'fear' in the sense that there is a specific threat and a definite object – it is not 'fear' of attack by a neighbour, for example, or indeed by a particular neighbouring state, as would be the focus in much traditional security studies.[20] Here the better term is anxiety or, better still, *dread*: Giddens talks specifically of 'dread in Kierkegaard's sense'.[21] And Kierkegaard is key to Davidson's understanding of the agoraphobia that people such as Susan endure; she titled chapter 3 of her book 'Fear and Trembling in the Mall'.[22]

Ontological security understood in this way depends upon both a practical consciousness, and the everyday routines that reproduce and are reproduced by it, in order to function. As Giddens puts it, 'the development of relatively secure environments of day-to-day life is of central importance to the maintenance of feelings of ontological security. Ontological security, in other words, is sustained primarily through routine itself.'[23] Thus, 'all individuals develop a framework of ontological security of some sort, based on routines of various forms. People handle dangers, and the fears associated with them, in terms of the emotional and behavioural "formulae" which have come to be part of their everyday behaviour and thought.'[24] And of course, although Giddens writes in terms of the individual, for him that individual is one that is embedded into an intersubjective whole in the period of high modernity; the individual cannot be understood separately and asocially. This commitment to routines is part of the socialization of the individual. This provides a sense of 'safety' for the individual, the necessary aspect of the working of social systems.

Giddens draws most explicitly on Laing when discussing the nature of self-identity. Here, both authors agree that there are key elements to that which they would describe as a 'normal' sense of identity. There has to be a biographical continuity, which is both easily grasped reflexively and communicable. There is a narrative which is

[19] Giddens, *Modernity and Self-Identity*, p. 37.
[20] A distinction made by Brent J. Steele in 'Ontological Security, Shame and "Humanitarian" Action', paper presented at the 2004 ISA Conference, Montreal, March 2004, at www.allacademic.com [accessed August 2009].
[21] Giddens, *Modernity and Self-Identity*, p. 37.
[22] Davidson, *Phobic Geographies*, p. 54.
[23] Giddens, *Modernity and Self-Identity*, p. 167.
[24] *Ibid.*, p. 44.

fragile, because of course it is only one reading of events and may be
subject to other, 'hostile' readings; but it will also be robust, in that
it will be able to withstand (and thereby give meaning to) significant
changes in the social environment. This, of course, fundamentally
problematizes the self; as Giddens made clear in a classic statement,
'We are, not what we are, but what we make of ourselves.'[25] There
is no core identity: as Catarina Kinnvall puts it, 'Rather than representing some kinds of "core selves", these self-narratives become
"as-if selves", through which we present ourselves "as-if" we were
bearers of lasting identities.'[26] This is built in and through a web of
trust relations (the outlines of which would probably be developed in
early childhood), to enable the individual to operate within a cocoon
that protects and filters out dangers to the self in everyday life. The
ontologically secure individual has trust in particular items (social
tokens, as Giddens describes them) and individuals (professionals and
experts), and does not worry about the collapse of that trust. And this
allows for a self-integrity, an ability to be 'alive', that is, to act within
the scope of those elements under reflexive control. The social structure created allows the ontologically secure individual to map his or
her decisions on a predictable basis, in relation to his or her reading
of his or her own biography.[27]

What Giddens adds that is particularly relevant to the framework
initiated through the work of Laing is in relation to those elements of
society that help to build trust, and the way in which self-identity is
seen as in motion. Giddens is interested in the effects of late modernity, and the factors that relate here to ontological security are the trust
mechanisms of tokens and experts. Part of the sense of collective trust
is that tokens have value with those that we have not met or do not
even know of – and money is, of course, the most obvious example. I
may travel from Inverness to Ipswich, or from Armagh to Anglesey,
and know that my money will be accepted by people I do not know,
and who I will never meet again. Expert systems, which invoke professional expertise – doctors, for example – play a similar role; we

---

[25] *Ibid.*, p. 75.
[26] Catarina Kinnvall, 'Globalization and Religious Nationalism: Self, Identity,
and the Search for Ontological Security', *Political Psychology* 25(5),
2004: 748.
[27] Giddens, *Modernity and Self-Identity*, pp. 53–4, 58, 61; Laing, *The Divided
Self*, e.g. p. 142.

trust the experts to provide some predictability for our own lives to a certain extent. If I am unwell, I am not alone; there is a health system upon which I can naturally draw. These mechanisms help to provide ontological security, but they are in constant need of regrounding. The fear is that the failure of such mechanisms will undermine enormous structures of trust and, thereby, of ontological security.[28] What is also crucially important is the way in which self-identity is reproduced through routine: not a fixed, never-changing state, but a routine that can be reflexively reconstituted in the light of the new. As Brent Steele comments, routines can 'both constrain (discipline) and enable (quasi-emancipate) social agents'.[29]

An ontologically secure person may see his or her security threatened by 'critical situations', which Giddens defined in his *The Constitution of Society* (1984) as 'circumstances of a radical disjuncture of an unpredictable kind which affect substantial numbers of individuals, situations that threaten or destroy the certitudes of institutionalized routines'.[30] Critical situations are crises, events and processes that are constructed into fundamental moments in time requiring a choice about response. Of course, they are social crises, shocks to established beliefs and ways of doing things, rather than purely exogenous and objective in nature. Critical situations emphasize the fragility of ontologically secure entities: that established, everyday routines that allow a foundation to life can be interrupted; that trust structures – tokens, experts' roles – may lose their centrality; that agency may be questioned, as the actor considers means of acting that conform to his/her self-identity; and that the sense of biography could suffer temporal dislocation. It is in the construction of critical situations that the robustness or otherwise of the ontologically secure is put to the test.

So ontological security is structured around four specific claims. First, that self-identity is based on a sense of biographical coherence,

---

[28] On this, see Derek Gregory, 'Presences and Absences: Time Space Relations and Structuration Theory', pp. 185–214; Peter Saunders, 'Space, Urbanism and the Created Environment', pp. 215–34; and Anthony Giddens, 'A Reply to my Critics', pp. 249–301, in David Held and John B. Thompson, *Social Theory of Modern Societies: Anthony Giddens and His Critics*, Cambridge University Press, 1990.

[29] Brent Steele, '"Ideas That Were Really Never in Our Possession": Torture, Honor and US Identity', *International Relations* 22(2), 2008: 246.

[30] Giddens, *The Constitution of Society*, p. 61.

comprehended by the individual and communicable to others; that it allows for a sense of agency, that is the subject of reflexivity, of self-monitoring; and that this self-identity is performed in, through and by an everyday routine. Second, this self-identity, and the actions that it leads to, is produced in a cocoon of trust structures, notably in the role of social tokens, and confidence in professional experts, that nevertheless require constant regrounding. Third, the ontologically secure agent is able to act in conformity with his/her sense of self-integrity; the ontologically secure agent has a firm sense of the appropriate and the acceptable. Finally, no matter how ontologically secure the agent may be, there is always a fragility as well as a robustness to that position; there is always an awareness of the polar opposite, ontological insecurity, in which dread is dominant. The ontologically secure individual can never be always secure in that position.

To be content in one's ontological security is not the same as survival. Of course, in one sense physical survival is the pre-eminent driver; but concern about that is not the norm of everyday life under late modernity. As McSweeney puts it, 'If a street mugging worries us, the realist story implies, how much more will an ICBM twenty minutes after launch from its base … [however] most of us do not live our lives in the terror of the London Blitz, but in the presence of the network of risk attendant on ordinary life.' He writes that physical security is only primary if we live in circumstances 'where this level of security is empirically the most pervasive and common concern'.[31]

Yet there are a variety of circumstances in which the appropriate and the acceptable might lead to the destruction of the self; in which the alternative to self-destruction is ontological insecurity, which is by its very nature unacceptable. That is, ontological security might lead to pain and death; and similarly, ontological insecurity might lead to the same outcomes for a particular individual. One would, perhaps, expect the latter – that ontological insecurity and destruction would be connected. In his classic study, Durkheim concluded that the phenomenon of suicide was a social fact, the product of a growing normlessness in society, the sense that if the old certainties are being lost, depression and demoralization might grow in the

---

[31] Bill McSweeney, *Security, Identity and Interests*, Cambridge University Press, 1999, p. 153.

individual.[32] Durkheim saw the problematic resting in the marginal-ization and weakening of social ties, and of course his analysis has been widely critiqued in the more than one hundred years that have passed since its publication. But from our perspective, what Durkheim was identifying were the ways in which ontological insecurity might develop in the individual owing to the impact of societal discourses and practices, and the ways that such changes might be profoundly damaging to the security of the individual. And yet, it is also the case that the maintenance of ontological security can lead to destruction. Certainly, the blowing of whistles to signal to the First World War soldier that it was time to leave the trenches and charge at the enemy, into artillery and machine gun fire, would represent for each individ-ual the most dramatic of critical situations. The routines of army life would be about to be left behind; and the promise of the biographical certainties of the return to home life would be at ultimate risk. For some, a few, the stakes were too great; they were unable to perform the role of soldier. But for the great majority, it was appropriate and acceptable to put the survival of the self at risk. And in that, it was the structure of the nation that provided one pillar of those calcula-tions around survival and ontological security; as Benedict Anderson put it, 'it is this fraternity that makes it possible, over the past two centuries, for so many millions of people, not so much to kill, as willingly to die for such limited imaginings'.[33] To fail to perform, to fail to charge, offered the collapse of ontological security associated with the 'coward', the 'failure', the 'un-British'. Such outcomes would have been viewed with dread. And so men 'went over the top' with whatever courage they could muster. As Arthur Barraclough later recalled, 'Our heart would be cursing and there would be all sorts of stuff going up in fright. But I always used to just stand still for a minute and just say this little prayer. I'll never forget it. "Dear God, I am going into grave danger. Please help me to act like a man and come back safe." '[34] Not only going into battle, but also just going to

---

[32] Emile Durkheim, *Suicide: A Study in Sociology*, London: Routledge, 2002; first published as *Le Suicide: Etude de sociologie*, Paris, 1897; first published in English by Routledge and Kegan Paul, 1952.

[33] Benedict Anderson, *Imagined Communities: Reflections on the Origin and Spread of Nationalism*, 2nd edn, London, Verso, 1991, p. 7.

[34] Arthur Barraclough, quoted in 'The Last Tommy Gallery', *BBC History* (undated), at www.bbc.co.uk [accessed June 2010].

war filled some with dread. Rowland Hurley wrote to his sister the
day before he went to France, telling her about his new baby; there
were more than a dozen in the family. He told her, 'in papers look for
21 King's Royal Rifles, 9585 Sgt Hurley', obviously fearing that this
would be the way she would find out about his death. He finished
his letter: 'If anything happens, do what you can for Kiddies.'[35] That
was on 12 August 1914; just over a month later, he was dead. To put
survival first would have deeply infringed the ontological security of
both Barraclough and Hurley; they just could not do it.

The framework established by Giddens has been explored in empirical terms by a number of authors. Rose Boucaut, for example, used
the framework to examine bullying in the workplace. She found that
'[w]hen people work within an organisation they become socialised
into the routines of that workplace. An interruption of these routines,
for example when introducing change, may cause discomfort to a person's ontological security.'[36] Deborah Padgett used ontological security as the key concept to understand different strategies to manage
those with severe mental health issues in New York City in the 1990s,
finding that those who benefited from a 'housing first' strategy showed
stronger signs of ontological security than those who were part of a
'treatment first' strategy.[37] In a similar vein, Dupuis and Thorns (in
a much cited article) argued that the routines created by home occu-
pancy were a major contribution to the ontological security of older
New Zealanders.[38] Noble analysed the theme of 'home' and ontological security, but from the perspective of the migrant subjected to
racism in Australia, and the consequent creation of ontological insecurity for some.[39] The framework established by Giddens has led also to

[35] Unpublished letter by Rowland Hurley to his sister Lily, dated 12 August 1914.
[36] Rose Boucaut, 'Understanding Workplace Bullying: A Practical Application
of Giddens' Structuration Theory', *International Education Journal* 2(4),
2001: 68.
[37] Deborah K. Padgett, 'There's no Place Like (a) Home: Ontological Security
among Persons with Serious Mental Illness in the United States', *Social
Science & Medicine* 64(9), May 2007: 1925–36.
[38] Ann Dupuis and David C. Thorns, 'Home, Home Ownership and the
Search for Ontological Security', *Sociological Review* 46(1), February
1998: 24–47.
[39] Greg Noble, 'The Discomfort of Strangers: Racism, Incivility and
Ontological Security in a Relaxed and Comfortable Nation', *Journal of
Intercultural Studies* 26(1/2), February 2005: 107–20.

extensive work in the social policy and medical professions. In another example, Danermark and Möller examined the impact of processes of trust and social recognition on the ontological security of deafblind people.[40] And in a conceptual and empirical study, Crossley examined the way in which serious illness impacts upon ontological security.[41]

This brief examination of the way in which ontological security is deployed across medical, social policy and psychological disciplines illustrates that ontological security has become a focal point for research in trans-disciplinary ways. Not only has the concept been used in sociology – for example, Turner's argument that new debates about citizenship can be seen in terms of ontological security issues – but also, increasingly, in international relations.[42] Giddens moved the debate from Laing's individual-in-social-context analysis to the societal domain; given the nature of the academic study of international relations, the task has been seen to be to connect these societal claims to states and to interstate relations. Perhaps first discussed in the study of International Relations by Jef Huysmans and Bill McSweeney, other studies have followed: notably Steele, Mitzen, Krolikowski and Kinnvall, all of whom will shortly be discussed.[43]

A significant contribution is Brent J. Steele's *Ontological Security in International Relations*.[44] Steele wants to establish a distinction between ontological security and more traditional accounts of security, in which the former takes on a primary role.

---

[40] B. D. Danermark and K. Möller, 'Deafblindness, Ontological Security, and Social Recognition', *International Journal of Audiology* 47, Suppl. 2, November 2008: S119–23.

[41] M. L. Crossley, '"Let Me Explain": Narrative Employment and One Patient's Experience of Oral Cancer', *Social Science and Medicine* 56(3), February 2003: 439–48.

[42] Brian S. Turner, 'The Erosion of Citizenship', *British Journal of Sociology* 52(2), June 2001: 189–209.

[43] See Jef Huysmans, 'Security! What Do You Mean? From Concept to Thick Signifier', *European Journal of International Relations* 4(2), 1998: 226–55, especially p. 242.

[44] Brent J. Steele, *Ontological Security in International Relations*, New York: Routledge, 2008. See also a version of this work in Brent J. Steele, 'Ontological Security and the Power of Self-Identity: British Neutrality and the American Civil War', *Review of International Studies* 31(3), 2005: 519–40.

While physical security is (obviously) important to states, ontological security is more important because its fulfilment affirms a state's self-identity (i.e. it affirms not only its physical existence but primarily how a state sees itself and secondarily how it wants to be seen by others). Nation states seek ontological security because they want to maintain *consistent self-concepts*, and the 'Self' of states is constituted and maintained through a narrative which gives life to routinized foreign policy actions.[45]

Steele argues that ontological security can be challenged by circumstances in which a state does not behave according to its own sense of principles; in such circumstances, there is a sense of shame that animates revisions of identity and/or policy. Such revisions occur during 'critical situations' and thereby it is in crises that gaps can open up between actors' actions and their self-integrity, leading to what Steele described as shame. He argues, for example, that NATO's intervention into the Kosovo wars was produced by a sense of shame over historical memories and experiences.[46] Thus the 'Kosovo action' could be seen, for example, to relate to repentance for 'Rwanda', and through understanding how the 'visceral' images of violence impacted upon a sense of moral right and wrong in western countries (which could also be seen through the lens of shame for the Holocaust).

Far more widely cited is 'Ontological Security in World Politics: State Identity and the Security Dilemma', in which Jennifer Mitzen argued that it was possible to move from the individual and group levels that can be found in the works of Laing and Giddens, to the state level.[47] She argues that ontological security is the security of the self and, like Steele, that it can be seen as distinctive from security as survival. The key to this is the achievement of routine, but this routine can be either reflexively or rigidly followed. Routine is valuable; so valuable to the self, that states might privilege routine over other values, such as escaping from conflictual relations even when physical cost and harm is involved. Mitzen argues that it is this means of routine underscoring identity that can explain why states can continue in conflictual relations that would otherwise appear to be irrational:

---

[45] Steele, *Ontological Security*, pp. 2–3; italics in the original.

[46] *Ibid.*, p. 115.

[47] Jennifer Mitzen, 'Ontological Security in World Politics: State Identity and the Security Dilemma', *European Journal of International Relations* 12(3), 2006: 341–70.

routines, regardless of their rationalist content, secure identities. To support this line of argument, she proposed that the realist–rationalist argument, that states have egoist 'personalities' and that the state is a rational decision maker, could be generalized. For Mitzen, 'since rational action emanates from preferences or desires, states cannot be rational actors without having a sense of stable identity'.[48] Yet at the same time, the example that she gave for the social reality of onto-logical insecurity was not at the state level: 'people in the US found it difficult to do anything: go to work, cross a bridge, ride the subway … the sense of uncertainty and threat was pervasive.'[49] As a scholar in international relations, it is perhaps inevitable that Mitzen would read Giddens through the perspective of international relations schol-arship, rather than more directly through sociology. There seems to be a desire for the work to be seen as mainstream International Relations, which requires the concept to be connected to other theor-etical work in the discipline. She assumes states to be rational: 'since my goal is to engage realist IR theory, which treats states as rational actors, I develop the concept of ontological security with respect to rational agency.'[50]

The value of 'Ontological Security in World Politics' as an article is that it allows the reader to see how the concept of ontological secur-ity could be transposed from the individual level with Laing, through the sociological with Giddens, to the national/international level with Mitzen's work. This approach is taken up by others: Zarakol, for example, with reference to the 'state denial of historical crimes' in Turkey and Japan.[51] Giddens develops Laing's focus on individuals with psychological difficulties to the societal level, suggesting more fully that it is society that provides the framework that can solve the ontological security problems of many of its members, since society is

---

[48] An amplification of the argument, Mitzen in 'Jennifer Mitzen on ontological security, multilateral diplomacy, and states' addiction to war', *Theory Talks*, 18 February 2009, at www.theory-talks.orgl [accessed July 2009]. On this, see Alexander Wendt, 'State as a person', *Review of International Studies* 30, 2004: 289–316; emphasis added.

[49] Jennifer Mitzen, 'Anchoring Europe's Civilizing Identity: Habits, Capabilities and Ontological Security', *Journal of European Public Policy* 13(2), 2006: 273.

[50] Mitzen, 'Ontological security', p. 345.

[51] Ayse Zarakol, 'Ontological (In)Security and State Denial of Historical Crimes: Turkey and Japan', *International Relations* 24(1), 2010: 3–23.

an intersubjectively shared ordering of the environment which allows for the 'cocoon' that individuals (hopefully) experience early in life to be scaled up.

The contributions of both Steele and Mitzen are important in connecting the broad work on ontological security in psychology and sociology with international relations; this can be seen as part of the process whereby ontological security theory is introduced to a variety of other disciplines. But in so doing, both Steele and Mitzen have a powerful 'other' in sight: traditional international relations theory and, in particular, realism. Neither author takes ontological security purely on its own terms; both relate it particularly to international relations concerns – explaining state behaviour (in terms of shame leading to action for Steele, in terms of routines leading to harmful outcomes for Mitzen). In doing this, they separate the social institution of the state from other social institutions. But what if we did not make such a separation?

The approach that these authors follow – which is to extrapolate theory that is focused on the individual and social context to the state level – has been critiqued by Roe and Krolikowski.[52] This theoretical extrapolation from individual to state occurs in the work of Steele and Mitzen in the sense that, for both, states as well as individuals seek ontological security. Therefore for Steele, states can feel shame in the same way as individuals; and for Mitzen, states can be attached to physically harmful routines, because routines are so important in affirming identity. For Roe, the distinction is between values (which are shared by both individuals and states) and needs, which operates only at the level of individuals. The alternative that Krolikowski proposes is to see the referent as the individual again, not the state; and to see the state as a potential provider of ontological security to the individual, while also recognizing that the state and nation face profound challenges in the late modern era.

Beyond the study of international relations, Roger Silverstone discussed human defences against chaos and dread in an article in *Media, Culture and Society*. In a classic reading of ontological security, he

---

[52] Paul Roe, 'The "Value" of Positive Security', *Review of International Studies* 34, 2008: 777–94, especially the discussion at pp. 784–6; Alanna Krolikowski, 'State Personhood in Ontological Security Theories of International Relations and Chinese Nationalism: A Skeptical View', *Chinese Journal of International Politics* 2(1), 2008: 109–33.

described the importance of routines. He wrote that '[t]he institutions which we have inherited and which we still struggle to maintain: family, household, neighbourhood, community, *nation* ... are those institutions which have historically been the containers of, and provided resources for, our ability to sustain that defence [against chaos and dread]'.[53] Silverstone went on to add television to the list of routines, particularly, as Cohen and Metzger suggest, among those in developed societies who are the least mobile, the least healthy and/or those with the fewest social interactions.[54] Another clear source of the routine so important to the achievement of ontological security would be the workplace, and there is a significant literature on the destabilizing effects of unemployment, the casualization of labour and the impact of workplace restructuring on ontological security.[55] But in this list of social institutions, it is clear that the 'nation' is a key part: not something separated or bracketed away from society as in the work of Steele and Mitzen, but something mutually constituted with it. One obvious form of routine is in the performance of traditions, and these are both public and private in form; we can identify 'the increasingly interdependent traditions of both family and nation' that Silverstone describes.[56] Rather than considering 'merely' the state, international relations can connect with the ontological security literature by considering the issue at the level of the nation.

One author who has written in this vein from within international relations, and upon whom Krolikowski draws, is Catarina Kinnvall.[57] Giddens argued that ontological security has to be seen in the context of – constructed by and through – high modernity, and from this Kinnvall emphasizes the destabilizing function of globalization in terms of the effects of scale, speed and cognition. She argues that these factors impact dramatically on the human condition: 'As people

[53] Roger Silverstone, 'Television, Ontological Security and the Transitional Object', *Media, Culture and Society* 15, 1993: 573–4.
[54] Jonathan Cohen and Miriam Metzger, 'Social Affiliation and the Achievement of Ontological Security through Interpersonal and Mass Communication', *Critical Studies in Mass Communication* 15, 1998: 41–60.
[55] See for example William S. Brown, 'Ontological Security, Existential Anxiety and Workplace Privacy', *Journal of Business Ethics* 23(1), January, 2000: 61–5.
[56] Silverstone, 'Television', p. 593.
[57] Catarina Kinnvall, *Globalization and Religious Nationalism in India*, New York: Routledge, 2006.

feel increasingly uncertain about their daily life, the search for security takes on ontological and existential dimensions.'[58] Her work has
been in part connected in theme to much of what has taken place
in a variety of disciplines. Drawing on authors such as Dupuis and
Thorns, Kinnvall emphasizes the importance of 'home'

as a bearer of security ... found in its ability to link together a material
environment with a deeply emotional set of meanings to do with perman-
ence and continuity ... It is a place where one knows and accepts certain
values, rules, and behaviour, but it is also a place from which one can open
the door and go out into the world ... Ontological security is maintained
when home is able to provide a site of constancy in the social and material
environment ... Home, in other words, is a secure base on which identities
are constructed.[59]

Thus, 'when home as a category of security is lost as a result of rapid
socio-economic changes, then new avenues or a new home – a new
identity – for ontological security are sought'.[60] This may involve
homesteading (a commitment to occupying a piece of land and making
oneself self-sufficient), engagement with an exile community through
shared places of assembly, or even local identity-based groups committed to prevent change or to return to previous times, through violence
if necessary. This focus has been important to Kinnvall in particular
in her analysis of Sikh communities. She argued that 'for many diaspora Sikhs ... the struggle for a home (even abroad) became intim-
ately linked to homeland politics. Imagining the nation, especially
in its religious form, has become a way for many migrants to solve
a crisis of ontological security and existential identity.'[61] In her analysis of Hindu constructions, Kinnvall suggested that 'Hindu nationalism, although complex and multifaceted, supports the notion that
religion and nationalism, in combination, act as powerful responses
to the individual quest for ontological security in a rapidly changing
world'.[62] Thus the institutions of nation and religion in their various
forms interacted around the development of collective structures of

[58] Kinnvall, *Political Psychology*, p. 746.
[59] Kinnvall, *Globalization*, p. 31.
[60] Kinnvall, *Political Psychology*, p. 747.
[61] Kinnvall, *Globalization*, p. 172.
[62] *Ibid.*, p. 137.

ontological security within which the individual could be (relatively) free of dread. Collective identities can therefore assist the individual to reaffirm a threatened self-identity.

Such collective structures were, of course, the focus for Benedict Anderson, in particular in *Imagined Communities: Reflections on the Origin and Spread of Nationalism*. He had been inspired to write the book in the light of 'The armed conflicts of 1978–79 in Indochina … I was haunted by the prospect of further large scale wars between the socialist states.'[63] Twenty years on from the publication of the first edition, Nils Ole Bubandt returned to the focus on identity and security issues in the region, this time with a focus particularly on Indonesia. Bubant brought together the imaginary with the need for ontological security. He argued that the 'political imaginary' in terms of 'the political cultivation of localism by former bureaucrats with some sort of "traditional legitimacy" … [is] constructing an alternative political imaginary in which what they see as a truly democratic tradition ensures "ontological security"'.[64] The importance of the imagined community to ontological security is strong, yet this connection needs to be worked through.

Anderson defined the nation as 'an imagined political community – and imagined as both limited and sovereign'.[65] He saw the nation as imagined, in that in even the smallest nation, the individual would not know his or her fellow countrymen and women, but nevertheless he or she still believes in the communion shared with them. And part of that communion is a shared narrative about the past of that community or nation, where it came from, what it stood for, and shared readings about the key defining moments. As Anderson points out, even the newest imagined community imagines itself as antique: 'The more the ancient dynastic state is naturalized, the more its antique finery can be wrapped around revolutionary shoulders. The image of Suryavarman II's Angkor Wat, emblazoned on the flag of Marxist Democratic Kampuchea' being a prime example.[66]

---

[63] Anderson, *Imagined Communities*, p. xi.
[64] Nils Ole Bubandt, 'Vernacular Security: Governmentality, Traditionality and Ontological (In)Security in Indonesia', DIIS Working Paper no. 2004/24, Copenhagen: Danish Institute for International Studies, 2004, p. 2.
[65] Anderson, *Imagined Communities*, p. 6.
[66] *Ibid.*, p. 160.

That the imagined community is limited refers to the extent of the community. Even among the most populous nation there is a sense of boundary, even though such a limit may be flexible and negotiable. Beyond that boundary, other communities lie. That is, within the imaginary of each community is a concept of other communities, of others with whom there can be a whole range of different forms of relationship. In what Giddens refers to as late modernity, all imagined communities have boundaries, have Others, and are not communities imagined to be coterminous with the whole of humanity. In previous eras, it was possible for some to imagine a world entirely Christian, or entirely Islamic. In the late modern age, with humanity divided nationally, such global imaginings are much harder not only to hold, but particularly, to perform. This does not mean that there cannot be solidarism; but it is a solidarism between different communities, rather than within a single whole.

The imagined community is sovereign in the sense that it emerged with the modern period, with the construction of the world into national structures and powers; as Anderson puts it, 'the concept was born in an age in which Enlightenment and Revolution were destroying the legitimacy of the divinely-ordained, hierarchical, dynastic realm'.[67] And it is a community in the sense that there is the horizontal attachment; regardless of religion, political affiliation, region, there is still an imagining that binds together those who have never met, and will never do so.

The currency for being a part of the imagined community is cultural and, thereby, socially constructed. Even language barriers are not fixed. Of course, 'the major states of nineteenth-century Europe were vast polyglot polities, of which the boundaries almost never coincided with language-communities. Most of their literate members inherited from medieval times the habit of thinking of certain languages – if no longer Latin, then French, English, Spanish or German – as languages of civilization.'[68] And indeed, in times of migration it can be clear that 'Language is not an instrument of exclusion: in principle, anyone can learn any language. On the contrary, it is fundamentally inclusive.'[69] It is not language per se that is exclusive, but the social tokens of the time and place: accent, skin colour, or practices of worship.

---

[67] *Ibid.*, p. 7.   [68] *Ibid.*, p. 196.   [69] *Ibid.*, p. 134.

So our conception of ontological security is tempered by the insights from Anderson's imagined communities. Unlike the recent trend in some aspects of international relations, what is to be secured ontologically is the individual, and in the following the state is not extrapolated theoretically from the individual level. Within the imagined community of the British, there is an institution that provides a structure for individual self-identity, which helps to play into a sense of biographical coherence, comprehended by the individual and communicable to others. An individual's sense of self will be structured in part through their sense of Britishness. This is structured through routines, with that sense of Britishness being performed through everyday tasks and discourses, such as in the performance of national traditions or, on holiday, in performing within the comfort of national roles. The agency of the individual can be reflexively constructed through (and indeed against) this sense of Britishness, which can be the subject both of self-monitoring, and of social surveillance. That Britishness is not and has never been purely coterminous with the citizens of the state. Britishness, indeed any such imagined community, can be denied to others – by themselves, and by others. The limited nature of the imagined community described by Anderson can be limited within the state, and thereby can relate to others within the state, as well as to others beyond the state. State citizenship and imagined community are related, but are not coterminous. Britishness is based on a whole series of social tokens – the pound sterling, indeed the image of the monarch on the currency – as well as on relations with experts, whether they be difficult relations (Members of Parliament), or much easier, more accepting ones (professionals within the National Health Service). Britishness helps to create the sense in the individual of what is appropriate and acceptable: the sense of what is the British thing to do – about being British. This trope can be called upon in all sorts of circumstances, to instruct the individual both about the nature of his or her self-monitoring, and to simply perform the role of being British for its own sake. Yet, of course, we know that even the individual who feels the most ontologically secure, drawing upon the institution of Britishness, still faces fragility even though there is in his or her view a fundamental robustness to that position. There is still the awareness of the dread that comes with ontological insecurity; of the vulnerability of the institutions upon which security lies which, in the context of many individuals who live in the United Kingdom, and indeed for some who live beyond the state, is a particular notion of Britishness.

This book is, then, an account of Britain as an imagined community, of Britishness as an institution – evolving, always in motion – that offers to individuals a contribution to the achievement of their ontological security; while also, at times through processes of particular forms of Othering, being profoundly ontologically desecuritizing to the life of others. As with other imagined communities, Britishness has been constantly in motion, and has constantly articulated itself through that which it is not, i.e. through describing others. It has also often been imagined as antique. Imagining a past – even if that past was often given a higher normative value (i.e. things were better then …) has been a key part of the myth generation of the imagined community. And Britishness, as with other national identities, has often been expressed by key agents to allow people to understand, to be able to communicate, that which binds them together.

What, then, can be the means by which we uncover imaginings of Britishness? Three images of that identity are examined in what follows. First, is the ways in which the British have imagined themselves by articulating who they have not been. Britishness has always necessitated a series of others, but one particular other image – that of the Dutch in the seventeenth and eighteenth centuries – allows us to see the power of the self in other imagery. The second picture is drawn by examining particular elements of Britishness at play in the 1930s. Britishness as 'always-antique' is an important trope, but this was given particular emphasis in relation to a specific golden past; a project shared by both conservatives and socialists. And the third picturing of Britishness is more contemporary: examining an exhibition at the *British Library* held in 2008–9, which in many ways sought to reinscribe British identity through reference to the specifically British archive.

Imagining Britishness 1: Cruikshank's Hollanders

The National Portrait Gallery in London holds a hand-coloured etching by Isaac Cruikshank, published by Samuel William Fores on 1 April 1795, entitled 'A New Dutch Exercise'.[70] Mary Dorothy

[70] The image can be found on the National Portrait Gallery website, at www.npg.org.uk [accessed August 2009].

George, writing about the image for the British Museum, wrote that the work was 'a satire on the sluggishness of the Dutch Government and people, and on the hostility of the Dutch towards their English allies' in the context of the Revolutionary Wars.[71] Cruikshank's image was of 'eight Hollanders', and much of it was political in character: the image entitled 'Reverence Treaties!!' shows a Dutchman with a torn paper reading 'Alliance Treaty' hanging from a pocket, ripped as the man uses a portion to light his pipe. This was a reference to the 1788 British–Dutch Alliance that was deemed easily broken by the Dutch in favour of the French, who had occupied the Netherlands and set up a puppet regime. Another image shows the British disgust at the Dutch military: under the image 'Stand to your Guns!!' a terrified Dutch soldier runs away from the enemy, dropping his gun in his desperation to escape. But what is interesting in the satire is not simply the commentary on the politics of the situation. Rather, it is the way in which Cruikshank showed the British view of the Dutch. All eight 'Dutchman' are overweight; half are drunk; most smoke to excess; one attempts forlornly to follow fashion, but fails; most seem lazy, unable to follow through on commitments. Not only have the Dutch failed the British, but the British, Cruikshank seems to be saying, should expect such an outcome from such a people. The British at war were all the opposites of the Dutch: virile, active, honourable, sober, responsible. And the identity of the artist was important too. Cruikshank, though living in London, had been born in Scotland; his art symbolized the *Britishness*, as opposed to merely the Englishness, of the identities in contradiction.

Part of that past has been the establishment of what 'we' are in contradistinction to that which we are not. Self-identity is a relational concept, and related as much to that which we are not as to that which we are. Thus, Cruikshank's condemnation of the Dutch was not only condemnation of what they had done (or rather, had failed to do), not simply of their *behaviour*, but, more importantly, of their *character*. And in this way, he could (re)establish in the mind of his British audience all those characteristics that were good in the British identity. Cruikshank was no mere cheerleader for the war against Revolutionary France; his work included satire on the political and

---

[71] M. Dorothy George, 'Catalogue of Political and Personal Satires in the British Museum', VII, 1942, at www.archive.org [accessed August 2009].

military leadership in London as well. But in his satirical work on France, he was also able to draw distinctions between 'Frenchness' and 'Britishness'.

When Benedict Anderson argued that language is fundamentally inclusive – because, in principle, anyone can learn any language – he is correct; but a language is more than just the structure. A language has within it echoes of past otherings. That is, by looking carefully at language practices, we can become archaeologists of past relationships. In the first half of the twentieth century, one might 'mafick' rather than 'celebrate'; to 'mafick' was 'to exult riotously, as on the relief of Mafeking in 1900'.[72] By creating and deploying the verb 'to mafick', the British could mark their imperial extent and victory over others. And those others might well be 'beyond the pale', a reference to a fence of painted wood enclosing a safe area – here, very probably, a reference to the ancient 'Pale of Dublin'. But even today, British people may still say 'pardon my French' in certain circumstances after swearing – the point here being that profanity and the French language are coterminous.[73] A 1936 Dictionary defines 'to take French leave' as 'to go away without warning'; with obvious connotations of cowardice.[74] Of course, many British people still understand the term 'Frog' to represent the French (meaning 'frog eater') and have done so probably since the French Revolution; but a century before that, the 'frogs' were not the French, as that derogatory term was rather applied to the Dutch (referring to 'frog land' – that is, marshy land where frogs live). Indeed, the second image of Cruikshank's *Hollanders*, 'Advance with Spirit', shows the fat Dutchman yawning, stretching his arms, with a frog by his feet. As Peter Silverton suggests, it is possible that 'when the French took the place of Britain's favourite enemy [from the Dutch], the racial slur [frog] moved over with them'.[75]

As seen in the work of Cruikshank, the Dutch have been a notable – though, from the perspective of the twenty-first century, bizarre – target. At times, the British and Dutch had close relationships, notably

---

[72] *Modern Standard Dictionary and World Atlas*, London: Odhams Press, 1936, p. 697.

[73] See for example Eric Partridge, *A Dictionary of Catch Phrases from the Sixteenth Century to the Present Day*, 2nd edn, Routledge, 1985, p. 364.

[74] *Modern Standard Dictionary and World Atlas*, p. 236.

[75] Peter Silverton, *Filthy English: The How, Why, When and What of Everyday Swearing*, London: Portobello Books, 2009, p. 237.

after the Glorious Revolution, when the English, Scottish and Dutch shared the same monarch. Similar ideas were transferred easily, such as the 'rule of thumb' as a unit of measure; in Dutch, the word for thumb, *dium*, also means inch. But far, far more common are phrases and attitudes towards the Netherlands, focused around the wars and competitions of the seventeenth century, which created a number of phrases still in use today. One such example is 'Dutch Courage': at a time of bitter naval fighting in Europe, Dutch sailors were particularly feared. They were presumed to be fighting with 'Dutch courage' – i.e. drunk – in order to explain their ferocity; their courage, being based on alcohol consumption, was therefore essentially false. Related to this, a 'Dutch agreement' was one entered into when drunk. If we 'go Dutch' (or have a 'Dutch treat', or a 'Dutch date'), the assumption is that the costs will be shared equally by the participants. Unexceptional in the twenty-first century, in earlier times this was equated both with miserliness, and with bad manners (particularly towards women). In a further unfortunate reference to gender politics, the British would refer to a 'Dutch widow', which meant a prostitute; or a 'Dutch doll', which meant of 'mixed race'. And then there is 'Dutch uncle', some-one not actually related who gives unwanted and harsh advice. A 'Dutch oven' is not simply a casserole dish, or cocotte; it refers also to the practice of flatulence in an enclosed space – the point here being the revolting nature of the cuisine of the Netherlands. And then, of course, there is 'double Dutch' – something completely incomprehensible, which makes half as much sense as the Dutch language.[76] In a 'Dutch auction' prices get lower rather than higher – clearly seen as lacking common sense to the British.

Perhaps we should expect other nationalities to be recorded as the subject of affirmations of Britishness. The polar opposites of the Dutch tropes are those that the British, at particular times, wanted to see in themselves, both collectively and individually. The British didn't need

---

[76] A significant number of texts record these phrases. Among those drawn upon for these sections are Glynnis Chantrell, *The Oxford Dictionary of Word Histories*, Oxford University Press, 2002; Alex Games, *Balderdash and Piffle: English Words and Their Curious Origins*, London: BBC Books, 2006; Georgia Hole, *The Real McCoy: The True Stories Behind Our Everyday Phrases*, Oxford University Press, 2005; and Myron Korach, *Common Phrases, and Where They Come From*, Guilford, CT: The Lyons Press, 2002.

'Dutch courage'; there was a natural heroism, clear in the reading of history that saw heroes such as Nelson at the Battle of Trafalgar, or Scott striving to reach the South Pole. Britons did not enter into 'Dutch agreements'; they behaved in responsible, sober ways. The British would not 'go Dutch' (in the past) for fear of impoliteness in terms of hospitability (although in more recent decades 'going Dutch' has been, of course, reclaimed by feminists). There would be no need of a 'Dutch wife' for the upstanding British, and again, politeness and decency were the opposites of the 'Dutch uncle'. Indeed, compare the British alternative use of 'uncle' – to say 'Bob's your uncle' is to mean that all is fine and well (although, originally, this had been part of criminal language – 'bob' here being a shop lifter's accomplice: once the item was in his or her hands, the deed was done – hence 'bob' meant safe).[77] And as to the 'Dutch oven' – well, the British rarely made grand claims of their cuisine. The function of this particular phrase was the well-worn one – which we shall see again – that of exhibiting bad odour. The Dutch are ridiculed in other aspects of the language. A 'boomkin' is Dutch for a little tree; originally a term of abuse for a Dutchman (short, squat), this has entered the English language as 'bumpkin'.[78] 'Builders even call a piece of wood or metal used to repair or patch up poor workmanship a "Dutchman." '[79] And many years ago, if in trouble with a marriage partner, employer, or teacher, one would be 'in Dutch' with them.

Many, if not all, these phrases are alive in British English today, but of course in times past there would have been a great many other references in the language to the Dutch. Francis Grose's *Dictionary of the Vulgar Tongue* (1811) gives some interesting examples: a 'butter box', for example, is defined as 'a Dutchman, from the great quantity of butter eaten by the people of that country'. Here, Dutch greed and excess was implicitly contrasted with the British character. Then there was 'Clinkers', which were 'a kind of small Dutch bricks; also irons worn by prisoners; a crafty fellow.' The 'Dutchness' of the bricks was connected to criminality. Pursuing the theme of the Dutch as inhospitable are also 'Dutch feast', 'where the entertainer

---

[77] See for example Nathan Bailey's *Canting Dictionary*, 1736, available online at www.fromoldbooks.org [accessed August 2009].

[78] Chantrell, *The Oxford Dictionary of Word Histories*, p. 73.

[79] Adrian Room, *A Dictionary of True Etymologies*, Law Book Co. of Australasia, 1986, p. 31.

gets drunk before his guest'; 'Dutch concert', 'where every one plays or sings a different tune'; and finally, 'Dutch comfort', meaning 'thank God it is no worse.' In all, there are twenty distinct references to the Dutch, and, of course, for the purposes of the *Dictionary of the Vulgar Tongue* these were not meant to represent all relevant references to be found in mainstream discourse.[80] In addition to the references discussed so far, at various times the following have also been in use: Dutch act (suicide); a Dutch bargain (an agreement made when consuming alcohol); Dutch talent (a nautical phrase referring to an act lacking common sense, being carried out by force rather than intelligence); and, of course, 'I'm a Dutchman if I do' (meaning that I will never do that, because being a Dutchman is beyond that which is acceptable; a similar phrase is 'well, I'm a Dutchman', indicating very strong surprise).

Perhaps one of the most frequent invocations of the Dutch in Britain lies in the myth of the *Flying Dutchman*: a sea captain neglects God in his struggles against the forces of nature and is punished by being condemned to sail the seas forever; for sailors, the sight of the *Flying Dutchman* is traditionally taken to indicate their own imminent death. But what is particularly interesting is the rereading of the myth at particular moments. Thus, at a time of particular hostility to the Dutch during the struggle for Belgian independence (1820s), the *Flying Dutchman* made an appearance in the guise of Edward Fitzball's *The Flying Dutchman; or, the Phantom Ship*, performed in 1829 and 1830. The Dutchman himself – Vanderdecken – is mute (part of his bargain with Rockalda, the aquatic demon-queen) and represented by the actor 'blacking up' – to further the image of the alien. Vanderdecken is condemned to never landing, to returning every hundred years to view the family long gone. In so doing, he seeks to seduce Lestelle, who turns out to be his great-granddaughter. Through these tropes – Dutch, African, incest – the unacceptability of the Dutch identity was reinscribed. But as with many texts, there were other readings readily apparent to the audience. Fitzball's play was an act of resistance against the idea of the state emigrating the poor and unemployed to the colonies (and here, in particular, to the Cape

---

[80] Francis Grose, *1811 Dictionary of the Vulgar Tongue*, 1811, originally 1785, reproduced by Project Gutenberg, at www.gutenberg.org/etext/5402 [accessed August 2009].

Colony). As J. Q. Davies puts it, 'Fitzball's Vanderdecken embodied the radical idea of the emigrant as demon-victim' and was therefore read as political commentary on the imperial project of the day.[81]

With references to the Dutch embedded in the language and thereby in the arts, it is perhaps inevitable that this would also be the case in British jokes. In England, with the Restoration of the Crown, underground jokes and songs were allowed back into the open, and one of the best sources of these materials is the collection known as *Rump Songs*. Here we see, of course, much hostility to the Protectorate and to Cromwell, but also we see the views of other nations. That is, there is an internal other: Cromwell, and the Puritans, as greedy materialists:

> He dives for Riches down to the bottom,
> And cryes, my Masters, when he had got um,
> Let every tub stand upon his own bottom,
> Which no body can deny.[82]

And there is also an external other, notably again the Dutch. In 'A Medley' on 'The English', verse four reveals contemporary views:

> If the Dutchman or the Spaniard
>   Come but to oppose us,
> We will thrust them out of the Main-yard,
>   If they do but nose us;
> Hans, Hans, think upon they sins,
> And then submit to Spain they Master,
> For though you look now like Friends,
> Yet he will never trust you after;
> Drink, drink, give the Dutchman drink,
> And let the tap and kan run faster,
> For faith, at last I think,
> A brewer will become your Master.[83]

---

[81] J. Q. Davies, 'Melodramatic Possessions: The Flying Dutchman, South Africa, and the Imperial Stage, ca. 1830', *Opera Quarterly*, 21(3), 2005: 496–514, at http://oq.oxfordjournals.org [accessed August 2009].

[82] Cited in Laura Lunger Knoppers, 'Sing Old Noll the Brewer: Royalist Satire and Social Inversion', *The Seventeenth Century*, 15(1), April 2000: 45.

[83] Alexander Brome, *Rump: Or an Exact Collection of the Choycest Poems and Songs Relation to the Late Times and Continued by the Most Eminent Witts from A1639 to 1661*, London: Henry Brome and Henry Marsh, 1662, reproduced on *Google Books* at http://books.google.co.uk [accessed August 2009].

Some eighty years later, in 1739, with the production of a collection of jokes, *Joe Miller's Jests*, named after a then-famous actor, the range of Dutch jokes was explored more fully. A classic example is joke 810: 'An Irish soldier ... being asked if he met with much hospitality in Holland? Oh yes, replied he, too much: I was in the hospital almost all the time I was there.' This plays into the trope of Dutch inhospitality, and perhaps also into the violence associated with 'Dutch courage'.[84] On a similar theme, number 596 reads as follows:

George the First, on a journey to Hanover, stopped at a village in Holland, and while the horses were getting ready, he asked for two or three eggs, which were brought him, and charged two hundred florins. How is this? said his majesty, eggs must be very scarce in this place. Pardon me, said the host, eggs are plenty enough, but kings are scarce. The king smiled, and ordered the money be paid.[85]

Here the miserly Dutchman (being the 'host', importantly) is met by the good-humoured British monarch – though of course the 'journey to Hanover' line reminds those listening that this king was as much German as British. But then again, the joke could also be seen as part of the Anglicization of the Hanoverians.

The image of Britishness that Cruikshank illustrated was one that was constructed in counterpoint to a threatening other figure. Through the enemy figures or alter egos of, for example, the Dutch, a construction of Britishness was formed and communicated, and helped to shape the institutions around which individuals could form their own sense of ontological security through such routinized practices as singing songs and telling jokes.

Imagining Britishness 2: pictures from the 1930s

The contents of Britishness clearly altered in form and perspective at different times and in different places. The resonance of the hostility to the Dutch that was still live to the audience of the *Rump Songs*, of Joe Miller, or of Isaac Cruikshank, had dissipated by the 1930s, with

[84] Frank Bellew (ed.), *Joe Miller's Jests*, London: T. Read, 1739, reproduced on *Google Books* at http://books.google.co.uk [accessed July 2009], p. 164.
[85] *Ibid.*, p. 122.

just the remnants of that past othering left in phrases and idioms. For those reflecting the norms of Britishness in the 1930s, there was work to be done with a number of elements of identity, such as the countryside and the sea, both of which played a role in constructing the narrative of an ancient and decent Britishness. A good deal of this can be seen in the work of the British Documentary Movement.

Led by John Grierson, with a variety of colleagues often working together but also sometimes breaking down into internecine conflict, the British Documentary Movement worked with and through the British government in complex ways.[86] 'The state became involved in film production largely because of a belief that motion pictures could have an impact on a mass audience thought to be immune from other types of appeal.'[87] Yet through its various forms – the Empire Marketing Board (EMB) Film Unit (1927–33), established by John Grierson and Stephen Tallents; the General Post Office (GPO) Film Unit (1933–9), which operated from the disbandment of the EMB; and its successor, the Crown Film Unit (1939–52) – it was able to inject a social democratic strand of thinking into a series of films during a decade of Conservative rule. 'The characteristic Grierson documentary dealt with impersonal social processes; it was usually a short film fused by a "commentary" that articulated a point of view.'[88]

The Movement often focused on the lives of the working class, and suggested that the quality of those lives ought to be improved. A classic example is *Drifters* (1929, director John Grierson), which focused on sea fishing to 'express the reality of the way in which "simple heroic labour" was transformed into a market commodity'.[89] Another example is *Children at School* (1937, 23 minutes, director Basil Wright), which contrasts the education of children in fascist countries (marching and drill) with more lofty aims. The film seeks to show how well children can be educated in Britain, focusing on a

---

[86] For a detailed account see Paul Swann, *The British Documentary Film Movement, 1926–1946*, Cambridge University Press, 1989. Swann provides a fascinating reading in which he suggests that various agents within state structures sought to provide more scope to the Movement, but were often frustrated by tactlessness on the part of the film makers.

[87] *Ibid.*, p. vii.

[88] Erik Barnouw, *Documentary: A History of the Non-Fiction Film*, 2nd edn, Oxford University Press, 1993, p. 99.

[89] Ian Aitken, *Film and Reform: John Grierson and the Documentary Film Movement*, London: Routledge, 1992, p. 110.

modernist development; and then spends the last part demonstrating how rare such good facilities are, showing the viewer the desperate state of the majority of Britain's schools. By implication, the viewer is drawn into the endorsement of higher standards of educational provision as a right for all children, and to stand for the British contrast to fascist conformity.

Most famous in this style is *Housing Problems* (15 minutes, 1935, directors Arthur Elton and Edgar Anstey), which showed the sheer degradation of Britain's slum housing, with occupants speaking their own words directly to camera. Grierson persuaded the Gas Light and Coke Company to sponsor the film, which called for the provision of government-financed housing (of course, a key demand of the Labour Party) on the grounds that this would lead to an increased demand for gas.[90] Some of the films became enduring works of art, perhaps none more so than *Night Mail* (25 minutes, 1936, directors Harry Watt and Basil Wright), with its imagery of moving the post between England and Scotland by rail, and its verse by W. H. Auden, with the classic and memorable opening lines:

> This is the Night Mail crossing the border,
> Bringing the cheque and the postal order,
> Letters for the rich, letters for the poor,
> The shop at the corner and the girl next door.

Colls and Dodd argued that these 'British documentary films represent the nation in two ways. They are said to be Britain's contribution to the cinema; and they represent "us" to ourselves and to others.'[91] It is in this latter sense that the works of the British Documentary Movement are important in this analysis.

Four of the films created by the British Documentary Movement will be taken not to illustrate their social democratic or aesthetic credentials, but rather to reveal a particular sense of Britishness. The first, *Industrial Britain* (1931, 20 minutes, director Robert Flaherty), extolled the skill of the individual British workman in being at the heart of British industrial leadership globally. The second, *Farewell Topsails* (1937, 8 minutes, director Humphrey Jennings), examined

---

[90] Barnouw, *Documentary*, pp. 94–5.
[91] Robert Colls and Philip Dodd, 'Representing the Nation: British Documentary Film, 1930–45', *Screen* 26(1), 1985: 21.

the china clay industry in Cornwall. The third, *Today We Live* (1937, 23 Minutes, directors Ruby Grierson and Ralph Bond), was made at the behest of the National Council of Social Service and both recorded and dramatized its work in providing skills and centres for community life. And the fourth, *Britain at Bay* (1940, 7 minutes, director Harry Watt), sits right at the end of the period, on the cusp where the war was about to become extremely violent for the British themselves.[92] The central contribution was, at times of great difficulty – owing to economic depression and, later, war – to focus and reflect thoughts of a longer-term narrative in relation to land, sea and the people themselves.

The importance of the land – specifically, of rolling countryside marked by farms and wheat fields – was marked throughout all these short films. *Industrial Britain* is introduced by a national narrative. To images of a windmill and a spinning wheel, of fields being harvested and of swans on water, with idyllic music playing, the narrator (Donald Calthrop) explains to the viewer: 'The old order changes, giving way to new. Half the history of England lies behind these scenes of yesterday. The history of daily work done, of people who carried on through the centuries growing things, making things, transporting things between the English villages and the English towns.'[93] The reference to 'England' rather than 'Britain' is marked (Grierson himself was a Scot, though living in London), particularly given that the title of the film was *Industrial Britain*. But the reference to 'half the history' was to mark that this ended some time ago, at the time of the Industrial Revolution, for with the images moving to that of the coal miner, the narrator explains that 'here is the symbol of the new order: steam and smoke. There is power behind it. And behind the power is coal.'[94] The country has moved from the idyll of the past to the present dirty and dangerous modern age and, perhaps, from England to Britain. But through it all, a constancy remains: the professionalism and care of the craftsmen (very clearly, all those with a 'modern' craft are presented as men). The character of the working man is thereby inscribed as part of the national identity, allowing Britain to be a

[92] These and many other films are available on *Land of Promise: The British Documentary Movement 1930–1950*, London: British Film Institute, 2008.
[93] Observation of 'Industrial Britain' on *Land of Promise*.
[94] *Ibid.*

world-leading modern power. 'Industrial Britain' is, as Aitken has argued, 'a romantic celebration of industrial craftsmanship'.[95]

Although *Industrial Britain* focuses mostly on the way in which the land has been changed, there are at the beginning some images of the sea, of seafaring as being part of that past idyll. The sea is the theme of *Farewell Topsails*. The sadness of the narration by J. D. Davidson was for the recent lost age. 'Once there were hundreds [of topsail schooners]; now there are only half a dozen left.'[96] The period of this decline is not specified, but whereas the lost idyll of *Industrial Britain* is centuries ago ('half the history of England lies behind these scenes ...'), that of *Farewell Topsails* could be measured in decades. In the older viewer, it probably evoked the 'halcyon' days of the late Victorian and early Edwardian periods. Some of the imagery is played out to the sounds of a former sailor's accordion playing 'My Bonnie Lies over the Ocean', a Scottish folk song in a Cornish port, giving a wider sense of Britishness. Davidson laments: 'No more will they heel gracefully over, under the freshening breeze. They're gone, and their crews with them.'[97] But the importance of the sea to the nation was being transformed. *Farewell Topsails* presaged a far deeper loss, just ten years later, at the end of the War. Hundreds of warships were scrapped (thirty-seven aircraft carriers alone) or their production cancelled, while the Admiralty, a separate institution of state for 336 years, was abolished and folded into the new Ministry of Defence which was, as Andrew Marr noted from the perspective of the twenty-first century, 'the last act in the ruthless liquidation of the organization that had been central to British identity for as long as Britain had been a single nation'.[98] Linda Colley notes how the sea was 'imagined as a telling symbol of identity' in quoting a clergyman preaching in celebration of the Act of Union: 'We are fenced in by a wall which knows no master but God only.'[99] *Farewell Topsails* marks not only the end of the topsail schooner, but also the end of a period when the sea was a central element in the national identity.

[95] Aitken, *Film and Reform*, p. 121.
[96] Observation of 'Farewell Topsails' on *Land of Promise*.
[97] *Ibid.*
[98] Andrew Marr, *A History of Modern Britain*, London: Macmillan, 2007, p. 15.
[99] Linda Colley, *Britons: Forging the Nation 1707–1837*, Yale University Press, 2005 (first published 1992), p. 17.

By contrast, in *Today We Live* a morality tale about engaging and making a difference in a time of economic hardship was presented, focused on the present, and with a clear expectation that the future would be better (not least, in that mass employment would return). But the strangeness of the present had to be explained; things had been better, and would be again, so how to make sense of the Depression? The narrator, Howard Marshall, reminded the viewer of the key narrative, of the move from pre-modern to modern Britain: 'Not long ago, the wealth of Britain lay in the fields and farms and estates of the countryside. Change came only with the seasons ... The church was the centre of social life. Then came a change, not in the seasons, but in power ... The centres of wealth passed to the new areas of activity around the coal fields.'[100] Unlike in *Industrial Britain*, here the language was of 'Britain' and not 'England'; and also in contrast, whereas *Industrial Britain* marked this change centuries ago ('half the history ...'), *Today We Live* made it far more contemporary – 'Not long ago ...' To older viewers, this could have been read as reference to the great agricultural depression of the 1880s, which changed the British countryside in profound ways, rather than to some much earlier unspecified time. Crucially, *Today We Live* focused on the experiences of those still living. The problems that this more recent industrialization had brought were made explicit: 'Thousands of houses were built without plan or conscience, to shelter the increasing population. Today, these houses are the slums and shame of Britain.'[101]

Both *Farewell Topsails* and *Today We Live* had managed to connect the profound change in life to a period comprehensible to individuals either directly, or through their family's history. An excellent literary example of this is the semi-autobiographical work of A. G. Bradley, who wrote of 'country life in the serene, confident, untroubled days before the collapse of the 'eighties – and the permanent break-up of old conditions. In short, the peaceful atmosphere of Trollope's novels.'[102] Bradley gave this work the evocative title of *When Squires and Farmers Thrived*. What had been lost, in *Today We Live*, was that sense of well-being attributed to an earlier age, and the narration

---

[100] Observation of 'Today We Live' on *Land of Promise*.
[101] *Ibid*.
[102] A. G. Bradley, *When Squires and Farmers Thrived*, London: Methuen, 1927.

was every bit as explicit as Bradley had been. 'The war memorials across the country, in village and town, not only stand for sacrifice of life on foreign soil, but mark the climax and close of a long era of English social life.'[103]

The final film is in many ways the most powerful. *Britain at Bay* was made at the moment after the 'Fall of France' in 1940, when the British saw themselves as facing the Nazi threat alone. The narration, by J. B. Priestley, was rich and brought together many of the themes of the earlier films. To the (now) familiar images of farms and countryside, Priestly intoned: 'For nearly a thousand years, these hills and fields and farmsteads of Britain have been free from foreign invasion. They've not even known civil war for close on two hundred years. We have been a fortunate people.'[104] The narrative of a long-lived and blessed people was then mixed with the problems of the modern period: 'These [modern industrial] towns are anything but perfect dwelling places.' But even then, there was hope of rural redemption: 'Not far away from even the blackest towns was always one of the most beautiful, peaceful countrysides in the world.'[105]

The exposition of the current state of the domestic world, and the position of the current generation trans-historically, was then counterpointed with the threat from Europe. To images of Nazi conquest, culminating in the Fall of France, Priestley explained: 'This has left Britain alone, at bay. It's not the first time she's been at bay [here, images of the White Cliffs of Dover came into view] against a conquering tyrant, [image of the ocean] for we were equally alone against the full might of Napoleon, who ruled an area greater than Hitler rules now.'[106] The historical fortitude of Britain was called upon and signalled in the image of the White Cliffs; Britain's good fortune in its position, and its command of the seas, was signalled by the ocean image. 'The future of the whole civilized world rests on the defence of Britain.'[107] In a sister film entitled *If War Should Come*, viewers were told that 'Democracy will triumph!'[108] *Britain at Bay* raised the stakes still higher – the future of civilization itself. And the future of Britain, and thereby of civilization, would depend 'first, of course,

---

[103] Observation of 'Today We Live' on *Land of Promise*.
[104] Observation of 'Britain at Bay', *ibid.*
[105] *Ibid.*   [106] *Ibid.*   [107] *Ibid.*
[108] Observation of 'If War Should Come', *ibid.*

on the Navy.'[109] The sea, and the command of it assumed across the generations to be part of the national heritage, was called upon as the key deliverer at the moment of ultimate crisis not only of the state, but of Britishness itself.

The work of the British Documentary Movement, progressive in so many ways, also reflected and constructed a conservative sense of always-British, a people still connected to the special British land and sea, despite the contemporary challenges of modern life. It thereby reflected and constructed a sense of Britishness that contributed to the ontological security of individuals, by presenting the Depression as one-off, to be faced down by an extraordinary nation of 'nearly a thousand years' into which all could, perhaps, fit their own personal narrative; and also in relation to the sense of the British as the ultimate nation, defending civilization itself, in standing against the Nazis.

Imagining Britishness 3: Taking Liberties

One way of capturing the contemporary meta-narrative of Britishness is to examine the Taking Liberties exhibition, held at the British Library from 31 October 2008 to 1 March 2009.[110] It was, in many ways, an elite and establishment exercise of rearticulating the nature of identity, endorsed by the Prime Minister, held at the cultural heart of the nation. The purpose of the exhibition was to 'Explore the 900-year struggle for Britain's freedoms and rights'.[111] The strapline proclaimed the key elements of that meta-narrative: that there has been an entity called 'Britain' for 900 years – that the British therefore have an inter-generational connection with all that has taken place throughout that time: it is 'our' history. And that which has taken place has not been a series of random events; it has been the purposeful pursuit of 'freedoms and rights'. There was something profoundly democratic and egalitarian about that pursuit, as it was about securing those 'freedoms and rights' for all. But that pursuit has not been easy; it has been a 'struggle' against hostile (and clearly in this sense anti-British) forces. That sense of struggle, and indeed the sense of

---

[109] Observation of 'Britain at Bay', *ibid.*
[110] I visited the exhibition on 24 November 2008.
[111] Taking Liberties exhibition, British Library, at www.bl.uk/takingliberties [accessed June 2009].

radical struggle, was visually communicated by the selection for the exhibition of a raised and clenched fist as its visual symbol. When Prime Minister Gordon Brown opened the exhibition, he did so making the British meta-narrative, and the need to communicate it to the British, very clear:

I hope that in the course of people coming round this exhibition, and in the course of young people particularly, they will see that these great traditions of liberty, our tradition of social responsibility, our belief in tolerance and openness as a society, and our commitment to democracy are the essence of what it is to be British in every part of the United Kingdom, that we build on these great traditions that have been established over a thousand years, and in doing so we create a better democracy, a more compassionate society and a stronger Britain for the future.[112]

These themes were carried through the eight rooms of the exhibition at the British Library.

In the first room, Magna Carta was placed in a central position, giving an impression of that document as *the* foundational moment of this 'British' 'struggle' for 'freedoms and rights'. Indeed, to powerfully reinforce the point, the room was entitled 'Liberty and the Rule of Law: Ancient struggle for equality before law for all'. Magna Carta was, socially, the only choice for such a centrepiece to the opening of the exhibition. In the course of debates about creating a 'British Day' public holiday in 2006, it was the day commemorating the signing of Magna Carta that topped a poll of 5,002 people held by *BBC History Magazine*.[113] The problem, of course, is that, as Benedict Anderson had argued, 'The barons who imposed Magna Carta on John Plantagenet did not speak "English" and had no conception of themselves as "Englishmen", but they were firmly defined as early patriots in the classrooms of the United Kingdom 700 years later.'[114] Taking Liberties

---

[112] Gordon Brown, 'Speech, at the British Library', 29 October 2008, at www. number10.gov.uk [accessed August 2009].

[113] However, perhaps this was due to a split vote on a World War II commemoration; Magna Carta received 27% of the vote, but VE Day and D-Day together received 35% (21% and 14% respectively). See 'Magna Carta Tops British Day Poll', *BBC News Online*, 30 May 2006, at http://news.bbc.co.uk [accessed August 2006].

[114] Anderson, *Imagined Communities*, p. 118.

continued this process of inscribing the barons as these 'early patriots'. But of course, a contradiction lies in this reading, for even if the barons could be read retrospectively as 'English', they certainly could not be read as 'British'. The 5,002 voters on the *BBC History Magazine* poll were supporting a barely English event for a British National Day. The solution reached by Taking Liberties was to surround Magna Carta with a variety of other, national, texts. Thus, the English Law of the Forest sat next to the Scottish Ayr Manuscript, which was next to the Welsh Hywel Dda. The impression is of a range of medieval attempts to establish these 'freedoms and rights' across the British Isles, with Magna Carta perhaps the symbol that could be seen to unite all these efforts, rather as 'Britain' could be projected as the summation of the English, Scottish and Welsh nations. The selection of documents would have been a fine judgement. The 'Law of the Forest', for example, was a companion to Magna Carta; whereas the latter managed relations between monarch and nobles, the latter was aimed at – in the words of the exhibition 'the rights of ordinary people'.[115] Thus, the Law of the Forest was given to represent the democratic and egalitarian values ascribed to Britishness over this 900-year period.

The representation of the Ayr Manuscript played a similar function – emphasizing that 'The lord king wishes and orders that common law and common justice be done as well to poor people as to rich people according to the old laws and liberties justly used before these times.'[116] When the Scottish Parliament announced its exhibition For Freedom Alone in 2005, although the Ayr Manuscript was present, pride of place was given to the Arbroath Declaration.[117] In the latter, it was declared that 'as long as but a hundred of us remain alive, never will we on any conditions be brought under English rule. It is in truth not for glory, nor riches, nor honours, that we are fighting, but for freedom – for that alone, which no honest man gives up but with life itself.'[118] Arbroath's anti-English sentiments were on display in Room Four, entitled 'United Kingdom?', which spoke of 'constantly

[115] 'Law of Forests', Takings Liberties, at www.bl.uk [accessed March 2009].
[116] Translated and reproduced at 'Ayr Manuscript, 1318', National Archives of Scotland, PA5/2 (folio 44), at www.scottisharchivesforschools.org [accessed August 2009].
[117] '"For Freedom Alone" Exhibition Details Revealed', *Scottish Parliament*, 14 June 2005, at www.scottish.parliament.uk [accessed August 2009].
[118] Translated and reproduced at 'Defining Moments in History', *National Archives of Scotland*, www.nas.gov.uk [accessed August 2009].

contested national identities'. However, in this room Arbroath sat alongside the Act of Union, and various representations of the Union flag. It would be easy in that context to read the Arbroath Declaration as a statement against English imperialism, rather than being in essence anti-British.

A particular element of the meta-narrative was provided in the discussion of Hywel Dda. Both the Law of the Forest and the Ayr Manuscript were lauded for their provision of rights on an egalitarian basis. Hywel Dda was represented as being particularly significant in the struggle for gender equality:

Some of the provisions regarding women seem quite enlightened for the time. For instance, if a marriage broke up after seven years or more, the woman was entitled to half the joint property. An unfaithful husband had to pay his wife a fine of five shillings the first time and a pound the second time – respectively the equivalent of three weeks', and three months', wages for a craftsman.[119]

Yet this gender dimension is entirely absent in the National Library of Wales representation of Hywel Dda's law, with the Library concentrating instead on the importance of the imagery in the text and, of course, the national importance of Welsh laws by a Welsh king.[120]

Room Two of the exhibition developed the themes of 'Parliament and Rights', with the rather repetitive sub-theme of 'Parliament and the People', although in essence it was a collection of materials drawn from the Civil War and the Protectorate. More persuasive in terms of the meta-narrative was Room Three, 'The Right to Vote', with the clear indication that the 'struggle' for voting rights had been long (the exhibition began with documents on eighteenth-century electoral corruption) and was 'only recently achieved'. Material on radicalism and Peterloo, on the Chartists and the Suffragettes reached a peak with a letter from Christabel Pankhurst to Henry Harben, dated August 1913, in which Pankhurst wrote that she was 'game' for 'riot and violence' if necessary for the suffragette cause.[121] The proximity

---

[119] 'Laws of Hywel Dda', Taking Liberties, at www.bl.uk [accessed August 2009].

[120] 'Peniarth 28: A Latin Text of the Laws of Hywel Dda', National Library of Wales, at www.llgc.org.uk [accessed August 2009].

[121] Letter by Christabel Pankhurst, August 1913, Taking Liberties exhibition, Add.MS58226.f.z6, observed 24 November 2008.

of Britain to revolution at various points since the Civil War was a key theme: that the 'struggle' for rights against 'anti-British' forces had been that profound. The themes of progress towards and reaction against general rights dominated the rest of the exhibition. The remaining rooms focused on issues such as human rights, freedom from want, and freedom of speech and belief.

The exhibition was important not only in the sense of seeking to (re)create a particular reading of Britishness as combative, justice-focused, inclusive and long-standing. It also sought to measure (or instruct) the nature of that reading among exhibition attendees and those who visited its website via an interactive programme.[122] From this, we get an insight into the way in which the values of Britishness being promoted by the exhibition are reflective of, and are internalized by, the viewing public. One of the main symbolic tokens of Britishness, the monarchy, is shown – just – to be holding onto majority support, with 52.4% of respondents in favour of the monarchy, and some 47.7% seeking a post monarchical nation. Reflecting the emphasis on 'freedom' in the exhibition, 51.8% declared themselves against any amount of time in detention without trial. Some 50.4% declared themselves in favour of some form of English parliament, but 71.9% were against any form of Cornish autonomy, indicating that Cornwall is perhaps seen as an English, rather than a British, entity. Finally, following a series of commentaries including one by a former suffragette, Olive Wharry, 84.6% of respondents replied that some form of law-breaking is legitimate in order to change 'bad laws'. The British, then, are through this exhibition, radical, committed to freedom, constructed also through their sense of sub-nationalities within the state, and still engaged with the admittedly contested symbol of a monarch. Above all, there is a great engagement with the idea of a British story, some 900 years in the making.

The guest curator for the exhibition was Linda Colley, Princeton scholar, and friend of Prime Ministers. On the back of her book *Britons: Forging the Nation 1707–1837*, she was courted by the Labour Party elite.[123] Read by both Tony Blair and Gordon Brown, she was seen as 'providing apt historical guidance for dealing with

---

[122] See 'Taking Liberties Interactive', at www.bl.uk [accessed August 2009].
[123] Colley, *Britons*.

present anxieties'.[124] Tony Blair invited her to deliver the Millennium Lecture, and in 2009 she was appointed a CBE in the Queen's New Year Honours List (Diplomatic and Foreign Office section) for services to historical studies. At the opening of Taking Liberties, Brown commented: 'I think we all owe a debt of gratitude to Linda Colley who has brought this exhibition together, she is an amazingly successful historian, her book – *The Britons* [sic] – has been one of the great books of the last few decades.'[125]

Colley has become known for arguing that 'Britishness' was a project constructed during and after the 1707 Act of Union. Following Benedict Anderson, 'Britain' and 'Britishness' were imagined communities, imagined on top of and alongside other imagined national (Scottish, Welsh, English) and regional identities. Colley argued that all governments, all states, are based on certain fictions: of the ancientness, specialness, the divineness of the people, nation and/or rulers. 'If the fiction is to work and compel mass belief, rulers and governments may also be obliged at times to sacrifice a measure of the freedom and power they would otherwise enjoy.'[126] This new Britishness was dependent upon a core identity being threatened:

[T]he overwhelming Catholicism of large parts of Continental Europe, and especially France and Spain, provided a newly-invented Britain with a formidable 'other' against which it could usefully define itself. The real and imaginary threat represented by French and, to a lesser extent after 1707, Spanish forms of government, religion, and military power allowed the different Protestant traditions of Scotland, Wales and England to come together in a common union of self-preservation, anxiety, and defiance.[127]

This identity formation created integrating and divisive identity structures. For much of the eighteenth century, British Catholics were subject to specific constraints: punitive taxes; being forbidden to possess weapons; being discriminated against in education,

---

[124] Stephen Howe, 'Linda Colley: I Don't Even Know if I'm British Any More', *The Independent*, 21 September 2002, at www.independent.co.uk [accessed August 2009].
[125] Gordon Brown, 'Speech, at the British Library'.
[126] Linda Colley, *Taking Stock of Taking Liberties: A Personal View by Linda Colley*, London: British Library, 2008, p. 26, here following the argument of Edmund Morgan.
[127] Colley, *Britons*, p. xvi.

in property ownership and, of course, in freedom of worship; and not being allowed to vote, nor to stand for public office. 'In other words in law – if not always in fact – they were treated as potential traitors, as un-British.'[128] This contrasted strongly with the position of non-Anglican Protestants: 'in practice, English and Welsh Protestant dissenters were able to penetrate almost all levels of the political system up to and including Parliament itself, and so too were Scottish Presbyterians'.[129] Not only was there an integrating effect for all those who were Christian non-Catholics, but there was also the powerful integrating effect of empire. For example, Colley argued that '[m]any of the Scotsmen who made successful military or civilian careers in the colonies at this time [the latter half of the eighteenth century] came from Jacobite families or had at one time been Jacobites themselves'.[130] For Colley, this all had obvious conclusions for the contemporary British state:

As an invented nation ... heavily dependent for its raison d'etre on a brutally Protestant culture, on the threat and tonic of recurrent war, particularly war with France, and on the triumphs, profits and Otherness represented by a massive overseas empire, Britain is bound now to be under immense pressure ... The Other in the shape of militant Catholicism, or a hostile European power, or an exotic overseas empire is no longer available to make Britons feel that – by contrast – they have an identity in common.[131]

Thus, the conclusion that she reached in the early 1990s about Britishness, and the one that spoke so clearly to the emerging Labour Party hierarchy, was that as a consequence of the loss of enemies within and without, and of the differences provided through empire, 'the predictable result has been a revival of internal divisions among them.'[132]

Taking Liberties insisted on a 900-year-old Britishness; that is, an inter-generational series of relationships binding those who are 'British' today with those engaged in the 'struggles' for liberty in a particular place over the period since the Norman Conquest. William

---

[128] *Ibid.*, p. 19.   [129] *Ibid.*   [130] *Ibid.*, p. 131.

[131] Linda Colley in Matthew Reisz, 'Citizenship Papers', *Times Higher Education*, 23 October 2008, at www.timeshighereducation.co.uk [accessed August 2009].

[132] Colley, *Britons*, p. 7.

the Conqueror's mark on history has long been taken as that of creating the new state, as marking the foundational moment for the country. When in 1600 Robert Speed produced a map of 'The Invasions of England and Ireland with al their Civill Warrs', he began the history some 500 years earlier, to record all 'since the Conquest'.

> And to begin with the first battell in this plot which was the first beginning of gouernment of this state as it yet continueth. Such was the attempt of William Duke of Normandy against King Harold the sonne of Earle Goodwin, who preuailed so against him in fight at Battaile in Sussex (a place so called by this euent) as the said Duke was afterward King of this Land, and brought the whole nation vnder his obedience, as it hath beene continued to his posterity euer since.[133]

Dating 'Britain' to 1066 has been the norm, the common sense; but in linguistic terms, the victory of the Normans saw the relegation of the English language to the periphery of the everyday usage by the poor and the dispossessed. King Harold was the last king to use English for 300 years, until perhaps Richard II deployed a knowledge of English to defeat Wat Tyler's Peasants' Revolt in 1381. And, of course, the sense of 'Britain' that animated the Norman and Plantagenet kings was not one of the nations of the islands in harmony, but one of English imperialism, symbolized by the wars leading to the de facto annexation of Wales, the wars against the Scotland of William Wallace and Robert the Bruce, and successive invasions and occupations of Ireland, as well as hundreds of years of occupation and war in France. An aged Britain has also been conjoined with the notion of specific British liberty – a value constructed into the identity at the birth of the United Kingdom at the beginning of the eighteenth century, and one reflected subsequently in poem and song.

> Oh happy Britain! we have not to fear
> Such hard and arbitrary measure here;
> Else could a law, like that which I relate,
> Once have the sanction of our triple state,
> Some few that I have known in days of old
> Would run most dreadful risk of catching cold.

---

[133] Walter Goffart, 'The Genesis of John Speed's Maps of Battles in England and Ireland', *The Seventeenth Century* 19(2), October 2004: 170.

> While you, my friend, whatever wind should blow,
> Might traverse England safely to and fro,
> An honest man, close buttoned to the chin,
> Broad-cloth without, and a warm heart within.[134]

William Cowper's 'An Epistle to Joseph Hill, Esq', part of the more famous *The Task* and published in 1785, elegantly captured the elements of Britishness and the commitment to liberty.

Taking Liberties ensured that the tokens of Britishness – Magna Carta, and the like – would be (re)woven into the national narrative. By creating space for interactivity, and in hosting 'Study Days', it allowed individuals to perform their identities during the event and subsequently. Citizens were tasked with learning of their cultural past, and with deciding how British certain contemporary measures – such as detention without trial – actually were. As if to symbolize the nature of the Britishness that the exhibition sought to illustrate, at the grand opening there were no complaints when the Prime Minister's speech was delayed ... by his audience with the Queen.[135]

The ontological security of Cruikshank, Grierson and Colley's Britishnesses

Ontological security 'entails having a consistent sense of self and having that sense affirmed by others'; it is 'a security of social relationship, that is to say a sense of being safely in cognitive control of the situation'; it is 'a security of being, a sense of confidence and trust that the world is what it appears to be'.[136] The sense of ontological security derived from Giddens's work is structured through four issues. First, self-identity is based on a sense of biographical coherence, which is communicable and allows for agency, performed in everyday routine. Second, this is embedded in trust structures, notably in social tokens and in professional experts. Third, agency conforms to the sense of

---

[134] William Cowper, 'An Epistle to Joseph Hill, Esq', in *The Task and Other Poems*, Kila, MT: Kessinger Publishing Co., 2004, p. 161.

[135] See Anthony Barnett, 'British Library Opens Taking Liberties', *openDemocracy*, 30 October 2008, at www.opendemocracy.net [accessed August 2009].

[136] Zarakol, 'Ontological (In)Security and State Denial Of Historical Crimes', p. 6; McSweeney, *Security, Identity and Interests*, p. 156; Kinnvall, *Political Psychology*, p. 746.

self-integrity, of the appropriate and the acceptable. Fourth, even the most ontologically secure individual has a sense of the polar opposite condition. In this context, the nation creates a framework – here, Britishness – within which everyday life can be constructed and performed. This national identity is rarely the predominant element in the lives of individuals; but it is sometimes, and for many more it is one of the foundations. And the works of each of the three examples examined here contributed to that sense of ontological security, in different ways and at particular times. All three examples had close relationships with the British state: but each had an independence of action as well. They were able to reflect particular senses of Britishness, but were also involved in communicating those senses through their remediations.

In relation to the first of the elements of ontological security, we can see biographical narratives of the nation embedded in each of the three examples. One of the purposes of Taking Liberties is, of course, to create that shared sense of inter-generational struggle for rights, dating back from Magna Carta. And therefore the various protestors –abolitionists, Chartists, suffragettes – have in common that sense of liberty that pervades Britishness (in the eyes of the exhibition) throughout the ages. The contemporary generation is invited to view all favourably, as contributors to the Britishness of today and thereby direct contributors to our own individual ontological security. The images, comments and jokes about the Dutch in the work of Cruikshank, or in Grose or Joe Miller, or the Rump Songs, precisely connected these generations together, from the 1600s to the 1800s, providing a sense of national continuity – the British 'we' being constituted, and thereby behaving, differently from the Hollanders. And of course, many of the works of the British Documentary Movement began with reference to the long history of the country. In these readings, that there has been a *Britain* for many, many generations, and that this has been a good thing for the people who lived on the British Isles, has been part of the starting point for what is to be said next.

For the British Documentary Movement in particular, aspects of this ongoing biography referred to the land – unchanged for a millennium, until recent upheavals – and to the sea. Both were a core element of the British story, along with a sense of the future. When tasked with persuading parents that, in the summer of 1939, evacuation of their children in the face of the potential bombardment of cities should not be questioned, even though the parents might not see those children again for years, the documentary makers produced (to the stirring national music of Elgar) images of smiling children in the countryside, and explained that 'here in the country, children are safe and happy.'[137] In *If War Should Come*, the image of the forever British/English farmland was fallen back upon. And as *Britain at Bay* built to the climax at which Priestley quoted Churchill's 'We will fight them on the beaches' speech to further images of the farmland, he made key foundational claims about the British. 'These people of ours – as easy-going and good natured as any folk in the world – who've asked for nothing belonging to others, but only for fair dealing among nations.'[138] To the twenty-first-century ear, these are extraordinary claims. 'Easy-going … folk' chimes poorly with the sense of place inherit in a rigid social class system. 'Asking for nothing belonging to others' does not ring true in the light of the enormous empire then ruled by the British. But the ever-thus narrative of the nation dominated, providing for the citizens some sense of security in their individual lives.

In relation to trust structures, the second element of ontological security, again each imagining provided different resources. We see this in Taking Liberties with the emphasis on the role of the intellectual in leading change. In the exhibition, particular emphasis was given to John Locke, Thomas Paine, Mary Wollstonecraft and William Blake in leading the way on human rights; and in terms of freedom from want, to Charles Booth and William Beveridge. Great figures, great experts could produce important changes in the nature of everyday life and, when their cause was that of the people, the message was that they had done so. Isaac Cruikshank could be relied upon to shape and reflect upon the role of particular experts – sharply, for example, in the extraordinary image of 'The Man-Mid-Wife.' Reinforcing gender roles, Cruikshank's picture is of a half-woman, half-man image: the woman 'who offers a feeding cup and is featured in a domestic setting' while the man 'holds forceps … and on the shelves are more horrific instruments as well as love potions ("for my own use")'.[139]

---

[137] Observation of 'If War Should Come' on *Land of Promise*.
[138] *Ibid.*
[139] Maria L. H. Emory, *Mother and Child Care in Art*, London: Royal Society of Medicine Press, 2007, p. 42.

As Marcia Emory puts it, 'The contrast and conclusions are clear.'[140] His work also sought to reinforce the limits of the acceptable. For example, Napoleon was frequently pictured as greedy and foolish, and thereby as less threatening. Cruikshank drew him as a baby in 'Crying for a New Toy', sitting on the floor, shouting petulantly 'I will have it, I will, give me the Crown', and being told by the Old Nurse, 'Well Child, you shall have it, but I don't think you'll be a bit better for it nor quieter when you've got it.'[141] In 'Frith the Madman Hurling Treason at the King', Edmund Burke is shown as bedraggled, mad and utterly ineffectual.[142] In 'Iohny Mac-Cree in the Dumps' he ridiculed Henry Dundas, the first Scot since the Act of Union to make it to the highest levels of British politics (Home Secretary, Secretary of War), who upon his resignation in 1805 was charged with misappropriating public funds. Importantly in the caricature, Cruikshank showed Dundas rejected by fellow Scots; he declares 'That my Countrymen turn their backs on me! Then its all up with Iohny Mac Cree', and in so doing Cruikshank was able to strengthen the core unionist, British, narrative.[143] And in the work of the British Documentary Movement, we also see the emphasis on the role of key expert groups, most notably in *Today We Live*. The film sought to give bureaucracy a human face, here in particular the National Council for Social Service with its practical commitment to supporting communities during the Great Depression. The 'image of the expert was enlarged in later films', such as in *Britain at Bay*, with its emphasis on the professionalism of the armed services.[144] And throughout, in films that demanded better housing and schooling, it was clear that the professional expert knows best.

These imaginings then allowed predictable patterns of everyday behaviour to follow: practical reliance on experts, and the

---

[140] *Ibid.*

[141] Isaac Cruikshank, 'Crying for a New Toy', 25 January 1803. Reproduced, at http://commons.wikimedia.org [accessed August 2009].

[142] See F. P. Lock, *Edmund Burke, 1784–1797*, Oxford University Press, 2006, p. 342; and John Barrell, *Imagining the King's Death: Figurative Treason, Fantasies of Regicide, 1793–1796*, Oxford University Press, 2000, with image of the caricature at p. 92.

[143] Isaac Cruikshank, 'Iohny Mac-Cree in the Dumps', National Galleries of Scotland and at www.nationalgalleries.org [accessed August 2009].

[144] Swann, *The British Documentary Film Movement, 1926–1946*, p. 116. On this aspect of 'Today We Live' see also Aitken, *Film and Reform*, p. 139.

performance of identities through the telling of jokes and stories, and in the singing of songs. The third element of ontological security is that people behave with self-integrity. That is, these psychological struggles define that which is acceptable and appropriate, which informs practice. People would behave in predictable, and shared, ways relating to their perceptions of their ontological security. Adrian Randall describes the practice of many master clothiers in the West Riding of Yorkshire of also owning small holdings as having a number of economic advantages (such as being a ready source for credit, and a source of income to ride out lows in the demand for cloth). However, those small holdings also provided a 'psychologically important sense of stability and security'.[145]

The final element in the structure of ontological security is the sense that it is not permanent, and may be threatened. In this vein, Adrian Randall quotes a Staffordshire clerical magistrate, Alexander Haden, bemoaning the role of the judiciary in supporting high prices and profiteering at the expense of the impoverished, in a private letter in 1795. Comfortable in his own ontologically secure position, he worried that 'the poor are almost shut out from the possibility of procuring the common necessaries of life ... Want of employ and the very shameful and exorbitant price of corn have brought them to utmost distress: so that unless some restraint can be laid upon the farmer and miller it will be impossible to preserve the public peace.'[146] He objected to the 'enriching of one part of the community and supporting them in the most glaring act of oppression at the expense of the comforts, happiness and even the existence of the other'.[147] The point, of course, was that the ontological insecurity of the poor would bring violence (the impossibility of preserving 'the public peace'), which would impact upon all classes. We can see similar concerns with ontological security in the films of the British Documentary Movement. For example, to images of poverty and unemployment in *Today We Live*, the narrator tells us that 'there are fundamental problems which strike at the

---

[145] Adrian Randall, *Before the Luddities: Custom, Community and Machinery in the English Woollen Industry, 1776–1809*, Cambridge University Press, 1991, paperback edn 2004, p. 223.

[146] Alexander Haden in a letter dated 10 June 1795, quoted in Adrian Randall, *Riotous Assemblies: Popular Protest in Hanovarian England*, Oxford University Press, 2006, p. 232.

[147] Alexander Haden in a letter dated 16 June 1795, quoted *ibid.*

very root of our existence.'[148] Even though a good portion of the film concerns the relatively comfortable lives of the rural English middle class, such comments indicate the sense that even in such places the dread of ontological insecurity lies.

The changing construction of identity necessarily leads to changing practices, and, of course, the four elements of ontological security are most important in how they interact. Linda Colley, guest curator of Taking Liberties, argued that the abolition of slavery came about because the manifest infringement of liberty involved did not accord with the self-image, the integrity, of being British, which was based on a construction of freedom. Describing slaves as 'British citizens' was, Colley argues, an 'adroit abolitionist strategy. It played on how large numbers of ordinary Britons – and many among the British ruling elite – wanted to see themselves and their state: as conspicuously benevolent, particularly free, a beacon and example to the world.'[149] This evokes the importance of shame in Brent Steele's writing about ontological security at the state level. Colley argued further in *Britons* that a major transformation in the national identity of the British occurred in the early nineteenth century, brought about, and also symbolized, by the Battle of Waterloo and the growth of empire. Colley argued that

[i]n a very real sense, war – recurrent, protracted and increasingly demanding war – had been the making of Great Britain. But Waterloo finally slew the dragon; and the immediate reaction among many Britons was less complacency than disorientation. How was Britishness to be defined now that it could no longer rely so absolutely on a sense of beleaguered Protestantism and on regular conflict on the Other in the shape of Catholic France?[150]

It was, Colley argues, that the British state itself was a product of this Other; that England and Scotland had united in order that the Protestants in both countries might work together to preserve that Protestantism in the face of a hostile Europe. And further, that union with Ireland in 1800 had been a direct consequence of the fear of French invasion, and of Irish Catholic support for the Catholic French against the Protestant British. 'Even more than the earlier Act

---

[148] Observation of 'Today We Live' on *Land of Promise*.
[149] Colley, *Taking Stock of Taking Liberties*, p. 27.
[150] Colley, *Britons*, p. 322.

of Union with Scotland, the immediate cause of this new political arrangement had been fear of French military intervention.'[151] And the fear of the Catholic Other abroad intersected with the fear of the Catholic Other at home; there had been Jacobite wars in 1708, 1715 and 1745, and scares of such wars in 1717, 1719, 1720, 1721, 1743, 1744 and 1759. But with Waterloo, all of that had ended; it left Britain without that major, continental, Catholic Other. It left Britain united with a major Catholic country, in Ireland. How might that arrangement actually work in practice, now that the threat had gone? With the defeat of Napoleon, Britain had been left as 'indisputably the foremost European power. Moreover, the ensuing division of the spoils at the Congress of Vienna ensured that the British Empire emerged from the war the largest the world had ever known.'[152]

That which Britain had been constructed to mean, therefore, was up for renegotiation after 1815. It had once been based on a cohesive Protestantism in the face of powerful Catholic Others, but now Britain had emerged from being beleaguered to being the foremost power. Once determinedly Protestant within, it now connected with large numbers of (Irish) Catholic citizens. Once the raider of the outside world for resources, it now ruled enormous swathes of land, and the peoples that lived there. And in what was once a highly elitist society, the mobilizations of so many people in so many ways in the war against Napoleon now led to demands from those people for change, expressed through, for example, 'successive waves of petitions weighed down with signatures' to Parliament.[153] Thus Britain after 1815 was not one of unbridled joy, but one of deep collective searching for new meaning, and what Colley describes as a 'profound loss of direction'.[154] It must have been a time, for some individuals, when Britishness failed to contribute to their ontological security. But the Britishness project gripped the nation and came to be symbolized through three transforming pieces of legislation: removing restrictions on Catholics, abolishing slavery and reforming Parliament. Colley argues that '[t]he rate of political change in Britain in the two decades after Waterloo suggests that there *is* a relationship – albeit a complex one – between mass involvement in a war effort and the widening of political rights and participation'.[155] In the period between 1828

[151] *Ibid.*   [152] *Ibid.*, p. 321.
[153] *Ibid.*, p. 363.   [154] *Ibid.*, p. 322.   [155] *Ibid.*, p. 371.

and 1833, there were 3,000 petitions arguing for or against Catholic emancipation, another 3,000 on parliamentary reform and 5,000 on the abolition of slavery.[156] That these issues touched individuals on what the nation meant to them is clear. And in this work and reform, new values were attached to Britishness that were to provide contemporary supports to the contribution of the nation to ontological security. The old order was out: 'By passing Catholic emancipation in 1829, Britain's rulers unavoidably compromised Protestantism's value as a national cement ... [but] Peaceful and orderly constitutional reform and pioneering and successful abolitionism would serve for many as further and conclusive proofs of the superior quality of British freedom.'[157]

Thus, in different ways, Cruikshank, Grierson and Colley all reflect and perpetuate the ways in which the national identity, socially transmitted, can provide means of support for the ontological security of individuals. And much of this is through the imagery and tokens that come to represent that permanent and fixed sense of nation that contributes to the ontological security of those individuals. This can be seen in three, interrelated contemporary dimensions: shared topics for conversation; shared social practices; and a shared recognition of the meaning of images. There are shared discursive norms; British people traditionally would expect to talk about the weather when meeting, for example, and would not expect to talk about politics or religion. Then there are shared social practices: the expectation of a turkey and a tree at Christmas, evoking the feast of medieval times. Or going to the pub, and drinking British (or Irish) beer, connecting to a sense that this is part of normal national behaviour for generations. Of course, not everyone acts in these ways, and even those who do, do not do so always; but there is a 'norm' that is recognized. In the past, practices would have included celebrations of royal occasions (monarch's birthdays, coronations, weddings and anniversaries), and these do still take place. A more contemporary reading would be pride in the National Health Service, and the expectation that it is normal to put the future of the individual – his or her health – safely in the hands of those professionals.

[156] *Ibid.*, p. 362. On the issue of slavery, Parliament had voted to abolish the trade in 1807 (Slave Trade Act), but it was not until the Slavery Abolition Act of 1833 that slavery itself was abolished.

[157] Colley, *Britons*, p. 361.

Part of the sharing of social practices includes food: roast beef, fish and chips, and possibly curry. A vital social practice is the currency, evoking through its imagery both the longevity of the state with the monarch, and the great figures of Britain's past. Contemporary British banknotes showcase individuals whose contributions would make their representations at home in Taking Liberties. On the £5 note, Elizabeth Fry; female, Quaker, prison and social reformer. On the £10 note, Charles Darwin, intellectual reformer of science and religion. The £20 note has an image of Edward Elgar, the great composer of imperial music, and on newer notes Adam Smith, Scottish intellectual of the Enlightenment. Finally, the £50 note shows both James Watt and Mathew Boulton, Scottish and English partners in the Industrial Revolution.

And then there are the images that evoke the stable, peaceful, ever-Britain: cricket on the village green; the mother of parliaments, symbolized by Big Ben; the Tower of London and the Crown Jewels. Also symbols of triumph in a just cause – the Spitfire, and the Lancaster, or the Tommy, the First World War soldier who suffered owing to a class injustice that is no more. And this can have national dimensions: the White Cliffs of Dover, the kilt and bagpipes, the daffodil and Eisteddfod. Regional dimensions have declined, but still it is more common to see people wearing local football shirts in the United Kingdom than it would be in many other countries. There are performances and behaviours that are routine, appropriate and acceptable means by which dread is kept at bay.

Perhaps some of this is most obvious in relation to Britons abroad. A survey of British holidaymakers by the travel company Airtours in 1999 found that:

- 50% ate only fish and chips and English breakfasts when abroad
- 14% of men took their football team's shirt with them
- A small hardcore have also taken the Union Flag
- 34% of Britons have taken an umbrella abroad
- 21% have packed a cagoule
- 1% took English teabags with them.[158]

This was deemed to be problematic, reflecting a determination to keep to everyday ways of living, without sharing in local behaviours

---

[158] 'Sun, Sea and Sand for Brits Abroad', 14 July 1999, *BBC Online*, at http://news.bbc.co.uk [accessed August 2009].

and norms. In subsequent commentary on the BBC message board, 'Ed' from 'England' explained that 'in general, it tends to be the working classes who give the English a bad name overseas. The reference to football shirts proves this.'[159] Class, as a defining aspect of Britishness, was clearly brought to the fore. Kevin Paulaskas wrote: 'I am an Englishman living and working in Boston with an American wife and I am proud to be English and will show it in any way possible i.e. Football Shirt, Union Jack, Cross of Saint George, English Beer, Tea Bags etc. Why not be proud of who you are.'[160] Some seek to evoke those symbols consciously to mark their national identity, to reinscribe that which is providing for them an important pillar in their own ontological security. Diana Kozuh, a British citizen living in America, wrote that 'when I travel I have to limit my intake of "foreign food" because I don't want to spend my time in the loo and my money on diarrhoea medication.'[161] As in many cultures, 'othering' is equated with 'unclean', all the more notable for a Briton living abroad.

Yet it is perhaps with the Britons living permanently abroad that the struggle with the contribution that the national makes to ontological security is most pronounced. Caroline Knowles and Douglas Harper wrote of the lives of the British expatriates in Hong Kong, after the return to Chinese rule. We learn of Ellen, who 'returned to Britain annually throughout her now grown-up children's childhood. The entire family would go to the rural north of Britain. Here they would stay in a rented cottage ... Ellen's version of a "proper" British life involves animals and rural landscape as well as family connection and provides a counterpoint to a thoroughly urban existence in Hong Kong.'[162] Knowles and Harper showed the ways in which the expatriates maintained their sense of Britishness; in their inability to speak Cantonese; in their struggle to get 'British'-style meat (sufficient lamb, for example); in their refusal to travel in similar ways to the local population; in their structured meetings with Chinese people; in visits 'back' to the UK; in their structured communications

[159] 'Are Brits Too British Abroad?', *BBC Online* discussion board, 26 July 1999, contributions undated [accessed August 2009].
[160] *Ibid.*   [161] *Ibid.*
[162] Caroline Knowles and Douglas Harper, *Hong Kong: Migrant Lives, Landscapes and Journeys*, University of Chicago Press, 2009, p. 145.

'back' – the card list of 200 people to receive Christmas cards and a standard letter detailing the family's year. Through all these routines and practices, they maintain their sense of Britishness.

In research published in 2006, the Institute for Public Policy Research argued that 5.5 million British citizens reside permanently outside the United Kingdom, representing nearly 10 per cent of the population. The top four countries of such residence are Australia (1.3 million), Spain (761,000), the United States (678,000) and Canada (603,000); no other country has a permanent residence of Britons over half a million.[163] On the website British Expats we can learn a good deal of the motivations for such a radical transformation in the lives of so many individuals; much of the language is about 'escaping' the homeland.[164] Yet the relationship is not that simple; it is not just about rejecting all that is wrong with the state, because the national inscriptions are deep on the individual, and connect with the sense of ontological security. Of the forty-three posts to the Australia section of *British Expats* following England's victory in the 2009 Ashes cricket series, thirty-nine explicitly celebrated the English win over the new homeland; other posts debated whether 'England' actually represented 'Britain' in the world of cricket, and whether it was sufficiently inclusive of the nations of Great Britain. But as 'Pompey Blonde' put it, 'the longer I'm here the more I support England!'[165]

Connection with the nation, expressed most conveniently through food as above, or sport as in this example, illustrates that for those migrating dissatisfaction with the opportunities in the state do not necessarily disconnect the individual from the sense of the nation. When 'Wigan Warrior' wrote asking for information about an area in Australia to which he and his family were moving, he received a reply which began 'I'll answer you – even though you are a pie eater' – thus making sure that the British sporting affiliations were marked, as Wigan's rugby club has the nickname 'the pie eaters'. With

163 The data has been visualized by the BBC: See 'Brits Abroad', at http://news. bbc.co.uk [accessed August 2009].
164 See for example, 'Splatt' [Member name], 'Spain, Sun and Signs', *British Expats*, 17 February 2009, at http://britishexpats.com [accessed August 2009] who wrote of 'escaping England'.
165 'Pompey Blonde' had lived in Sydney since April 2005; post at 'England Regain the Ashes', *British Expats*, posted 23 August, at http://britishexpats. com [accessed August 2009].

common identity thus marked, and affinity thus demonstrated, the reply explained that the area 'is generally a "white christian" area, I'm not being racist – just stating it how it is i.e. there is no significant Muslim, Chinese, Indian, etc.'.[166] Here, implicitly, a contrast was being drawn with the imagined home of the 'Wigan Warrior', with an implicit assumption as to one of the motives for migration.

'Shoz in Aus' wrote of the family return to Britain after two and a half years in Australia as a failed migration. Seeking to explain this, she wrote: 'We like the feeling that things are actually happening here. Somehow I feel so much more ALIVE.'[167] Laing had written that the ontologically secure person 'may have a sense of his presence in the world as a real, alive, whole ... person'.[168] 'Shoz' was evoking precisely this description of being in the nation, as opposed to being geographically separated from its norms and practices. Finally, 'Professional Princess' wrote that during the application for a visa to migrate to Australia she had felt many emotions, but 'they all boiled back down to a strong dislike of the UK.' However, as the prospect of emigrating became a reality:

I was at Lambeth embankment on business and as I glanced up I spotted the Houses of Parliament and Big Ben. Lots of boats sailed slowly down the Thames. I had seen it a hundred times if not more, but this time I really saw it. Staring round at all the old buildings, the history, the sun shining, the tacky souvenir shops at the bridge, I grabbed my mobile phone and called the one person I pour my feelings to – my Mum. 'Mum, I'm looking at Big Ben and the Houses of Parliament, I have never noticed how beautiful London is!' ... [I] watched the VE day celebrations on TV, I really wish that I had gone to see it live in London instead of watching it on TV. Seeing those proud war vets choking with emotion ... Our history is so incredible, I can't believe we are contributing to it in our own small way.[169]

When Laing had written of the ontologically secure individual being 'in a temporal sense, a continuous person', he could have been

---

[166] 'Red_V_Roger' post 22 August 2009, *British Expats, at* http://britishexpats.com [August 2009]; a member of the site for over two years.
[167] 'Shoz in Aus', '6 Weeks Back in England', *British Expats*, 9 June 2006, at http://britishexpats.com [accessed August 2009]; emphasis in the original.
[168] Laing, *The Divided Self*, p. 39.
[169] 'Professional Princess', 'What Makes Britain "Great"', *British Expats*, 18 August 2005, at http://britishexpats.com [accessed August 2009].

describing 'Professional Princess'. She saw the images of London and Britain, of the nation's past, in a new light: one that described to her a role and identity, one made more alive by her then-desire to migrate.

The nation, and hereby Britishness, therefore has an important function in offering a structure for the ontological security of the individual. But those functions and imaginings, in bringing together many, will have consequences for 'others'. The next chapter examines how the structures that provide ontological security for some can lead to ontological insecurity for others; it examines the social process of the securitization of identity.

2 | A post-Copenhagen securitization theory

Introduction

Ontological security is not, as we have seen, a condition enjoyed by all individuals. And the denial of identity structures to particular groups may be a root of the ontological insecurity of some individuals, or at least might significantly increase their sense of dread. That is, the securitization of identities is a crucial issue for the understanding of ontological security. The securitization of identity leads to the securitization of subjectivity – the intensified search for and/or attribution of a single, stable identity, 'regardless of its actual existence'.[1] How are identities securitized, leading to the construction of ontological insecurity for some individuals?

This chapter seeks to establish the new mainstream in non-American security studies work produced in the English language, not in order to follow securitization theory slavishly, but rather to establish it as the new grammar for security studies. That grammar is then redeployed in different ways: that is, the four key elements of securitization theory are amended to produce a 'post-Copenhagen securitization theory'. However, this is not sufficient in and of itself, because there are three elements that need to be developed in the context of this 'post-Copenhagen' project, elements that are not privileged in the Copenhagen School's framework. In turn, these elements focus on the roles of identity, spatiality and temporality. Securitizations reconstitute all three elements, and this is accounted for in this new 'post-Copenhagen securitization theory', which enables us to understand more fully dread and ontological insecurity.

The development of new approaches to security studies – even when building on, rather than rejecting, previous frameworks – raises issues

---

[1] Catarina Kinnvall, 'Globalization and Religious Nationalism: Self, Identity, and the Search for Ontological Security', *Political Psychology*, 25(5), 2004: 749.

of method, data sources and ethics, and each of these elements is considered at the end of this chapter.[2] What is at stake is understanding not only how particular constructions of national identity might contribute to the ontological security of individuals, but also how the performance of rituals and routines associated with that identity might increase dread in others: that is, understanding how ontological security for some might lead to, or even necessitate, securitization of the identity of others. Examples can be found in many cultures, and in many times. As far as the British were concerned, during the sixteenth to eighteenth centuries performing the national identity meant, for many, performing anti-Catholic routines. Catholics were discriminated against by law; and a number of Catholics were executed purely for being Catholics. One such person was John Wall, born in 1620, arrested in Rushock, Worcestershire in 1678 on mistaken identity by officers searching for a debtor. Wall was clearly not that man, so he was instead interrogated in connection with the so-called Popish Plot, engineered by Titus Oates to enhance his own political position by whipping up anti-Catholic agitation. Wall was manifestly not guilty of treason and, despite the agitation, was found not guilty. All he had to do to secure his release was to swear an oath of allegiance to the king – which he was happy to do – and also to swear the oath of supremacy, by which the king was declared the head of the church. Refusal to perform this routine act was to cost Wall his life. His ontological security – although, of course, not his physical security – lay in remaining loyal to the Pope and to his faith. Ontological security for the English state (and for the Scottish – see the fate, for example, of John Ogilvie) lay in performing executions of individuals, with dread of their Catholic faith and continental allies a motivating factor.[3] Indeed, this was one of the uniting cultural factors that, subsequently, allowed a *Britain* to be formed.

[2] Of great importance in opening security studies to these forms of analysis were Barry Buzan *People, States and Fear*, 2nd edn, Boulder, CO: Lynne Rienner, 1991; and David Campbell, *Writing Security*, 2nd edn, Minneapolis: University of Minnesota Press, 1998.

[3] On John Wall, see John Kenyon, *The Popish Plot*, London: William Heinemann, 1972. However, as Kenyon shows, public revulsion, at these executions was in part that they were *un*-British in character (p. 206). Wall, and thirty-nine others, were made saints by the Pope in 1970.

Securitization theory, beyond the Copenhagen School

The nature of security studies, as a sub-discipline of international relations, has been deeply contested for many decades. However, certainly in the past twenty-five years, there has been an intensification of the arguments over what security might be seen to comprise. Steve Smith has argued that since the early 1980s security has become 'genuinely a contested concept'.[4] In this context, inevitably there have been determined attempts to represent groups of theories as like-minded. One such representation of this is the contrast between 'traditional' and 'non-traditional' security; between military security issues and those that include 'societies and human collectivities. Consequently, issues like infectious diseases, environmental degradation, trafficking in illegal drugs, people smuggling and trafficking and others are being discussed in academic circles as pressing concerns with security implications.'[5] Another representation sought to create a distinction between realism, liberalism and 'critical theory' (which here comprised Frankfurt School-inspired work, and post-structural work).[6] A third take makes a distinction between international relations (and thereby security studies) in America and Europe.[7]

A different form of representation for the sub-field of security studies would be to emphasize the development of a coherent brand of critical security studies in the period since the middle of the 1990s.[8]

[4] Steve Smith, 'The Increasing Insecurity of Security Studies: Conceptualizing Security in the Last Twenty Years', in Stuart Croft and Terry Terriff (eds.), *Critical Reflections on Security and Change*, London: Frank Cass, 2000, p. 96.

[5] Mely Callabero-Anthony and Ralf Emmers, 'Understanding the Dynamics of Securitizing Non-Traditional Security', in Mely Callabero-Anthony *et al.* (eds.), *Non-Traditional Security in Asia: Dilemmas in Securitisation*, Aldershot: Ashgate, 2006, p. 1.

[6] Most famously, of course, John J. Mearsheimer, 'The False Logic of International Institutions', *International Security* 19(3), Winter 1994/5: 5–49.

[7] Most notably, Ole Waever, 'The Sociology of a Not So International Discipline: American and European Developments in International Relations', *International Organization*, 52(4), 1998; but see also c.a.s.e collective, 'Critical Approaches to Security in Europe', *Security Dialogue* 37(4), 2006: 443–87.

[8] See in particular Keith Krause and Michael Williams (eds.), *Critical Security Studies: Concepts and Strategies*, London: Routledge, 1997; and Ken Booth (ed.), *Critical Security Studies and World Politics*, Boulder, CO: Lynne Rienner, 2004.

Under this umbrella we might identify three different and yet related types of theory.[9] The first is the work of the Copenhagen School, with its key 'brand' concept, securitization, focusing on the way in which states construct security issues beyond the realm of normal politics. The second is the Welsh School with its leitmotif, emancipation and with a normative demand for action to emancipate individuals. And the third is the Paris School, with its key focus on *insécurisation*, the concern with the means by which elites and government authority lower the threshold of acceptability of others, and where a variety of discourses are connected into a variety of insecurities, allowing the transfer of practices from one policy arena to another. For example, the 'c.a.s.e. collective' seeks to constrain that which comprises critical security studies to these three sets of theories and ideas.[10] However, it is possible to consider an additional candidate for membership of this family of 'critical security studies'. That contender, human security, has but a loose attachment to critical security studies. Critical in the sense of being non-state in focus, it does not share an epistemological connection to the other schools of thought in terms of a focus on the constructed nature of social reality. It is perhaps a matter of taste as to whether it should or should not be included in this family of theories.

Imagining critical security studies in this way gives the sense of a vibrant field of intellectual interchange. However, there is no clear agreement that we have a coherent grouping of theories under this label. Ken Booth resists putting the Welsh School alongside those theories that are state-centric (by which he means the Copenhagen School) or alongside others that reject positivism (i.e. the Paris School); for Booth, 'There is no problem with a critical theorist adopting positivist procedures.'[11] For Aradau, the lack of political responsibility in the Copenhagen School means that it is a theory that cannot be related to other approaches that concern themselves with the normative.[12]

---

[9] Based on Stuart Croft, 'Conclusion', in Paul Williams (ed.), *Security Studies*, London: Routledge, 2008.

[10] c.a.s.e collective, 'Critical Approaches to Security in Europe'.

[11] Ken Booth, *Theory of World Security*, Cambridge University Press, 2007, p. 194.

[12] Claudia Aradau, 'Security and the Democratic Scene: Desecuritization and Emancipation', *Journal of International Relations and Development* 7(4), 2004: 388–413, especially p. 389.

For Floyd, there are fundamental distinctions between the concept of human security and the work of the Copenhagen School.[13] Another way of imagining the field would not focus on picturing four (or three) schools of thought engaged in an interchange, as has been laid out immediately above. Rather, the field would be envisaged as comprising one dominant approach, with three (or two) niche areas of research. For it is the Copenhagen School that has achieved that position of dominance; for example, at the 2008 International Studies Association Annual Convention, over thirty papers focused in some way on the Copenhagen School, and fewer than six on the Paris and Welsh schools. That is a partial representation; the vast majority of those presenting such papers were based in European (or Oceanic) institutions. But when this is viewed alongside the range of publications and recently completed doctorates emerging in the non-American English language world, it is reasonable to suggest that the Copenhagen School has become as mainstream as it is possible to get.

Securitization theory has become a widely deployed term in the study of international security since the mid 1990s.[14] One of the three main concepts of the Copenhagen School (the others being the sectors of security and security complexes), securitization has had a long and detailed theoretical genealogy constructed for it, drawing on authors as diverse as Derrida, Schmitt, Waltz and Austin.[15] Securitization is, in a classic Copenhagen School definition, 'the discursive process through which an intersubjective understanding is constructed within a political community to treat something as an existential threat to a valued referent object, and to enable a call for urgent and exceptional

---

[13] Rita Floyd, 'Human Security and the Copenhagen School's Securitization Approach', *Human Security Journal* (5), Winter 2007: 38–49, at www.peacecenter.sciences-po.fr [accessed July 2008].

[14] Although much has been written subsequently, the core texts are of course Barry Buzan *et al.*, *Security: A New Framework for Analysis*, Boulder, CO: Lynne Rienner, 1998; and Ole Wæver 'Securitization and Desecuritization', in *On Security*, ed. Ronnie D. Lipschutz, New York: Columbia University Press, 1995.

[15] See for example Rita Taureck, 'Securitisation Theory – The Story So Far (Part one): Theoretical Inheritance and What it Means to be a Post-Structural Realist', paper presented at the annual meeting of the International Studies Association, Town & Country Resort and Convention Center, San Diego, California, USA, 22 March 2006 www.allacademic.com [accessed June 2008].

measures to deal with the threat'.[16] Yet as well as its strict use by the Copenhagen School, securitization is also a term that is frequently used in a more lenient fashion, in which securitization as a term is stripped of its Copenhagen theory and is used to indicate simply that an issue has become the subject of debate in security terms.[17] Thus Gareth Morrell, of the Information Centre about Migration and Refugees, reflected on the 2006 Labour Party Conference as focused on 'tough talking value politics, applied particularly (but not exclusively) to *securitised* policy areas: terrorism, crime, immigration, asylum and some foreign policy (i.e. conflict not poverty)'.[18]

One way of understanding this distinction between the strict and lenient uses of securitization is to consider the work that the term 'security' does in both cases. In the strict sense, 'security' is performative: as Huysmans has put it, 'Rather than describing or picturing a condition it orders social relations into security relations.'[19] However, in the lenient use of securitization, 'security' is not considered to be performative in this sense, but is, rather, descriptive, merely labelling objects: Morrell in the above quote does not consider his discussion of securitized policy areas to be anything other than a labelling exercise, even if his practice must have other implications. In this book, I will follow the performative dimension of 'securitization', but will nevertheless deploy 'securitization' in a third way that is significantly different not only from the lenient fashion, where securitization is used as a stand-alone term, but also from the strict, Copenhagen School sense. In what follows, I use securitization in a 'post-Copenhagen sense', in which a number of the key elements of the school's concept are relaxed, and a number of new elements are added.

The idea of a 'post-Copenhagen' security analysis has been used before, in 2001, by Olaf Knudsen. He sought to critique the Copenhagen School – partly because even then he saw it as the new mainstream of critical security studies – on the grounds that it failed

---

[16] Barry Buzan and Ole Wæver, *Regions and Powers: The Structure of International Security*, Cambridge University Press, 2003, p. 491.

[17] *Ibid.*, p. 489.

[18] Gareth Morrell, 'Two Colliding or Colluding Discourses?', *Information Centre about Asylum and Refugees*, 29 September 2006, at www.icar.org.uk [accessed June 2008]; italics added.

[19] Jef Huysmans, 'Security! What do You Mean? From Concept to Thick Signifier', *European Journal of International Relations* 4(2), 1998: 232.

to focus on large-scale conflict, failed to maintain an objective core in threat conception, and failed to concentrate proportionately on the state.[20] This is not where my redeployment of securitization is situated, either epistemologically or in terms of critique. This is not an analysis of why the Copenhagen School is in any sense 'wrong'. Rather, it is an attempt to move from that new mainstream in critical security studies, to draw upon the commonly understood grammar of critical security that the Copenhagen School has developed, and to develop something related, but different, that will enable us to analyse how different structures of ontological security might clash. In order to do that, I seek to loosen the constraints on the theory in four key areas, and from there add on a greater focus in three additional areas – identities, spatiality and temporality.

Securitization theory as a mainstream endeavour in its strict, Copenhagen sense, rests on four central pillars of analysis: that securitization is a speech act; that although any actor with the necessary capabilities can securitize, in practice those capabilities are most often only held by the state; that the securitizing move works by raising the prospect of the survival of the in-group; and that a successful securitizing move may lead to the imposition of extraordinary measures, beyond the realm of normal politics, to safeguard the core group against the securitized threat. Securitization, in this strict sense, has been the subject of much debate and criticism.[21] As the new mainstream, the Copenhagen School represents a new common sense in critical security studies, and as such it represents a grammar for analysing security that is comprehensible to a wide range of scholars. I therefore use securitization theory as a starting point for

---

[20] Olav F. Knudsen, 'Post-Copenhagen security studies', *Security Dialogue* 32, 2001: 355–68.

[21] A sample of the critics would include Thierry Balzacq, 'The Three Faces of Securitization: Political Agency, Audience and Context', *European Journal of International Relations* 11(2), 2005: 171–201; Jef Huysmans, 'Revisiting Copenhagen', *European Journal of International Relations* 4(4), 1998: 479–504; Olav F. Knudsen, 'Post Copenhagen Security Studies: Desecuritizing Securitization', *Security Dialogue* 32(3), 2001: 355–68; Claire Wilkinson, 'The Copenhagen School on Tour in Kyrgyzstan: Is Securitization Theory Useable outside Europe?', *Security Dialogue*. 38(1) 2007: 5–25; and Hazel Smith, 'Bad, Mad, Sad or Rational Actor? Why the "Securitisation" Paradigm Makes for Poor Policy Analysis of North Korea', *International Affairs* 76(3), 2000: 593–617.

moving to a post-Copenhagen form of securitization in order to analyse ontological security by proposing amendments to each of these
four pillars.

The first pillar of securitization theory is that the process of securitization is that of a speech act. Given the intersubjective nature of
social reality, the nature of an issue can be changed from one where it
can be understood to be in the realm of politics, to one where it can be
called into the realm of security, by the performative nature of speech.
As Waever put it, the use of 'the security label does not merely reflect
whether a problem is a security problem, it is also a political choice,
that is a decision for conceptualization a special way. When an issue
is "securitized" the act itself tends to lead to certain ways of address-
ing it.'[22] In line with writers such as Williams and Hansen, the first
amendment to strict securitization theory would suggest that rather
than the importance of intersubjectivity being understood purely
through speech, meaning can also be transmitted by silence, and by
image.[23] That is, security meaning can be communicated through a
variety of texts and not just those that are explicitly formed by language. More significantly, this meaning changes the conceptual frame
from (purely) intersubjectivity to intertextuality. Intersubjectivity is
concerned with shared understandings that may be spoken explicitly,
or may be inherent (hence 'common sense'). But with intertextuality, whether explicit or inherent in a particular social context, such
meaning is communicated and shared not only directly through that
particular text, but also because a particular text is situated within a
whole series of other signs and texts.

An example of an intertextual reading of an image is Turner's
painting *The Fighting Temeraire*, completed in 1839.[24] The painting

[22] Ole Wæver, 'Securitization and Desecuritization', p. 65.
[23] See Lene Hansen, 'The Little Mermaid's Silent Security Dilemma and the
Absence of Gender in the Copenhagen School', *Millennium* 29(2), 2000:
289–306; Michael C. Williams, 'Words, Images, Enemies: Securitization and
International Politics', *International Studies Quarterly* 47, 2003: 511–31;
and Lene Hansen, 'The Clash of Cartoons? The Clash of Civilizations?
Media and Identity in the Danish 2006 Cartoon Case', paper presented at
the annual meeting of the International Studies Association 48th Annual
Convention, Hilton Chicago, Chicago, IL, 28 February 2007.
[24] The painting is in the National Gallery, and an image in on their website,
at www.nationalgallery.org.uk [accessed July 2008]. Thanks to William
Paterson and Adrian Randall for this example.

is of an old ship being towed in the sunset. But the intertextual message read by the early Victorian viewer was concerned with national glory, contemporary malaise and modernity. The ship in the painting – *The Temeraire* – had been an important one in the Battle of Trafalgar, and it was a newsworthy event that the ship was being towed to Rotherhithe to be broken up. The Victorian viewer would have read first in this picture an evocation of the heroism of Trafalgar, and second an epitaph for the subsequent decline of the British navy. Further, Turner had painted the sun in the wrong place in the sky, to evoke a romantic sense of the end of the sail age and the arrival of steam. Although a beautiful painting, it was surely the intertextual elements that led *The Fighting Temeraire* to win a popular vote in 2005 as BBC Radio 4's *Today* programme's 'Greatest Painting in Britain'. It was perhaps not the intertextuality of the decline of the British navy that led *The Fighting Temeraire* to win with 27 per cent of the vote, but that in the year of the two hundredth anniversary of the Battle of Trafalgar, the news about that anniversary created a context – an intertextual reading – for the painting's support 146 years after its completion.[25] It is in the construction of these intertextualities that national narratives can be entwined with those of the individual, contributing to the sense of ontological security.

The second pillar of the Copenhagen School is that the calling for the securitization of an issue through a speech act must be undertaken by the key agent in society, which in most contemporary cases is the state. It is fair to say that in the theoretical discussions of the Copenhagen School the securitizing actor is not seen to be exclusively the leader(s) of the state, but 'most securitizations are still performed by state actors, as these – unlike most other securitizing actors – have the capabilities to make securitizations happen'.[26] Perhaps the classic representation of the state-centric nature of securitization theory is Buzan and Waever's *Regions and Powers*, in which they justify the nature of the approach as 'not dogmatically state centric in its premises … state-centric in its findings'.[27] If we were to continue to develop

---

[25] There were in total 118,111 recorded votes. See 'The Greatest Painting in Britain Vote', BBC Radio 4 *Today*, 2005, at www.bbc.co.uk [accessed July 2008].

[26] Rita Floyd, 'Human Security and the Copenhagen School's Securitization Approach', *Human Security Journal 5*, Winter 2007: 41.

[27] Buzan and Waever, *Regions and Powers*, p. 71.

a less strict post-Copenhagen security study (and contra Knudsen), rather than privilege the state as the focal point for the call of securitizing it would be important to focus on the role of all socially powerful agents both in producing and in reproducing securitizations. This is perhaps more a point of practice than a theoretical difference with the Copenhagen School, but it is an important point, for it means that securitizations can be produced by actors such as those in television and the print media, by think tanks and non-governmental organizations, by religious bodies and by novelists. In short, it allows an analysis of the cultural sources of securitization to be undertaken.[28] It matters when a Prime Minister makes a securitizing move. But it also matters when major newspapers, religious figures and cultural commentators do so.

We need to conceptualize power as being concentrated not simply in the hands of government, but in a wider elite. This wider political and cultural elite would include politicians and other officials of the state, the most influential media, those notable in cultural positions of power, in those economic structures that are particularly influential, senior military and police figures, and the leaders of powerful religious bodies. Although there will, of course, be significant political differences between these various actors, to form an elite they must share a common discourse: a common sense of what comprises the collective identity, not just of the elite, but of the social whole, and consequently a shared view of that which threatens the whole. Securitizing moves, then, can be made from any direction from within this elite, and will reflect wider elite discourse. Classic elite theorists, such as C. Wright Mills, emphasized three mechanisms: an elite sharing similar social and educational backgrounds (and undoubtedly often race, ethnicity and gender); one based on interconnections between the highest echelons of the various bureaucratic structures that can lead to shared interests; and thereby, thirdly, informal coordination.[29] Thus, securitization through a speech act appears to be a process different from that envisaged by the Copenhagen School, should society be conceptualized in terms of a power elite. Governments might announce

---

[28] This is something that I attempted in relation to the United States in *Culture, Crisis and America's War on Terror*, Cambridge University Press, 2006.

[29] C. Wright Mills, *The Power Elite*, Oxford University Press, 2000 (first published 1956), pp. 19–20.

securitizations, but much work might well be done by other social agents; indeed, it might be a role for governments to ratify securitizations that have been made elsewhere in the elite. In democratic societies, securitizations cannot simply be declared by central government. They must be grown by elements of the whole elite, working and reconstructing discourses and intertextual readings, recasting collective memory and collective forgetting. In such ways, the contribution of the 'national' to ontological security can be recast and, if accepted, performed differently.

Third, in calling a security issue into being, for the Copenhagen School the caller mobilizes support among the audience by asserting that the survival of the in-group is at stake. This is the securitizing move, which 'is the move that takes politics beyond the established rules of the game and frames the issue as either a special kind of politics or above politics'.[30] A post-Copenhagen approach would relax this assumption. Although there is a central role for government and other socially powerful actors in behaving as norm entrepreneurs in the process of securitization, this does not reduce the audience – here, the wider society that is defined as being the in-group – to the role of bystanders. Rather, the wider audience itself performs various roles that are crucial to the politics of securitization. A successful securitizing move will see the audience reconstructed, (re)dividing into the categories called for by that securitization. Or it might see elements of the audience performing resistance to that securitization.

The shift here follows that from the previous discussion. If social power rests in a power elite – who are thereby able to make securitizing moves from a range of social positions – it does not follow that the sole identity in whose interests such moves are being made is that of the elite. The power elite will understand their identity in part as being co-constituted with a wider society, and it is that wider social grouping that must be mobilized as part of a successful securitization. That is, the securitizing move, to be successful, must be accepted as such by elite and audience. And in that acceptance, the performance of everyday routine alters, reflecting new contributions to the ontological security of individuals. But crucially, the audience is not fixed – as in, for example, the category of 'the electorate' – but itself may be reconstituted by the securitizing act. Thus, for example, German Jews

---

[30] Buzan *et al.*, *Security: A New Framework for Analysis*, p. 23.

who had entered Britain as refugees before the outbreak of the Second World War were reconstructed from 'victim' and 'future Britons' into 'actual' and 'potential' enemies once war broke out. These included some 4,000 women who were interned on the Isle of Man for a period of years. As Miriam Kochan concluded, 'There is no hard and fast, no sensible explanation of why some 4,000 women, many of whom had fled the Nazi terror, were treated as suspect and lost a period of their lives behind barbed wire.'[31] The process of securitization reconstructed the identity of these women – and reconstructed it again, as the majority were released after a couple of years, no longer constructed through the prism of a threat.

If the third pillar is about the nature of the production of a securitization, the final pillar of Copenhagen School theory examines the implications of a *successful* securitization. A securitizing move may, if accepted by the audience, legitimize the use of extraordinary measures in the interests of the threatened self, measures that are accepted as necessary by the audience: 'what is essential is the designation of an existential threat requiring emergency action or special measures and the acceptance of that designation by a significant audience'.[32] For a post-Copenhagen approach, the extraordinary measures that are brought forward by a successful securitization are not merely enacted by government, but are the product of wider performances in and throughout society: that is, the ways in which, in Judith Butler's sense, performatives – a 'process of iterability, a regularized and constrained repetition of norms' that exceeds the performer, *and* performances ('as bounded "act"') – are shaped in and by particular securitizations.[33] What is important is not only the enacting of new legislation, for example, but also the means by which everyday life is for the citizens – the audience – reconstituted in and through the performance of that securitization, whether it be through employment practices, through jokes, or by specific expressions of identity such as

---

[31] Miriam Kochan, 'Women's Experience of Internment', in David Cesarani and Tony Kushner (eds.), *The Internment of Aliens in Twentieth Century Britain*, London: Frank Cass, 1993, pp. 165–6. Or the case of John Kitsuse, one of the leading sociologists of social constructivism, who, despite being born in California, spent more than a year in an internment camp in Los Angeles for being a 'Japanese American'.

[32] *Ibid.*, p. 27.

[33] Judith Butler, *Bodies that Matter: On the Discursive Limits of 'Sex'*, London: Routledge, 1993, pp. 95 and 234 respectively.

those which occur in the field of sport. The audience thus co-produces the new social reality which, as a consequence, allows for a reconstitution of collective memory.

What occurs, then, is analytically a two-stage process. In the first instance, the practices of identity reconstruction need to be performed not only by the elite, but also by the audience. This is a process of the audience accepting, extending and deepening the securitizing move made by the elite. And then once there is a successful securitization, it is important for the audience to continue to perform the new identity constructions, reinforcing in the everyday that which has become the new social reality. And here, the link to ontological security is clear: ontological security is maintained through the performance of routine, and the national elements of that routine are altered through securitizations. A securitizing move may, of course, fail in the sense that it is not accepted, or that it is partially accepted and subject to resistance. But even if accepted, once there is a failure to perform that particular securitization is likely to wither, to be replaced or overlaid at some point by a new securitization. During the 1940s and 1950s, as McCarthyism took root in the United States, 'The nation's policymakers and the public had to be convinced that Communism was so bad and dangerous that it had to be driven out of American life.'[34] The performances that followed included imprisonments, harassment, job loss. But McCarthyism also died out, a victim of resistance and internal contradiction.

So a post-Copenhagen securitization theory would focus not only on speech but also on the intertextuality of images and silences; it would explicitly examine not only the securitizing moves of governments, but also those of other elite social agents in society; it would analyse the ways in which securitizing moves reconstruct audiences into in-groups and out-groups, and into those who accept the new securitization, and those who seek to resist; and it would focus on the ways in which extraordinary measures take place not only at the level of the state but also at the level of the everyday, by focusing on the performances of the securitization both in embedding that securitization by making the securitizing move everyday, and then in maintaining it subsequently in the everyday.

---

[34] Ellen Schrecker, *Many Are the Crimes: McCarthyism in America*, New York: Little, Brown, 1998, p. 120.

Reconstructions of identity, spatiality and temporality

Taken together, it is clear that in such a new post-Copenhagen securitization theory, redrawn to illuminate further the focus on ontological security, that identity becomes much more central. In terms of reconstituting identity, strict securitization has been criticized for assuming that the social production of security is sufficiently stable to be treated as an objective process.[35] However, it would be far more persuasive to understand securitization as a process rather than as an event, as a process in constant motion, and to understand that this motion is not unilinear. Thus, a successful securitizing move may lead to a variety of identity reconstructions. Of course, this is not to argue that all identities are based around securitizations; and in addition, of course, narrations of self and other do not break down to simple we-good/they-bad dichotomies.[36] Lene Hansen provides a variety of Self–Other constructions, which we might think of in terms of a typology. Her concern is to understand 'identity as constructed through processes of linking and differentiation' through particular signs.[37] Examination of those signs allows the reader to identify different forms of Otherness embedded within discourse and, in so doing, to examine which connect to structures of ontological security.

The most threatening form of other is the Radical Other, one that threatens the very existence of the Self. Here, the Other becomes increasingly understood as a dehumanized monster as the sense of threat grows. Hansen draws on the work of Connolly at this point, and it is worth expanding on Connolly's writing.[38] Connolly argues that life requires identity; we cannot make sense of the world, we cannot function fully, without becoming embedded in some identity formation.[39] However, such identity formation can only take place

---

[35] See for example Bill McSweeney, 'Identity and Security', *Review of International Studies* 22, 1996: 81–93.

[36] On the first point, see for example B. Rumelili, 'Constructing Identity and Relating to Difference: Understanding the EU's Mode of Differentiation', *Review of International Studies* 30(1), 2004: 27–47.

[37] Lene Hansen, *Security as Practice: Discourse Analysis and the Bosnian War*, London: Routledge, 2006, p. 45.

[38] *Ibid.*, pp. 46–51.

[39] This section is drawn extensively from William E. Connolly, *Identity/Difference: Democratic Negotiations of Political Paradox*, Ithaca: Cornell University Press, 1991.

in relation with other identity formations; identity constitutes itself in relation to, and in opposition with, other identities. This leads to Connolly's 'second problem of evil'; that is, that with every identity difference there are pressures (it is not inevitable) to move from identity difference into otherness, whereby the Other is constituted in normatively negative terms. As we malign the Other, indeed the more we do so, the more clearly our own identity is expressed and strengthened. And of course, in such a process ontological security structures – and hence practices – are reformed. This is not a dilemma that we can escape, because we cannot exist without identity; the best that can be achieved – and it is an important achievement – is to minimize the violence that can come with identity consolidation.

This, then, leads to Connolly's conception of what we may describe as the Radical Other. Connolly argues that 'we' may drive towards establishing a comfortable and fixed identity. However, because this is not attainable – because no identity can be fixed in such a way – 'we' remain vulnerable to what Anne-Marie Smith calls the 'lure of demonisation'.[40] Connolly sets out the problem as follows:

A powerful identity will strive to constitute a range of differences as intrinsically evil, irrational, abnormal, mad, sick, primitive, monstrous, dangerous, or anarchical – as other. It does so in order to secure itself as intrinsically good, coherent, complete, or rational and in order to protect itself from the other that would unravel its self-certainty and capacity for collective mobilization if it established its legitimacy. This constellation of constructed others now becomes both essential to the truth of powerful identity and a threat to it. The threat is posed not merely by actions the other might take to injure or defeat the true identity but by the very visibility of its mode of being as other.[41]

Connolly's concern is that although democratic structures may allow difference to be created and affirmed, they might also create the conditions for an identitarianism that is dogmatic in character.[42] In so doing, it allows violence, and the concealment of violence, by dogmatic and dominant identities.

---

[40] Anne-Marie Smith, *Laclau and Mouffe: The Radical Democratic Imaginary*, London: Routledge, 1998, p. 67.
[41] Connolly, *Identity/Difference*, p. 66.
[42] *Ibid.*, p. 159.

Quite clearly, the construction of Radical Otherness is an outcome of a successful securitization, and it is one that has profound implications for the ontological security of many. However, it is not the only form of Otherness that can be conceptualized, as Hansen has illustrated. There can be 'Hierarchical Otherness'. One example is that of the central and eastern European 'return to Europe' movement in the 1990s, whereby peoples expressed their shared identity (their 'Europeaness') and their desire to join the superior form (the Western European institutions of the European Union and NATO). Or there can be 'Temporal Otherness'. One example that Hansen draws is from the work of Ole Waever, who wrote of Europe's Other being fears of Europe's own past in its reactions to the wars in the former Yugoslavia.[43] For Waever, the Other was a transgenerational concern, the fear that those in the present might behave like those in the past. A variation on this is the Abject Other. Kinnvall discusses the ways in which attitudes to others may exist even when there are few of those others: anti-Semitism in Poland, when very few Jews live there; the phenomenon of strong anti-immigrant feeling when few immigrants live in the locale. As Kinnvall puts it, 'The other exists in our minds through imagination even when he or she is not physically present ... This implies that the enemy-other is not only created by the self, but has been a previous part of the self.'[44]

Hansen also draws attention to Doty's work on development discourse, which constructs a distance between those who have achieved particular levels of 'development', and those who must strive to achieve this state.[45] As well as Hierarchical Otherness, Temporal Otherness and Abject Otherness, we might also consider 'Neutral Otherness', in which being different carries with it no clear normative demands. A contemporary Briton, for example, may have no sense of what to make of an Andorran visitor, except that she is different. As Arash Abizadeh argues, 'It is one thing to say that identity presupposes

[43] Hansen cites Ole Waever, 'European Security Identities', *Journal of Common Market Studies* 34(1), 1996: 103–32.
[44] Catarina Kinnvall, 'Globalization and Religious Nationalism: Self, Identity, and the Search for Ontological Security', *Political Psychology* 25(5), 2004: 753.
[45] Hansen cites Roxanne Lynn Doty, *Imperial Encounters*, Minneapolis: University of Minnesota Press, 1996.

difference; it is quite another to say that it presupposes an external *other*.[46] The Andorran may be seen to be different, but she may not be othered in that process. But in comparison with the Andorran visitor, that same Briton may feel very different in relation to a Canadian visitor, with whom various cultural affinities may seem apparent. There is no necessary hierarchical relationship here, so this might be represented as Connected Otherness.

In addition, we might think of at least two other categories. In the early nineteenth century, Britons killed large numbers of the indigenous population of Tasmania.[47] They did so not because the Tasmanians represented a Radical Other; rather, they represented a Non-Human Other, whom it was possible to shoot 'like kangaroos' and poison 'like dogs', as Robert Hughes contentiously put it.[48] As well as the Non-Human Other, we can envisage a Sub-Human Other; the slave who has a role to play in society, but not a full one. It thus becomes possible to categorize a whole group of people as sharing singular characteristics, as was the case with African American slaves in the United States who, it was claimed by many whites, were 'innately patient, docile, possessive of a child-like simplicity ... imitator and non-moralist ... easily intimidated, incapable of deep plots'.[49]

So far, conceptions of Otherness that affect work on securitization, and hence on ontological security, seem to be limited to the category of the Radical Other. But they should not be seen simply so to do. There is another category of Otherness that is important, but it depends on different constructions that do not rely on enemy images; rather, they might emphasize the simplistic, unworldly or foolish images. Said wrote that 'Orientalism is fundamentally a political

[46] Arash Abizadeh, 'Does Collective Identity Presuppose an Other? On the Alleged Incoherence of Global Solidarity', *American Political Sciences Review* 99(1), February 2005: 45.
[47] Benjamin Madley, 'From Terror to Genocide: Britain's Tasmanian Penal Colony and Australia's History Wars', *Journal of British Studies* 47(1), January 2008: 77–106.
[48] Robert Hughes, *The Fatal Shore*, London: Vintage, 2003; see Henry Reynolds, 'Genocide in Tasmania', in A. Dirk Moses (ed.), *Genocide and Settler Society*, Oxford: Berghahn Books, 2005, p. 127.
[49] Herbert Aptheker's critique of such views, *American Negro Slave Revolts*, New York: Columbia University Press, 1994 (first published 1943), cited in Ellis O. Knox, 'Reviewed Work(s): American Negro Slave Revolts by Herbert Aptheker', *Journal of Negro Education* 14(2), Spring, 1945: 206–9.

doctrine willed over the Orient because the Orient was weaker than the West, which elided the Orient's difference with its weakness.'[50] A securitizing move, therefore, might produce not only a Radical Other but also an 'Orientalized Other' to be led, governed, moulded and taught. Hansen considers this when she writes about the exotic, mysterious, attractiveness of the 'Oriental' as discussed by Said, and she notes the importance of the Byronic Romanticization of the 'Balkan' during the nineteenth century.[51] The 'Orientalized Other', then, is one in which the Self is deeply engaged, sometimes attracted, sometimes frustrated. There may perhaps be harmless dimensions of this; but it is a context shot through with the political and with power, and may be frequently limiting and destructive. Securitizations may lead to the construction not only of a Radical Other, but also of an Orientalized Other.

These various types of Otherness can be represented as in Figure 2.1. No social group is fixed, which means that the securitizing move itself reconstitutes that very identity that the move is made to save. It is the securitizing actor, or rather here, in this representation, it is the threatened, securitizing Self, that constructs the Radical Other and the Orientalized Other and, in so doing, reconstitutes itself. Securitization, then, in a post-Copenhagen sense, is concerned with the performatives and performances of multiple identity reconstructions. An in-group reconstructs the out-group(s), and in so doing reconstitutes itself.

Yet in the call to a new post-Copenhagen securitization theory, in addition to these four amended pillars, and the focus on the reconstruction of identities, two further points must be added. These are drawn not only from the critiques of the Copenhagen School, but also from wider theorizing in the social sciences. Post-Copenhagen theory must focus on how securitizations reconstitute not only identity, but also the spatial and the temporal.

The spatial aspect speaks to the new focus in geography on critical geopolitics.[52] What is crucial in that context is that despite the tendency of the Self to try to achieve a fixedness, that fixedness is

---

[50] Edward Said, *Orientalism*, 3rd edn, London: Penguin, 2003, p. 204.
[51] Hansen, *Security as Practice*, pp. 40, 42–4.
[52] See, for example, Gearóid Ó Tuathail, *Critical Geopolitics: The Politics of Writing Global Space*, London: Routledge, 1996.

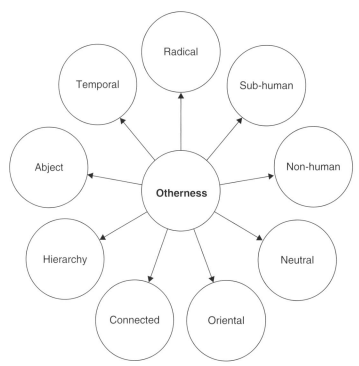

Figure 2.1 The range of Otherness

constantly challenged, in part by the constant reordering of the Other. That which is meant by 'Germany' changes over time: in the case of the British, from dynastic ally, to geopolitical challenger, to violent enemy, to vassal, to democratic ally, to emerging rival, and more, all within one hundred years from 1860 to 1960. And abstract spatial constructions may be added. Leslie Williams examines the ways in which the British press reported the Irish famine in the nineteenth century. In an examination of a cartoon in *Punch* of 1843, Williams notes that at the back of the image is a basket with 'Rint eggs' written upon it. Williams makes the following point: 'Accent and dialect were (and are) signifiers of class and ethnicity, usually implying either superiority or inferiority. Thus, *Punch*'s use of "rint" for "rent" to indicate an Irish dialect … indicated inferior character.'[53] A single

---

[53] Leslie A. Williams, *Daniel O'Connell, the British Press and the Irish*

term was able to communicate both nationality and its relative value to the reader through such intertextuality.

Gearóid Ó Tuathail has written of the 'Postmodern Geopolitical Condition', by which he means:

> where the boundaries that have traditionally delimited the geopolitical imagination are in crisis ... There is no necessary incompatibility between the postmodern geopolitical condition and the modern geopolitical imagination. In fact, the intensification of the postmodern geopolitical condition may provoke a deepening assertion of modern geopolitical imaginations and/or hybrid geopolitical imaginations that (con)fuse it with the deterritorialising tendencies associated with advanced modernity into new forms of geopolitical discourse.[54]

That is, we may see stronger assertions of spatial imaginings, precisely at the time at which those imaginings seem to be increasingly unpersuasive even among those most used to engaging in such imaginings. This connects with a wider focus on postmodern geography, to which Nigel Thrift gives full expression in a discussion of 'Space' which, he argues, has four characteristics: everything is spatially distributed, everything has 'its own geography'; there are no boundaries, all spaces are porous; all spaces are in constant motion; and 'there is no one kind of space'.[55] Threats from outside also impact on the inside as the boundary between the two breaks down. Spatial constructions are important in understanding the act of securitization, even though those spatial constructions – both through direct naming, and through more abstract terms – are themselves constantly in flux.

Securitization therefore reconstructs identities, both of the Self and of Others, and also reconstructs spatial imaginings. But what it also does is to reconstruct the temporal. Imagined communities, as Benedict Anderson has argued, call themselves into being. In part, this could be through securitizations. To paraphrase Anderson, I 'know' only a tiny percentage of my fellow British citizens; yet I am confident that their lives parallel mine, secure in the simultaneity of

    Famine: Killing Remarks, Aldershot: Ashgate, 2003, pp. 50–1.
[54] Gearóid Ó Tuathail, 'The Postmodern Geopolitical Condition: States, Statecraft, and Security, at the Millennium', *Annals of the Association of American Geographers* 90(1), March 2000: 167.
[55] Nigel Thrift, 'Space', *Theory, Culture and Society* 23(2–3), 2006: 140–1

our shared 'British' way of life – unless or until that identity, that self, becomes threatened through a securitization. At that time I intersubjectively reassess with my fellow in-group who does and who does not share my Britishness: the German-born Briton who becomes part of the out-group in 1914; the British communist who fights against fascism in Spain, but is recast as a threat during the Cold War; or the citizen of the United Kingdom who becomes the focus of suspicion because they have family links to Northern Ireland during the Troubles.[56] Similarly, when a securitizing move is made, it may be in terms of an imaged trans-historical link. As Yugoslavia descended into civil war, part of the argument was over the construction of 'old' identities. At the Battle of Kosovo Field in 1389, Milos Obilic assassinated the Ottoman Sultan. In 1989, that memory was invoked as Slobodan Milosevic, leader of the Serbs, stood on the battlefield to call Serbian nationalism to arms by saying, 'This great 600th anniversary of the Battle of Kosovo is taking place in a year in which Serbia, after many years, after many decades, has regained its state, national, and spiritual integrity. Therefore, it is not difficult for us to answer today the old question: how are we going to face Milos [Obilic].'[57] In such fashion, 'Serbia' became historic, valuable, worthy, and the assertion of a new Serb identity became a trans-generational ethical duty. Securitizations may reshape how we think of the temporal.

In these ways, I have developed a securitization framework that is post-Copenhagen in two senses. First, it loosens four of the key pillars of the Copenhagen School, broadening the focus on speech to wider communications including images and silences: enacting an examination of all social actors not just the state; analysing the impact on and involvement of the audience; and stressing the importance of the performatives. Second, it adds motion to understandings of identity, space and time, all of which are reconstituted in and through securitizations. This book is about the way in which the new terrorist threat has been securitized in the British elite, how that has created a Radical and an Orientalized Other, and how it has led to a reconstitution of Britishness. But before embarking on that part of the analysis,

---

[56] Benedict Anderson, *Imagined Communities: Reflections on the Origin and Spread of Nationalism*, 2nd edn, London and New York: Verso, 2002, pp. 22–36.

[57] Slobodan Milošević, 'Kosovo Polje Address', Vivovdan, 1989, at www.ocf. berkeley.edu [accessed September 2007].

it is important to discuss those sources that are appropriate to this theoretical framework.

Methods, sources, ethics

In order to understand the nature of contemporary securitizations in Britain, in which various members of the elite have performed securitizing moves around '(British) Islamic terrorism', it may be useful to have a discussion about the methods that will be deployed, on which sources and with what ethical implications.

Methods

In terms of method, I am seeking to identify the key identity signs in securitizing moves, and in responses to those moves.[58] It is not simply the call for action in the face of an existential threat that is important – though, of course, understanding the securitizing move is at the centre of the analysis – but also the work that such calls do in identity terms. These signs work in a relational way: the Self 'owns' the positive signs (civilized, rational), through ascribing the negative to the Other (uncivilized, irrational and so on). The positive signs are linked, and differentiated from the negative signs. Sometimes the signs relate to the Self implicitly; that is, the direct differentiation with that ascribed to the Other is left as a conclusion for the audience to draw and to share. Sometimes they are the product of deliberate construction of the Self.[59] Sometimes they are expounded at length; but over time, familiarity may lead to the use of identity shorthand.

An example of this can be taken from Prime Minister Tony Blair's Press Conference in the aftermath of the attacks in London of July 2005. He showed clearly that the enemy was a Radical Other that was therefore implacable in its aims: 'you only have to read the demands that come out from al-Qaeda to realise that there is no compromise with these people possible, you either get defeated by them or defeat them.'[60] He sought to construct a particular identity for post-bombing Britain:

---

[58] This section is developed from a close reading of Hansen, *Security as Practice*, pp. 1–92.

[59] See for example Richard Kiely *et al.*, 'The Markers and Rules of Scottish National Identity', *Sociological Review* 49(1), February 2001: 33–55.

[60] Tony Blair, 'Prime Minister's Press Conference', 5 August 2005, at www. number-10.gov.uk [accessed July 2008].

Since the 7th of July the response of the British people has been unified and dignified and remarkable. Of course there is anxiety and worry, but the country knows the purpose of terrorism is to intimidate, and it's not inclined to be intimidated. Of course too, there have been isolated and unacceptable acts of racial or religious hatred. But they have been isolated, by and large Britain knows it is a tolerant and good natured nation, it's rather proud of it, and it's responded to this terrorism with tolerance and good nature in a way that's won the admiration of people and nations the world over.[61]

Here, the call is to a united, tolerant, strong and admired identity, tested but more resolute for that testing. Failures to live by this creed – 'there have been isolated … acts of racial or religious hatred' – are 'unacceptable' and in the context of this message, profoundly un-British. He linked British values, and differentiated them from the Radical Other: 'We welcome people here who are peaceful and law abiding. People who want to be British citizens should share our values and our way of life. But if you come to our country from abroad, don't meddle in extremism. If you meddle in it or engage in it, then you're going to go back out again.'[62] Radical Others are not peaceful, law-abiding, mainstream, in the way that the British Self is. Again, he spoke of the 'duty … to share and support the values that sustain the British way of life. Those that break that duty and try to incite hatred or engage in violence against our country and it's [*sic*] people have no place here.'[63] Therefore in addition to the markers above, the Radical Other is violent and foreign in the sense of being non-British in character. And in a final statement, Blair made the signs clearer still, and shared with his audience an implicit sense of the Self in responding to a statement by Ayman Al Zawahiri claiming that the bombing attacks were the responsibility of al-Qaeda:

these very self same people who are making those remarks yesterday [al-Qaeda] are the people supporting the killing of wholly innocent people in Iraq, wholly innocent people in Afghanistan, innocent people anywhere in the world who want to live by the rules of democracy, and that's why when they try to use Iraq or use Afghanistan, or use the Palestinian cause as a means of saying we have justification for what we do, it is a complete obscenity, because what they are actually doing in countries like Iraq or

[61] *Ibid.*   [62] *Ibid.*   [63] *Ibid.*

Table 2.1. *Linked and differentiated signs in Blair's 5 August 2005*
comments

Linked signs – British Self	Differentiated signs – Radical Other
Peaceful	Violent
Supports the citizen	Murders the innocent
Democratic	Anti-democratic
Mainstream, tolerant	Extreme, marginalizing
Domestic (homely, comforting)	Foreign (strange, alien)
Decent values (unspecified)	Anti-British way of life

Afghanistan when the people have voted for democracy, is to try and stop
them getting it.[64]

By taking just this single speech, we can see how a network of
linked and differentiated signs begins to build up. The importance
of the linked signs is not only in terms of marking out the nature of
the enemy. It is also in describing some of the central contributions of
contemporary Britishness to the ontological security of individuals.
Of course, all these contributions could be contested; and all were,
to some degree, largely rhetorical. But this reflected and provided a
structure for understanding what is acceptable and appropriate in
everyday British life (see Table 2.1).

The first stage of the method is, then, to identify the linked and differentiated signs of identity, whether explicit or implicit, whether or
not deliberately deployed to co-constitute a social reality, and whether
fully spelled out or reduced – because of their multiple use over time –
to a shorthand (as with the 'Irish' example of 'rint' above). Second,
the texts need to be read for commentary in spatial or temporal terms.
In spatial terms, Blair spoke a great deal of the importance of the
'British Muslim community', but showed that 'it' existed in a particular place, alongside (rather than as a constituent part of) Britain.
He said 'it is very important in the light of the difficulty in trying to
do something like this that British Muslims should understand that

[64] *Ibid.*

they are our partners in getting this done'.[65] Here, the word 'partners' indicates the parallel space in which this 'community' was seen
to be operating. Again, he said 'The Muslim community, I should
emphasise, have been and are our partners in this endeavour. Much
of the insistence on strong action to weed out extremism is coming
most vigorously from Muslims themselves, deeply concerned lest the
activities of the fanatical fringe contaminate the good reputation of
the mainstream Muslim community in this country.'[66] A 'mainstream
Muslim community' is imagined, and given this particular identifi-
able and tolerated space in Britain: after all, Britain had 'responded to
this [Islamic] terrorism with tolerance and good nature'. In temporal
terms, this imagined 'mainstream Muslim community' is shown to
be separate over the long term: 'when you have people who have been
here sometimes 20 years or more and who still don't speak English,
that worries me'.[67] Of course, what these elements of the spatial and
the temporal show is that there is not simply a Radical Other, but
another form of Otherness under construction for this 'mainstream
Muslim community'. Taken together, these concerns created a web
of understanding about who we are and who they are, of Self and
Others, and of the nature of the problem. In addition, Blair went on
to describe a series of policy initiatives that would deal with the situation. That is, embedded within an analysis of Self, Other and threat
was a course of action that it would be necessary and responsible to
follow.

These signs are necessarily placed within a discursive context.
Henrik Larsen explains that 'discourses dictate what it is possible
to say and not possible to say. Discourses therefore provide the basis
on which policy preferences, interests and goals are constructed.'[68]
Discourse in this book is understood in this way, but also in a more
particular sense. There are a variety of individual texts through which
a securitizing move may be made, and through which securitizations
might be enacted. Those texts connect together into discourses, which
share common themes in relation to linked and differentiated signs
of identity, to the spatial and the temporal dimensions, and even in

---

[65] *Ibid.*   [66] *Ibid.*   [67] *Ibid.*
[68] Henrik Larsen, 'British and Danish European Policies in the 1990s: A
Discourse Approach', *European Journal of International Relations* 5, 1999:
453.

relation to proposals as to what should be done. However, although they share such commonality, they may well be situated in different discursive spaces. One source of some material for this book is the British National Party's message board; it would be extraordinary not to make distinctions between such a source and that of, say, the British government. But it is nevertheless important to see where there is such commonality (and of course difference) because, taken together, these discourses will comprise a meta-narrative, one that creates common sense about a particular topic. The task of a securitizing move is to reconstruct discursive space so that a new consolidated meta-narrative can take hold.

The construction of a meta-narrative may be due to a securitizing move; but it certainly will be due to the impact of a crisis. Here, 'crisis' is seen in its social dimension, echoing the critical situations that Giddens had described as 'circumstances of a radical disjuncture of an unpredictable kind which affect substantial numbers of individuals, situations that threaten or destroy the certitudes of institutionalized routines'.[69] It is not to argue that 'real' things do not happen – rather, that what is important for political analysis is the interpretation that is put to them. Ideas are rooted in our understanding of those particular events, of those crises that bring about changed perceptions and actions.[70] As Colin Hay put it, 'Crisis is the moment in which the unity of the state is discursively renegotiated and, potentially, reachieved and in which a new strategic trajectory is imposed upon the institutions that now (re-)comprise it.'[71] Thus the key element of a crisis is its discursive constitution, representing a point of rupture with that which has gone before. At this point, a variety of possible meanings could be constructed, but not an infinite variety; all possibilities must have a pre-existing form that can be drawn upon. The meaning that is ultimately agreed on for the crisis – which holds within it a clear course of action – is the decisive intervention. Thus there might be a variety of securitizing moves, based on pre-existing ideas and understandings, but the one that becomes the dominant is the decisive

[69] Anthony Giddens, *The Constitution of Society: Outline of the Theory of Structuration*, Cambridge: Polity, 1984, p. 61.
[70] See for example Terry Eagleton, *After Theory*, London: Penguin, 2003, p. 57.
[71] Colin Hay, 'Crisis and the Structural Transformation of the State: Interrogating the Process of Change', *British Journal of Politics and International Relations* 1(3), October 1999: 337.

intervention. This contestation of narratives is shaped by selectivity in relation to understandings of the crisis, and adaptivity in relation to what are understood to be the key elements of the crisis. The successful securitizing move, then, in addition to being articulated by key elements of the elite, will also be based on a narrative that is selected through its pre-existing status, and one that can be adapted to the crisis at hand. This decisive intervention – the successful securitization – produces a meta-narrative frame which contains within it a number of specific discourses. This meta-narrative frame represents a new strategic trajectory which solidifies into a period of stability. Thus, identities are called forward in response to crisis, and the successful securitization embeds performativity during the period of stability. Over time, contradictions will emerge, which come to discursively constitute the next crisis.

This means that it is important to look for securitizing moves in relation to particular moments of security crisis; to understand successful securitizations as part of a crisis cycle; and to emphasize the performative nature of those securitizations. We might conceptualize the crisis cycle as shown in Figure 2.2.[72] In relation to the contemporary British concern with terrorism, it means that we need to focus on two particular moments to understand the dynamic of securitization: the crisis of the attacks on New York and Washington DC in September 2001; and the crisis of the attacks on the London transport network in July 2005.

Sources

To understand the nature of securitizations in Britain in the early twenty-first century requires a clear strategy as to the selection of appropriate source material. The key focal point is on the meta-narrative discourse of the British elite with regard to the securitization of identities, which will then be analysed by the method outlined above. Lene Hansen offers four different routes for such a study. The first is the official discourse of the government; the second, a wider foreign policy debate including political opposition and the media;

---

[72] This is based on Croft, *Culture, Crisis and America's War on Terror*, pp. 76–81, which in turn is derived from figure 3 in Hay, 'Crisis and the structural transformation', p. 339.

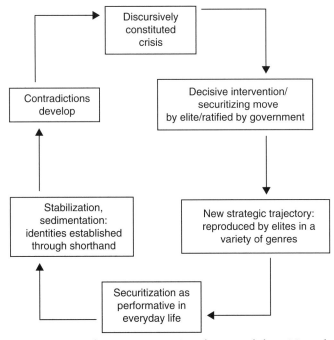

Figure 2.2 Post-Copenhagen securitization theory and the crisis cycle

the third, cultural representations (particularly in popular culture); and the fourth, what she describes as 'marginal political discourses' from non-governmental organizations and academia.[73] It is a very useful approach for thinking analytically about the nature of different research questions: however, the ambitious aim of this study is to try to cover all four to a certain extent. Core materials emanate from government spokespeople; from the popular media; from those in popular culture; and also in the discourse that is shared among a wider public. Drawing on this range of sources will enable the analysis to focus on securitizing moves across the social elite; to trace the contours of the meta-narrative and the extent to which is has become normalized throughout society (although it might still be contested); and to allow an examination of the ways in which securitizations become routinized in everyday life.

[73] Hansen, *Security as Practice*, pp. 59–64.

Of course, this relies upon an explicit notion of intertextuality: how particular texts draw upon and also recast other texts; and how this can legitimize both the 'new' text and the 'old' text. It is through intertextuality that, in a stabilized or sedimented phase, identities can be transmitted by shorthand. It allows us to draw upon and interrogate the power of metaphors in the communication of threat and identity. This can even allow us to draw upon the power of fiction in the imaginings of identity. David Dabydeen, born in Guyana but educated in Britain where he has worked throughout his career as author and educator, once said: 'Over the centuries our cultures have become so interwoven that you can't be a Guyanese without being a Brit, and you can't be a Brit without being a Guyanese, or a Caribbean.'[74] He gives full voice to this in his novel *Molly and the Muslim Stick*.[75] Young Molly is first sexually abused by her father at the age of fifteen in October 1933, a crime subsequently repeated not only by the father but by his friends. Brought up in Lancashire, she becomes a broken human being, seemingly descending into flights of fancy. But they are not abstract flights of fancy: her life becomes intertwined with Guyanese myth. Molly, or Guyana, is crushed and abused by, but also fundamentally constituted by, her father, or Britain, and by Britain's allies. Molly is an expression of what Dabydeen had said nearly twenty years earlier, 'you can't be a Brit without being a Guyanese'.

In drawing on sources that cover a wide range of different types of speaking, we are drawn to consider the different natures of genres. David Dabydeen, for example, writes differently according to whether he is writing in the genres of criticism, fiction, non-fiction, or poetry. The concept of genre is fundamental in cultural studies and film studies. A constructed way of understanding material, they are self-consciously employed by writers and directors to shape the nature of the output, and to organize forms of intertextuality. Daniel Chandler provided a clear examination of this by mapping the

[74] Cited in Jan Eijkelboom, 'David Dabydeen', *Poetry International Web*, 1999, at http://international.poetryinternationalweb.org [accessed July 2008]. Original source Wolfgang Binder, 'Interview with David Dabydeen 1989', in Kevin Grant (ed.), *The Art of David Dabydeen*, Leeds: Peepal Tree, 1997.
[75] David Dabydeen, *Molly and the Muslim Stick*, Oxford: Macmillan Caribbean, 2008.

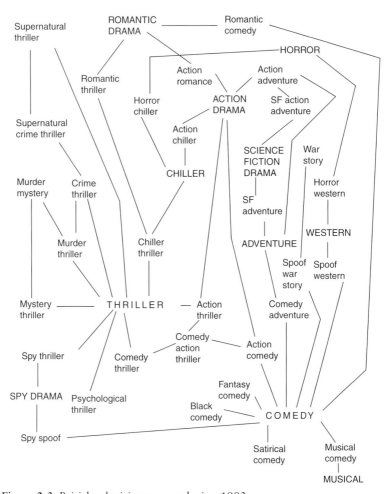

Figure 2.3 British television genres during 1993

different genres shown on British television over several months in 1993 (see Figure 2.3).[76]

Although there is much debate on the nature of genre, what is important for a political analysis is an understanding of the different forms of expression of ideas in different forms of writing. This enables the analyst to ensure that particular discourses are widely dispersed

[76] Daniel Chandler, 'An Introduction to Genre Theory', 1997, at www.aber. ac.uk [accessed July 2008].

across a range of social interactions, while also allowing a focus on the nature of a comment within the context of a particular genre. An awareness of genre forces the analyst to focus on the context for the text, and the context and speaker matter greatly when a 'joke' such as this is told: 'Two muslim [*sic*] women walking down the road with tight-fitting rucksacks, when one said to the other "does my bomb look big in this?" '[77] How ethically should such a joke be read and reproduced? When a self-identified Muslim comedienne tells a related joke, does that change how this should be read? 'I got on the plane to Denmark dressed like this, and this woman refused to sit next to me. So I said to her, "I'm going to sit on this plane and blow it up. And you think you're going to be safer three rows back?" '[78]

In deciding on the sources that will be drawn upon, Hansen's three rules will be applied. First, it must be a source with a clear articulation of the securitization in terms of identity. Second, the source must have clear authority, representing one of the elements of the social elite, regardless of the genre in which the communication is made. And third, it must be a source that is widely read.[79] However, there is one additional source that needs to be added. While Hansen's three rules make sense in terms of understanding the discourse of the elite, it is also important in a study of this sort to comprehend how securitizations impact upon the everyday. Inevitably, the everyday is not something that is of itself frequently widely read. One way into this conundrum is to look for sources that are shared in particular (often virtual) communities. While, of course, there are websites that discuss issues of security and identity, a far more powerful mode of common communication is through the telling and retelling of jokes. As we will see, the way in which jokes are constructed can be a powerful representation of the ways in which identity constructions are shared among those who live their lives beyond the elite. This means that we will have five broad categories of source material: first, texts of members of the elite – not only the government, but also other major figures in political and bureaucratic office; second, media coverage of issues shared in and through the major news sources, but also in

---

[77] Joke by 'Ploppy Pants' on the Yahoo! Answers board, at http://uk.answers.yahoo.com [accessed June 2008].

[78] 'Female Muslim comic Shazia Mirza talks to Ed Bradley', *60 Minutes*, 2 May 2004, at www.shaziamirza.org [accessed May 2008].

[79] Hansen, *Security as Practice*, pp. 82–8.

related coverage in newspapers and television of issues that might not
at first hand seem to be directly related; third, popular expressions of
identity and security, notably but not exclusively through the trans-
mission of jokes, and other expressions of voice from those outside the
elite; fourth, published material that might be fiction or non-fiction,
but which also speaks to these issues; fifth, wider sources of entertainment, whether film and television, or sport.

Ethics

A study such as this raises important ethical issues in three particular
senses. First, some of the material that is the source for the study is
offensive to some readings. An example may have been given above;
one or both of those 'jokes' may offend, and/or may contribute to
the marginalization of a particular (set of) community(ies). Although
there may be some debate about the offensiveness of those materials,
there are certainly other aspects of material that are around and that
could be the subject of this book about which there is no debate: they
are designed to be offensive. Of course, a classic example here is the
so-called 'Danish cartoon' crisis, provoked deliberately by the act of
creating a close link between 'offence', 'blasphemy' and 'comedy'.[80]
That crisis was initiated, apparently, as an act of resistance against
what is described as self-censorship about Islamic issues. The trigger for the work was that, according to the editor of the newspaper
that published them, Fleming Rose of *Jyllands-Posten*, 'at the end
of September [2005], a Danish stand-up comedian said in an interview with Jyllands-Posten that he had no problem urinating on the

[80] The issues are awkward, and defy such shorthand description. Blasphemy
for the Christian means insult to the divine; in the case of the cartoons,
the insult was to the Prophet Mohammed (pbuh) who in Islam is human –
indeed, it would be 'blasphemous' to suggest that he were divine. For a very
short overview, see Fred Halliday, 'Blasphemy and Power', *Open Democracy*,
13 February 2006, at www.opendemocracy.net [accessed July 2008]. There
is an offence of insulting the Prophet; however, it can only be enacted by
those of Islamic faith (i.e. not by non-believers). See Haider Ala Hamoudi,
'Blasphemy and the Ahmadiyya', *Islamic Law in Our Times*, 10 June 2006;
note that this is a self-avowed liberal perspective, and see also the discussion
that follows, http://muslimlawprof.org [accessed July 2008]. Yet even here
there may be an exception, with Wahabis less willing to make the distinction
between believer and non-believer.

Bible in front of a camera, but he dared not do the same thing with the Koran.'[81] Such a statement could have been read in many ways: that Muslims are more committed to their faith than Christians, for example; or that the Bible and the Koran hold a different status in their respective religions. It is not immediately obvious to most that whether a comedian would or would not urinate on a Holy Book would be a collective sign of self-censorship. It is also not at all clear why this particular comedian should be taken as a spokesperson for wider Danish, European and western society.

Nevertheless, the cartoons performed a role as a securitizing act. The point was not simply that they insulted the Prophet, but that they did so in particular ways – specifically by eliding a particular and pejorative identity of the Prophet with all Muslims, and the identity of all Muslims with terrorists. One can readily see how this could offend. As Minhaj Qidwai put it in the *Iran Daily*, 'The most controversial drawing shows Prophet Muhammad (May Peace Be upon Him) with a bomb in his turban, with a lit fuse and the Islamic creed written on the bomb. This shows that Islam is a religion propagating terrorism as per the propaganda of the West, and the Kalima shows its link with the religion.'[82] That is a crucial move: constructing a particular identity as a threat, as a Radical Other. As we will see later in this book, it is a move that has been replicated in Britain by a whole variety of sources, often deliberately offensive in tone. So how should this matter be managed in a scholarly text? Can contextualizing such materials be sufficient to neutralise the offence they might otherwise give?

It is unlikely that there will be a firm consensus on how to manage such problems. Some language and imagery will be insulting to various individuals regardless of context; and yet without such materials, it is more difficult to demonstrate arguments concerning securitizations. The ethics of republication are complex indeed. In this book, I will be drawing on offensive material explicitly, but will do so only in the area of securitizing moves. The intent is to illustrate how those of the Islamic faith are constructed as Radical Others, or as Orientalized

[81] Fleming Rose, 'Why I Published Those Cartoons', *Washington Post*, 19 February 2006, at www.washingtonpost.com [accessed July 2008].
[82] Minhaj Qidwai 'Blasphemous Cartoons Trigger Muslim Fury', *Iran Daily*, 13 February 2006, at www.iran-daily.com [accessed July 2008].

Others, as part of securitizing moves. Where there is material that is offensive but is linked only tangentially, it will not be included. This is an admittedly unsatisfactory compromise.

The second ethical issue is the concern that allowing social actors to speak security is a profoundly anti-democratic move. Who did *Jyllands-Posten* represent when publishing the cartoons? Surely ethically we should only want democratically elected governments to have the ability to securitize? As Wæver, Buzan, Kelstrup and Lemaitre argued, 'accepting other voices speaking for society will always involve a delegitimization of the state that "should" be the protector of society. It then becomes a problem that anyone can try to speak on behalf of society.'[83] This is precisely one of the dilemmas of a post-Copenhagen securitization theory which posits that a number of social actors within an elite can securitize. Wæver, Buzan, Kelstrup and Lemaitre go on to resolve their dilemma very straightforwardly: 'This could be a risk, but it seems to us a risk we have to take. This danger has to be offset against the necessity to use the concept of societal security to try to understand what is actually happening.'[84] This seems a reasonable position: if other actors are making securitizing moves, it is a process worthy of examination.

This leads to the third and final problem of 'speaking security'. In writing about security, the analyst commits a speech act and therefore co-constitutes the construction of a particular security issue and, in particular, a particular identity construction. Thus, as Jef Huysmans has argued, there is a normative dilemma: that the analyst produces security knowledge that might, in itself, have a securitizing effect.[85] The Copenhagen School had sought to use securitization as a basis for making judgements, thus making it possible 'to ask with some force whether it is a good idea to make this issue a security issue – to transfer it to the agenda of panic politics – or whether it is better handled within normal politics'.[86] One solution might be that set out by the Copenhagen School, and associated in particular with Ole Waever,

---

[83] Ole Wæver *et al.*, *Identity, Migration and the New Security Agenda in Europe*, London: Pinter, 1993, p. 188.

[84] *Ibid.*, p. 189.

[85] Jef Huysmans, 'Defining Social Constructivism in Security Studies: The Normative Dilemma of Writing Security', *Alternatives: Global, Local, Political* 27, 2002.

[86] Buzan *et al.*, *Security: A New Framework for Analysis*, p. 34.

for whom the resolution is to seek out desecuritizations, which leads to a repoliticization of an issue, with 'politicization' here meaning a return to the parameters of democratic politics.[87] But fundamentally, Waever accepts the dilemma as a dilemma – one to be managed rather than resolved.[88] This for Aradau is unacceptable; it is a refusal on the part of the analyst to accept political responsibility.[89]

The resolution to this dilemma in a post-Copenhagen securitization frame is surely a focus on revelation and contradiction. In terms of revelation, precisely one of the issues that is so important in the impact of successful securitizing moves is their translation into widely accepted 'common sense'. The work here is to render the familiar, strange; to take that which is accepted, and to interrogate it in terms of its own logic, and in terms of the social norms that it is co-constituting. In this way, the politics of everyday reality can be revealed and examined for their social impact. And in so doing, contradictions in discourse and material practice can be illuminated.

The final section in this chapter explains how the approach that has been outlined here can be deployed to understand the contemporary British concern with terrorism.

Britishness, terrorism and post-Copenhagen securitizations

This book will take a post-Copenhagen securitization theory approach to understanding the construction of contemporary security threats in the United Kingdom. Two moments related by socially constructed crises – '9/11' and '7/7' – are the social mechanisms through which the British Self has come to securitize the Radical Other – Islamic/Islamist/international terrorism – and to (re)construct an Orientalized Other, here being the 'British Muslim community'. These processes of constructing the Radical and the Orientalized Other have taken place through language and imagery, and the securitizing actor has been not just the government (indeed, at times some in government have tried *not* to securitize particular identities) but also a range of

[87] *Ibid.*, p. 206.
[88] Ole Waever, 'Securitizing Sectors? Reply to Eriksson', *Cooperation and Conflict* 34(3), 1999: 338.
[89] Claudia Aradau, 'Security and the Democratic Scene: Desecuritization and Emancipation', *Journal of International Relations and Development* 7(4), 2004: 388–413.

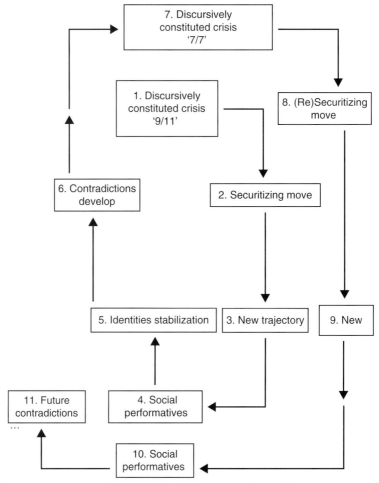

Figure 2.4 Crises and securitizations in the United Kingdom

other social agents, including the media, religious figures and aca-
demics/public intellectuals. This wider range of social agents are part
of the British elite which, given the nature of contemporary Britain,
largely functions as a London elite. It is not that this London elite are
purely located in the capital in a geographical sense; it is, rather that
'London' forms a conceptual space in which ideas are developed and
propagated. Although, to a certain extent, Edinburgh functions as an
alternative space (as do Cardiff and Belfast to a more limited degree),
on the central questions of security, and on the ability of a group to

securitize, London is the core. Of course, this is not the same as saying that *Londoners* are the focal point; it is those that operate in the structures of government, mainstream media, business and religion that form this elite.

The nature of this process of securitization, identity formation, performativity and reconstitution of identity in the United Kingdom can be represented by an adapted version of Figure 2.2, in which the twin crises of '9/11' and '7/7' work together to form a ratcheting effect upwards upon the processes of securitization (see Figure 2.4).

Over two reinforcing crisis cycles, the way in which the London elite has securitized a Radical Other, and constructed an Orientalized Other, forms the core of the analysis. The spatial and temporal aspects of these securitizations is at the heart of the sources examined in subsequent chapters. Consistent with the theoretical framework, what is important is not only the words and images of the elite, however, but also the ways in which securitizations impact and structure everyday life. The performatives of the securitizations are important and naturalized. Through these practices, the Self becomes reconstituted; and so I will return at the end to the contemporary nature of Britishness.

The next chapter examines how contemporary Britishness has been in motion, from a constructed foundational moment in the Second World War. This contemporary Britishness is important not only in creating a social construction worthy of protection against threat, but also in helping to create an identity (an Other) for that threat, as well as thereby contributing elements to the ontological security of individuals.

3 | 'Two World Wars and one World Cup': constructing contemporary Britishness

Introduction

'Two World Wars and One World Cup' has been for many years the song of choice for England's football supporters when the national team has played against Germany. It reflects the sense of twentieth-century triumph: in the Great War of 1914–18; in the Second World War; and in London in 1966, when England's footballers defeated West Germany by four goals to two to win the football World Cup. In terms of football, of course, it is a rather hollow chant. England's one World Cup triumph has been eclipsed by Germany's three (and another three defeats in the Final match); Germany defeated England in the 1970 Tournament, which is where England lost the World Cup; in the only two other competitive semi-final matches that England has ever reached (World Cup 1990, European Championship 1996) they lost to Germany; indeed, after the 1966 Final, England did not defeat Germany again in a competitive match for thirty-four years. It is a song that harks back to 'past glories', evoking particular temporal moments.

This song, however, reflects a deeper truth about British identity, which is that it has been in many ways constructed around, and against, German identity. The central reason for that concerns the moment at which what we consider to be contemporary Britishness was founded: in the ongoing mythologizing about the Second World War. Hostility towards, competition with, discussion about Germany all help to cement that Britishness.

This chapter discusses the nature of British identity first by examining the way in which the Other – the German – is so prevalent in British culture and debate. It then examines the centrality of the experience of the Second World War in the construction of Britishness, and assesses how Britishness has undergone successive waves of reconstruction, transmitted in and through popular culture.

Throughout this, 'Britishness' has been able to make contributions to the ontological security of individuals by creating some parameters in everyday life that become acceptable, and appropriate. This chapter thereby offers a genealogy of the resources offered by the national identity to individuals' ontological security in contemporary Britain.

The Germans: in football and in comedy

The nature of the peculiar antagonism that they might feel nationally from the British is often a mystery to visiting Germans – or to Germans whom meet Britons in other parts of the world. Hans-Friedrich von Ploetz, the outgoing German Ambassador to the United Kingdom in 2002, made much of his frustration towards British jokes based on stereotypes 'which just don't fit any more'.[1] His predecessor, Gebhardt von Moltke, complained of the British 'profound ignorance' of Germany.[2] Von Ploetz's successor, Thomas Matussek, complained, like Von Moltke, that the teaching of history in Britain seemed to end in 1945. He said: 'Most of the clichés are quite funny and I sort of like them, but when there is no knowledge about the reality of modern Germany, when clichés and stereotypes are taken for reality, then it gives reason for concern.'[3] In light of this, the next Ambassador, Wolfgang Ischinger, revealed no great state secret when he said:

Before my move to London in spring 2006, I was warned by my predecessors about the tough climate in London, especially with regard to regular attacks on Germany in the British tabloid press. 'Hitler and the Second World War' – those were the dominant themes, in the face of which no up-to-date assessment of the German–British relationship could hope to prevail.[4]

[1] Michael Kallenbach, 'Ambassador Is Not Amused by Jokes about Germans', *Daily Telegraph*, 3 July 2002.
[2] Gebhart von Moltke, cited in 'German Ambassador Decries UK "Ignorance"', *BBC News*, 12 October 1999, at http://news.bbc.co.uk [accessed April 2008].
[3] Cited in 'Xenophobia Slur on History Lessons', *BBC News*, 9 December 2002, at http://news.bbc.co.uk [accessed April 2008].
[4] Speech by Ambassador Wolfgang Ischinger to the Deutsch-Britische Gesellschaft, 17 February 2007, at www.london.diplo.de [accessed May 2008].

Ischinger's project was to convince the British that they had moved on from these negative views of Germany. But it is a project, rather than a reflection of social realities. Nick Clegg has written of a Britain 'still stuck in a childish rut of anti-German prejudice'.[5] Klaus Krischok would agree. Reflecting on a Goethe Institute survey that showed little familiarity with Germany among British youth, he said: 'It is interesting how stubborn stereotypes appear to be in Britain.'[6] The Goethe Institute had been attempting to 'market' the new Germany; the problems that they faced in Britain could be illustrated by a cinema advertisement in 2002 which showed Rik Mayall as Hitler, campaigning against the euro with the phrase 'Ein Volk, ein Reich, ein euro'.[7]

Football has played an important part in reflecting the national identity for many decades. For the English, the national football team has been in practice the only national institution, given the decline in congregations at the Church of England. At times, the separateness of national football style from that which took place on the continent was seen to show the 'inherent disposition of different races towards certain kinds of behaviour'.[8] Of all the nations of the football world, it is the Germans who are the focus of most English supporters' songs. Another choice example, to be sung not at German supporters, but at other Europeans, is 'If it wasn't for the English you'd be Krauts'.[9] Here, the sense of English superiority over all other Europeans is clear: 'we' saved 'them' from an appalling fate. Of course, the English are themselves descendants of Germanic tribes; and the British Royal Family was highly Germanic (the House of Saxe-Coburg and Gotha until they were renamed the House of Windsor in 1917 under the stresses of World War I). Another favourite was: 'We'll show the Krauts why they lost the last war.'[10] But Germany not only defines English superiority

[5] Nick Clegg, 'Don't Mention the War. Grow Up', *The Guardian*, 19 November 2002, at www.guardian.co.uk [accessed May 2008].

[6] Tony Paterson, 'Sorry, Germany, but the Joke's Still on You', *Daily Telegraph*, 7 August 2004.

[7] 'Comic Defends Euro Hitler Spoof', *BBC News*, 7 July 2002, at http://news.bbc.co.uk [accessed April 2008].

[8] Anthony King, *The European Ritual: Football in the New Europe*, Aldershot: Ashgate, 2003, p. 6.

[9] One reporting of this is contained in Sean Ingle and Barry Glendenning, 'If It Wasn't for the English You'd Be Krauts', *The Guardian*, 18 October 2007, at www.guardian.co.uk [accessed October 2009].

[10] See King, *The European Ritual*, p. 56.

abroad; it defines it at home as well. Another terrace favourite runs: 'I'd rather be a Paki than a Kraut.'[11] That is, on this view it is better to be a 'second-class' British citizen (a British Asian) than be a German. Thus it is that Germany's Otherness explains and defines the nature of Englishness both within and without the nation. As Giles Elliot, the *Fox Sports* writer, explained to his non-British readership ahead of the Germany versus England World Cup Qualifying match in 2001: 'The English have a problem with Germany.'[12]

In case it might be thought that this represents a minority interest, it is important to note that when England were defeated by Germany in the 1996 European Championships, some 20 million people watched on television: a third of the population of Britain, but undoubtedly a much higher proportion of the population of England. The song that represented the mood of the moment was undoubtedly 'Three Lions' (David Baddiel, Frank Skinner and the Lightning Seeds), which raced to the number one position in the British charts for two weeks and spent fifteen weeks in the charts in total. The theme of the song was that of footballing failure since 1996, laced with the optimism that failure must end soon (with the 'football's coming home' chorus).[13] A key line was:

Three Lions on a shirt
Jules Rimet still gleaming
Thirty years of hurt
Never stopped me dreaming

Here the 'three lions' represent the badge on the England football shirt; 'Jules Rimet' the name of the (former) World Cup trophy, won in 1966; 'thirty years of hurt', the failures since that World Cup victory; and, of course, 'never stopped me dreaming' representing the hope for an immediate change. The 'hurt' was of failure to win, not failure to defeat Germany; and indeed, the song became an anthem in Germany too, sung on the team's return to parade the 1996 European Championship Trophy in Frankfurt, with the song reaching number sixteen in the German charts.

[11] Recorded for example in 'Hooligans', *Panorama*, BBC, 10 August 2006, at http://news.bbc.co.uk
[12] Giles Elliot, 'Sven-no-phobia', *Fox Sports*, 29 August 2001, at http://msn.foxsports.com [accessed April 2008].
[13] Lyrics from 'Three Lions Vs Lightning Seeds', 1 June 1996, at http://homepage.ntlworld.com [accessed April 2008].

Much as 'Three Lions' did to reflect a different mood for the national sport, it could not hide the darker side of racism and violence: *Thirty Years of Hurt: A History of England's Hooligan Army* was the title chosen by Cass Pennant and Andy Nicholls for their book.[14] But the title is not only interesting for its use of the 'Three Lions' phrase: it is also noteworthy for the reference to violent gangs as 'hooligans', reflecting a different period of English Othering. In London in the 1890s, the term 'hooligan' was deployed to refer to violent conduct; it was closely associated with Irishness.[15] At that time, the Other to Englishness was not the German, but the Irish.

When 'Three Lions' was re-released in the UK for the 1998 World Cup, the 1996 failure was re-presented in new lyrics:[16]

Tears for heroes dressed in grey
No plans for final day
Stay in bed, drift away
It could have been all
Songs in the street
It was nearly complete
It was nearly so sweet

England had played the semi-final in grey rather than their usual white shirts; they were 'heroes' as their defeat had been by the 'lottery' of penalties. But this reconstruction of the narrative from the German Other to Othering the failure of the past – a temporal Othering – was not fully successful. Indeed, how could it be when Germany plays such an important role in the national identity? The 1999 European Champions League Final was between a British team and a German team; coverage in Britain focused greatly on wartime metaphors.[17] The 2006 World Cup Finals were held in Germany, and were the focus of much concern about the behaviour of the English fans. England's hostility to Germany is something of a mystery to German supporters. After all, in pure footballing terms, Argentina has been far more of a

[14] Cass Pennant and Andy Nicholls, *Thirty Years of Hurt: A History of England's Hooligan Army*, London: Pennant Books, 2006.
[15] T. F. Hoad, *The Concise Oxford Dictionary of English Etymology*, Oxford University Press, 1996.
[16] Lyrics from 'Three Lions 98 Vs Lightning Seeds', 20 June 1998, at http://homepage.ntlworld.com [accessed April 2008].
[17] See King, *The European Ritual*, chapter 1: 'From 1968 to 1999'.

challenge to Germany's teams – the two have twice met in the World Cup Final itself. Far more important though is the cultural hostility with the Dutch – something at one time shared by the British – which means 'that the rivalry between England and Germany on the football field is much more important to the English than the Germans'.[18] But English fans were warned, 'don't mention the war. In fact, don't imitate or make insulting reference to the war either.'[19] *The Sun* reported this colourfully: their headline was 'Don't Mention the Walk', with a photograph of John Cleese doing his famous Nazi marching impression from the BBC comedy series *Fawlty Towers*. As *The Sun*'s chief foreign correspondent put it: 'German cops will use sweeping powers to collar England fans doing Basil Fawlty-style Hitler impressions at the World Cup.'[20] Yet this is not only a football phenomenon. When English cricket teams were rebranded to cash in on the new 'Twenty20' version of the game, two counties settled on World War II imagery: Lancashire Cricket Club became the 'Lancashire Bombers' while Kent became the 'Kent Spitfires'. At the Aston Villa–Chelsea Premier League match in February 2009, Michael Ballack, being a German national on the opposition team, was treated to many versions of 'Ten German Bombers':

There were ten German bombers in the air, there were ten German bombers in the air, there were ten German bombers, ten German bombers, ten German bombers in the air …

And the RAF from England shot one down, and the RAF from England shot one down, and the RAF from England, RAF from England, RAF from England shot one down.[21]

And so on … down to zero 'German bombers'. Evoking the War – and thereby the spirit and victory – supporters will sing Vera Lynn's wartime

[18] From the discussion on the blog by Paul Scraton, editor of *Packed* magazine, based in Germany, at 'Two World Wars and One World Cup', 22 August 2007, at http://berlindiary.wordpress.com [accessed April 2008].

[19] 'England Soccer Fans Get World Cup Warning', *Deutsche Welle*, 9 February 2006, at www.dw-world.de [accessed April 2008].

[20] Nick Parker, 'Don't Mention the Walk', *The Sun*, 9 February 2006, at www.thesun.co.uk [accessed April 2008].

[21] Holte End, Villa Park, 21 February 2009; also, at www.gugalyrics.com [accessed February 2009].

classic 'We'll meet again' to supporters of teams facing relegation.[22] Football, Germany and *the* War are all tightly interwoven.

Throughout this chapter so far, the terms 'British' and 'English' have been used interchangeably. Indeed, at Villa Park it was important to note that the RAF was 'from England', not 'from Britain'. For so many English people, Englishness and Britishness have seemed to be one and the same for so long. Indeed, this seems to have been the case even for a Scottish Prime Minister: Gordon Brown frequently commented that if England were to secure hosting the football World Cup, 'It would be great for football, great for sport and great for *our country.*'[23] Scottish, Welsh and Northern Irish voices are not raised in such hostility to Germany in a football context; their great rival is often one and the same – England. But in some parts of the United Kingdom, traditional religious rivalries remain. Thus, for Glasgow Rangers supporters, 'I'd rather be a nigger than a Tim [Roman Catholic of Irish descent].'[24]

But the football hostility to Germany predominates, particularly given the weight of England within the United Kingdom, and the consequent weight of English football in relation to that of the other nations of the United Kingdom. However, even given this, the 'German' does appear in the other countries of the United Kingdom. Supporters of Glasgow Rangers are known by their rivals as the 'Huns'. Possibly this comes from a corruption of 'Hanoverian', representing the Protestant identity in the city (Glasgow Celtic are known as the 'Fenians' for similar, although of course contrary, reasons); however, Celtic supporters were also called 'Huns' in the past, possibly owing to their association with the purportedly pro-German Irish Republic during the Second World War. In short, 'Hun' is and has been a term of abuse in Scotland. That is also the case in Northern Ireland, given the power of both Celtic and Rangers to draw support there.[25] In

[22] Holte End, Villa Park, 19 April 2008; also, at Bill Howell 'Aston Villa 5 Birmingham City 1', *Birmingham Mail*, 21 April 2008, at www.birminghammail.net. Howell wrote: 'Vera Lynn was not known for her visits to Villa Park but her songs live on.'

[23] See for example Brown, quoted in 'Brown Backs 2018 World Cup Bid', *Sky Sports*, 6 June 2008, at www.skysports.com [accessed July 2008].

[24] Quoted in Patrick Barclay, 'Blurred Line between Bile and Banter', *Daily Telegraph*, 28 November 2004, at www.telegraph.co.uk

[25] For a particularly graphic representation see 'Nazi Rangers Huns', on *YouTube*, at www.youtube.com [accessed May 2008]. It shows shots of

addition, in Northern Ireland, the (traditionally Protestant) Belfast-based club Linfield are also referred to as 'Huns' by rival supporters.

If there is nevertheless a national partiality within the United Kingdom in this representation of the role of Germany in relation to football, there is none when it comes to Germany's role in British comedy. *The Sun* reported on the German police strategy for the 2006 World Cup using the metaphor of 'Basil Fawlty'. For decades, Britain's favourite situation comedies featured the Germans, much to the continued astonishment of Germans. 'The German response to the years of Adolf Hitler and the Second World War are complex and contradictory, but nowhere does humour play a part. It is, after all, hardly a piece of history that you can laugh off. That makes the unending British facility for Nazi jokes profoundly baffling to the Germans.'[26] Three television examples make the point: *Dad's Army*, *Fawlty Towers* and *'Allo, 'Allo!*

In the 1960s and early 1970s, *Dad's Army* showed those left behind in the general call to arms in 1940, those who were too old or too young, but those who were nonetheless called upon to defend the country in the Home Guard. Graphically, one of the most powerful elements of the series was the opening credits, in which a British arrow retreats from the continent in the face of three menacing Nazi arrows, showing the sense of British isolation. In the series, the German Other was usually absent, except for the fear of constant threat of invasion, of bombing, and the occasional brush with the possible enemy (a suspected spy, Italian prisoners of war). But in perhaps the most popular episode, 'The Deadly Attachment' (series 6, episode 1, 1973) the Home Guard platoon have a captured U-boat crew to watch, the captain of which is full of confidence, cleverness and menace (and, of course, the comedy German accent). The youngest Home Guarder, Private Pike, sings a little ditty: 'Whistle while you work, Hitler is a twerp, he's half barmy, like his army, whistle while you work.' The U-boat captain threatens to write the name of the culprit into his book for an official investigation once Britain has fallen to the Nazi

Nuremburg Rallies cutting away into shots of Rangers supporters; images of Rangers supporters giving Nazi salutes; and photo images of Ku Klux Klan members with a (superimposed) Rangers flag.

[26] Simon Barnes, 'Don't Mention the World Cup! (I mentioned it once and I don't think I got away with it ...)', *The Times*, 16 December 2005, at www.timesonline.co.uk [accessed May 2008].

conquest, and asks for the private's name. 'Don't tell him Pike,' the British captain instructs. The ease with which 'we' are outsmarted by 'them' is clear to all; and yet, of course, 'we' know that it doesn't matter, because 'we' will struggle heroically to victory with common sense rather than razor-sharp intelligence.

A second example comes from the 1970s, and it is one that provided a template for so much British comedy concerning Germany subsequently. In *Fawlty Towers*, which ran for two series (1975 and 1979), Basil Fawlty was a hotel owner, nagged by his wife and irritated by his 'Spanish' waiter, Manuel. In episode 6, 'The Germans', a family arrives at the hotel while Mrs Fawlty is away in hospital having an ingrown toenail removed. Basil struggles to cope, and things become worse when he receives a knock on his head. This allows him to reveal what 'we' really think without the need to be concerned with good manners, or the horror of embarrassment. When the family arrives and Basil hears them speaking German, he shows his surprise: 'Oh German! I thought there was something wrong with you.' 'Don't mention the war,' he tells his staff, a phrase that was to be frequently used in the episode, and one that has subsequently entered popular usage. At one point, when the family are distressed by Basil's continual references to 'the war', the German father argues with Basil over who started the argument: 'We did not start it,' the German father says. 'Yes you did, you invaded Poland,' replies Basil.[27]

The final example is *'Allo, 'Allo!*, which ran for eighty-five episodes from 1982 to 1992. Set in Occupied France, it featured a café with its owner and staff; Nazi occupiers including the Gestapo agent; the Resistance; and an English spy. All the actors performed with relevant 'national' accents. In *'Allo, 'Allo!* the Nazis – though threatening – are played for ridicule. The key German figure – Herr Flick of the Gestapo – shows little emotion; speaks in orders; wears a black coat, hat and gloves; walks with a limp. In 'The British are Coming'

---

[27] There are a number websites dedicated to the series: see for example www.fawltysite.net [accessed May 2008]. Interestingly, we receive a wider insight into racist attitudes in the episode. Basil shows physical shock at the sight of a black doctor. And later, the 'Major' gives Basil an insight into racist hierarchy. While remembering a conversation with his then date, at a cricket match, he tells Basil: 'The strange thing was that throughout the morning she kept referring to the Indians as niggers. No, no, no, no I said. Niggers are the West Indians. These people are wogs.' Cue much audience laughter.

he arrives at the German headquarters to see the colonel and is met by Helga:

HELGA: Do you have an appointment?
HERR FLICK: I am Otto Flick of the Gestapo.
HELGA: Oh, you don't need an appointment.

These three comedy series in different ways kept the Second World War, and peculiarly British images of the Germans, in the front rooms of the nation for some twenty-five years. As Jacques Peretti put it, 'When the war ended, Hitler came to live in Britain (spiritually, as it were), providing inspiration for much postwar comedy: from Monty Python and Spike Milligan to Freddie Starr.'[28] In 2009/10, Spike Milligan's *Adolf Hitler: My Part in His Downfall* played in theatres across the country – in Birmingham, Bradford and Bristol, among other places.

It is not only in such series that reference to the Second World War is often made. On his *Top Gear* television programme for the BBC in 2005, Jeremy Clarkson commented on making the Mini car more German: 'Give it trafficators that go like that ... [he moved his arms to mimic a Nazi salute]. A satellite navigation system that only goes to Poland ... And a fan belt that lasts for a thousand years.'[29] During the 2007 Rugby League World Cup, Radio Five Live produced a feature on the German team, and invited 'comic' comments; the most trans-mitted seemed to be 'Heil Kingston Rovers'.[30] Inevitably, the 'sick' jokes are the ones that are highly prized in parts of youth culture, such as: 'Some kid was playing up and being a right twat in Tesco, so his dad gave him a smack, so this German woman comes over and tapped the dad on the shoulder and said "in my country we don't smack our children" – he replied "well, in our country we don't gas our Jews"'; or, another example: 'I'm very proud of my Grandfather.

[28] Jacques Peretti, 'Don't Mention the War', *The Guardian*, 5 May 2007, at http://arts.guardian.co.uk [accessed July 2008].
[29] Cited in Allan Hall and Henry Meller, 'Clarkson's Blitzkrieg Offends the Germans', *Daily Mail*, 15 December 2005, at www.dailymail.co.uk [accessed April 2008].
[30] Thus imitating Hull Kingston Rovers comment made at various times during November 2008, when the World Cup was played. This despite the fact that Germany had not qualified for the Finals.

He shot down two German planes. Admittedly that was in 1972 but you can never be too careful.'[31] As Robin Gedye wrote in the *Daily Telegraph*:

The cartoonists' German is rosy-cheeked and creased with laughter as he sits at the trestle table, beer mug in hand, Lederhosen stained to a professional sheen. Or sun-bed tanned, his white hair swept back, we glimpse him as he glides past us in his Mercedes coupé at 140 mph. Sometimes he sports a swastika on his arm, a pelmet of greasy black hair covers an eyebrow and a pencil moustache his upper lip. The images carry an undertow of threat. The beer hall rabble, the once-blond Aryan master race now at the driving wheel of a ruthless economy.[32]

One such version was the cartoon by Jamie Turner for the 2005 general election: John Prescott (the minister responsible for local government) dressed in a Nazi uniform but with New Labour roses rather than swastikas, trampling on houses, carrying a notice declaring 'Final Solution: Destruction of Rural England'.[33]

The contemporary addition to this genre is the battle over sun-loungers. Much British popular culture around summer holidays is framed by the idea that German tourists get up early to reserve the 'best' sunbed by a pool; that the Germans, in short, are still imperialistically marking out their territory in foreign lands. In Majorca, there has been open competition and hostility between tourists in British and German hotels. Aggravation sometimes turns violent; more often, it is simmering. As Carole Cadwalladr noted, this is all about 'sunloungers, not Sudetenland. Fifty-five years after the end of the Second World War, this nationalistic faultline is repeated all over the Med.'[34] In Egypt an online review of a hotel at Sharm el Sheikh by a British tourist included the lament: 'Main pool couldn't get a sunbed ... Germans were on them from 3am and took most of the brollies

---

[31] Both recorded on the *Sickipedia* website, which collects jokes by email: see www.sickipedia.org [accessed April 2008].

[32] Robin Gedye, 'Auf Wiedershen, with Great Respect', *Daily Telegraph*, 12 July 1996, at www.telegraph.co.uk [accessed May 2008].

[33] The cartoon is reproduced on the *Channel Four News* website, at www. channel4.com [accessed July 2008].

[34] Carole Cadwalladr, 'Majorca: Battle for the Beaches', *Daily Telegraph*, 5 February 2001.

from round the pool I kid you not.'[35] And on a British cruise ship the captain banned the use of towels to reserve sunbeds on board with the comment: 'We don't want that kind of Germanic behaviour.'[36] As Cadwalladr noted in her report, the British joke about Germans placing towels on their sunbeds has no match in Germany. Mike Barber 'wasn't surprised to find you had to be at the pool by 7am to bag a sunlounger' for his family holiday in Greece, but the newspapers shared his outrage that his hotel was set up for German families.[37] The newspapers raged: 'British holiday family furious after being told "only German children can use resort playground and toilets".'[38] Poor Mr Barber was reported as saying, 'We were treated like second-class citizens.'[39] A good example of this was from the front page of *The Sun* published on 31 May 31 2008. The story is of an upset British holidaymaker who sued his tour operator because none of the activities at his hotel were in English; more importantly for the story, the activities ('even the TV …') were in German. This allowed *The Sun* plenty of opportunities to reinforce the trope. The story on page 6 was headed: 'Wish you were (not) herr'; and photographs were captioned 'Hans off' and 'Mein your language'. On arrival, the holidaymaker 'grew suspicious as he noticed all the unoccupied sunbeds draped with towels'.[40]

So in British culture, as manifest in English football and in British humour, the Germans are key targets. In this, the key focus is on the crimes of the 1940s: German expansionism, brutality, inhumanity with their 'cold' behaviour. An image of the Nazi period is transposed through these mechanisms to the current day. And yet no one actually pretends that this is a 'real' picture of contemporary Germany; there are no plays about contemporary Nazi behaviour in Germany, no speeches denouncing Germany's attempts to dominate Europe.

---

[35] 'Marion from Liverpool', from a holiday in August 2006, on the *Holiday Truth* website, at www.holiday-truth.com/holiday_truths [accessed May 2008].

[36] Christopher Wells, 'German Sunbed Joke Fury', *The Sun*, 8 May 2008, at www.thesun.co.uk [accessed May 2008].

[37] Andy Dolan, 'British Holiday Family Furious after Being Told "Only German Children Can Use Resort Playground and Toilets"', *Daily Mail*, 30 July 2008, at www.dailymail.co.uk [accessed July 2008].

[38] *Ibid.*   [39] *Ibid.*

[40] *The Sun*, 31 May 2008; front page scanned June 2008; other headlines and text from p. 6.

These imaginings of Germany do not translate into policy. Something different is going on here; and that something has nothing to do with contemporary Germany. It has everything to do with contemporary Britishness.

The foundations of contemporary Britishness

Britishness is important in providing one element of structure for ontological security. It has no independent or essential values, but the British have long associated their contemporary culture with traditions. It is part of the narrations of Britishness. The appeal to tradition comes in many forms: the institutions of the state, the representations of success, and in imagery. In terms of the institutions, the monarchy and Parliament are given long claims to traditional formats, as are newer institutions such as the BBC, with its claim to 'Reithian values'. In terms of representations, knighthoods are awarded, with echoes of medieval forms of authority, and awards that hark back to empire (the Order of the British Empire, or OBE, for example). In terms of imagery, soldiers in bearskin hats on guard duty around royal establishments, or the flag of the nation, claim significant lineage. Of course, all these claims can be countered. The House of Windsor, as already mentioned, came into existence only in 1917. The Houses of Parliament, with their great gothic architecture, were rebuilt in the nineteenth century. The BBC had moved far from the 'traditional' Reithian values by the 1960s.[41] OBEs were introduced only in 1917. Bearskin hats for officers of the Royal Scots Dragoon Guards were heavily modified in the early twentieth century, with the removal of the badge. The flag dates to 1801 – or, more strictly, to 1921, with the incorporation of just the north of Ireland. Of course, much earlier representations of these institutions can be found: there is still, for example, an award of the Most Noble Order of the Garter, the highest British order, which has stayed in essence unaltered since around 1348. One of the hallmarks of Britishness has been change in the context of the claim to tradition. However, the central argument of Hobsbawm and Ranger's *The Invention of Tradition* is that

---

[41] See Tim Gardam, 'Who's Afraid of Ideas? The Challenge to Television and Radio in the Digital Age', The Donald Baverstock Memorial Lecture, October 2006, at www.st-annes.ox.ac.uk/ [accessed May 2008].

although traditions might evolve over time, that which we call tradition might also have no continuity with the past, and may indeed by
quite deliberately invented. They called for awareness of how change
might be covered by the invention of tradition: ' "Invented tradition"
is taken to mean a set of practices, normally governed by overtly or
tacitly accepted rules and of a ritual or symbolic nature, which seek to
inculcate certain values and norms of behavior by reputation, which
automatically implies continuity with the past.'[42]

One classic example comes from the world of Scouting. Robert
Baden-Powell published the text that was to lead to the global scouting movement in 1908. In *Scouting for Boys*, Baden-Powell invented
a new activity.[43] Or rather, he pulled together a variety of different
elements, as there had been boys' movements for around twenty-five
years, from at least the foundation of the Boys Brigade in 1883. From
the turn of the century there had been other organizations, often
local, and regularly – as in Southport or Greenock – Baden-Powell,
as a national hero from the Boer War, had lent his name and support.
But the Boy Scout movement was bigger; national and international;
and not confined to a particular religion or social class. In that sense,
Baden-Powell's Boy Scout movement was, for its time, revolutionary:
avoiding class, and being an overwhelmingly civic, rather than a military, organization.[44] However, Baden-Powell constructed the movement not as new, but as traditional. He wrote:

'In days of old, when knights were bold', it must have been a fine sight to
see one of these steel-clad horsemen come riding through the dark green
woods in his shining armour ... Behind him rode his group, or patrol, of
men-at-arms – stout, hearty warriors, ready to follow their knight to the
gates of death if need be ... In peace time, when there was no fighting to
be done, the knight would daily ride about looking for a chance of doing a
good turn to any needing help, especially a woman or child who might be
in distress ... The men of his patrol naturally acted in the same way as their
leader, and a man-at-arms was always equally ready to help the distressed
with his strong right arm. The knights of old were the patrol leaders of the
nation, and the men-at-arms were the Scouts.

---

[42] Eric Hobsbawm and Terence Ranger (eds.), *The Invention of Tradition*,
Cambridge and New York: Cambridge University Press, 1983, p. 1.
[43] BP [Lieutenant General Baden-Powell], *Scouting for Boys*, New York:
Oxford University Press, 2004 (first published 1908).
[44] See for example Tim Jeal, *Baden-Powell*, New Haven, CT: Yale University
Press, 2001.

You patrol leaders and Scouts are therefore very like the knights and their retainers, especially if you keep your honour ever before you, and do your best to help other people who are in trouble or who want assistance. Your motto is 'Be Prepared' to do this and the motto of the knights was a similar one, 'Be Always Ready'.[45]

The Boy Scout, then, was not to be seen as something innovative and socially challenging; but rather as something always-British.

The claim of tradition is a device to create a call to legitimacy that cannot be countered: if something is 'traditional', we can't speak against it if one of the core elements of our claim to Britishness is our emphasis on the traditional. But, of course, much that was traditional has been changed over the course of British history: the abolition of slavery, and granting the franchise to women, being two popular examples. Sometimes these moves in tradition happen in particular periods of change, as happened in the 1940s, or in the 1820s and 1830s. In the latter period, change came in terms of the final abolition of slavery in 1833, in parliamentary reform in 1832, and in Catholic emancipation with the Catholic Relief Act of 1829. Another important period of change was the late 1940s, with the introduction of the welfare state and the national health system.[46]

If there is one value that has been associated with Britishness more than anything else, it has been the class system. It would, of course, be foolish to suggest that class became irrelevant after 1946, as it has been reinscribed rather than rejected as a marker of identity.[47] Indeed, evidence shows that there is no more social mobility in the United Kingdom now than there was before the First World War, and that social mobility in Britain compares very unfavourably to that in comparable developed countries.[48] A 2007 report for the Department of

---

[45] Baden-Powell, *Scouting for Boys*, with references throughout chapters 6 and 7, pp. 207–70.

[46] The classic text on the welfare state in Britain is perhaps Derek Fraser, *The Evolution of the British Welfare State*, Basingstoke: Palgrave, 2002, here in its 3rd revised edn.

[47] See for example Mike Savage, 'Changing Social Class Identities in Post-War Britain: Perspectives from Mass-Observation', *Sociological Research Online* 12(3), 2007.

[48] Jo Blanden and Stephen Machin, 'Recent Changes in Intergenerational Mobility in the UK: A Summary of Findings', report for the Sutton Trust, 2007, summary report, at www.suttontrust.com [accessed July 2008];

Work and Pensions reviewed studies and reflected that 'social mobility in the UK is limited and that it may have become more limited over time'.[49] Class was narrated, however, differently after 1945, and has entered into the way in which children are taught about the past. Woodlands Junior School in Kent has a website which sets out issues in British culture. On class, their view of the issue is mainstream: 'Britain was once a class-ridden society. Class was a staple part of the British way of life. Today, multiculturalism and a changing economy are gradually eroding the British class system, but some features of the system still remain.'[50] But of far greater significance for understanding the debate about contemporary Britishness has come with the narration of the early 1940s experience, in contradistinction to previously held British values.

The Second World War has become the foundational moment for contemporary Britishness; and it is for that reason that particular constructions of Germanness, as shown above, play such an important role in that contemporary Britishness. The British like, or need, to be reminded of what it was that made them great; and portrayal of Germany's Nazi past, in whatever format, has that effect. Surely this has something to do with Vera Lynn's feat in 2009 of achieving the number one position in the UK album charts with *We'll Meet Again: The Very Best of Vera Lynn* and, in so doing, preventing the re-mastered Beatles album as well as Arctic Monkeys and Kings of Leon from doing so. Dame Vera sold over 100,000 copies in the first three weeks after release.[51] Another contemporary of the Second World War also continued to enjoy great popularity into the twenty-first century. To Marguerite Patten's contribution of over 165 cook books, and sales of over 17 million, since her employment by the Ministry of Food

J. Blanden *et al.*, *Changes in Intergenerational Mobility in Britain*, Centre for the Economics of Education, Discussion Paper No: CEEDP0026, 2002; Gordon Marshall, 'Social Mobility? Plus ca change ...', *Prospect*, November 1995.

[49] Alex Nunn *et al.*, *Factors Influencing Social Mobility*, Department for Work and Pensions Research Report 450, Norwich: HMSO, 2007, p. 25, at www. dwp. gov.uk [accessed July 2008].

[50] Woodlands Junior, 'Social Class in Britain', at www.woodlands-junior.kent. sch.uk [accessed May 2008].

[51] Ben Leach, 'Dame Vera Lynn becomes Oldest Living Artist to Have Number One Album', *Daily Telegraph*, 13 September 2009, at www.telegraph.co.uk [accessed November 2009].

during the 1940s, was added a podcast in 2009 to show how quickly that staple of the 'British' Christmas, the pudding, could be made. Her authored contributions include *Feeding the Nation: Nostalgic Recipes and Facts from 1940–1954*, *Best British Dishes* and *Century of British Cooking*.[52]

The foundational moment for Britain in much contemporary debate had to be in the 1940s, as prior claims lack contemporary legitimacy. There can be no universal claim to the greatness of the British Empire at a time when freedom and self-determination seem to be such universal values. There can be no claim to the strength of rule of the country (and empire) when claims to meritocracy are stronger than those of the class system; and the experience of the First World War has been taken to show what happens when upper-class 'donkeys' are in charge of working-class 'lions'. And in any case, Britain's imperial past is littered with invasions, killings and mistreatment of local populations (as in the repression of the Mau Mau rebellion), unfortunate inventions (such as the concentration camp in South Africa), slavery and exploitation. Of course, this is not a balanced historical account of imperial Britain of the sort that Niall Ferguson would recognize.[53] It is, however, part of the backdrop to why the Second World War is so important to contemporary Britishness.

That moment has been inscribed in the collective British consciousness, and thereby it informs the individual as to the contribution that the national identity might make to his or her ontological security. The war was Britain's 'finest hour'. Winston Churchill's speeches – particularly three that he gave in the middle of 1940 – have etched themselves on the collective cultural psyche, not least in that they have been frequently replayed. The 'finest hour' speech came as France had fallen to the Nazis, and it was a call to face the imminent invasion of Britain.

What General Weygand called the Battle of France is over. I expect that the Battle of Britain is about to begin. Upon this battle depends the survival of

---

[52] Marguerite Patten, *Feeding the Nation: Nostalgic Recipes and Facts from 1940–1954*, London: Hamlyn, 2005; *Best British Dishes*, London: Grub Street, 2001; *Century of British Cooking*, London: Grub Street, 2001.

[53] Niall Ferguson, *Empire: The Rise and Fall of the British World Order and the Lessons for Global Power*, New York: Basic Books, 2003.

Christian civilization. Upon it depends our own British life, and the long continuity of our institutions and our Empire. The whole fury and might of the enemy must very soon be turned on us. Hitler knows that he will have to break us in this Island or lose the war. If we can stand up to him, all Europe may be free and the life of the world may move forward into broad, sunlit uplands. But if we fail, then the whole world, including the United States, including all that we have known and cared for, will sink into the abyss of a new Dark Age made more sinister, and perhaps more protracted, by the lights of perverted science. Let us therefore brace ourselves to our duties, and so bear ourselves that, if the British Empire and its Commonwealth last for a thousand years, men will still say, 'This was their finest hour.'[54]

The speech evoked everything that the Second World War has come to signify: the whole future of civilization depended on the outcome, though civilization here is 'Christian' in character rather than 'democratic'. The 'abyss of a new Dark Age' can only be resisted by the British: a threat to be faced alone as, with the Fall of France, only the British were left to confront the Nazi threat. So for the British, national identity has some basis for the claim to be exceptional; for it was the British that saved the world from Hitler. Many other national narratives might not share this perspective – not least Russian and American – but these are social facts, not objective ones. Churchill evoked this phrase again in his post-war memoir *The Second World War*, the second volume of which was entitled *Their Finest Hour*.[55] This was a theme that Churchill had developed a few weeks before the 'finest hour' speech. That Britain was alone induced fear: but also pride. He had said: 'I have, myself, full confidence that if all do their duty, if nothing is neglected, and if the best arrangements are made, as they are being made, we shall prove ourselves once again able to defend our Island home, to ride out the storm of war, and to outlive the menace of tyranny, if necessary for years, if necessary alone.'[56] The call was for duty, effort and common sense to be made the appropriate and acceptable response to war. And this was

---

[54] Sir Winston Churchill, 'Their Finest Hour', 18 June 1940, House of Commons, at www.winstonchurchill.org [accessed May 2008].

[55] Sir Winston Churchill, *The Second World War, 2: Their Finest Hour* London: Penguin 2005 (first published 1949).

[56] Sir Winston Churchill, 'We Shall Fight Them on the Beaches', 4 June 1940, House of Commons, at www.winstonchurchill.org [accessed May 2008].

evoked most powerfully in subsequent reproductions by the call to 'fight on the beaches':

We shall go on to the end, we shall fight in France, we shall fight on the seas and oceans, we shall fight with growing confidence and growing strength in the air, we shall defend our Island, whatever the cost may be, we shall fight on the beaches, we shall fight on the landing grounds, we shall fight in the fields and in the streets, we shall fight in the hills; we shall never surrender, and even if, which I do not for a moment believe, this Island or a large part of it were subjugated and starving, then our Empire beyond the seas, armed and guarded by the British Fleet, would carry on the struggle, until, in God's good time, the New World, with all its power and might, steps forth to the rescue and the liberation of the old.

Britain's strength, heroism and determination would see the ultimate evil defeated, and, spoken with the characteristic individuality of Churchill's voice, no wonder that these speeches would become so iconic, so well known to subsequent generations. Few could recite all of these lines: most Britons would know about the call to the 'finest hour', to 'fight on the beaches', and of course 'blood, toil, tears and sweat', the third of the three major speeches of 1940, when on becoming Prime Minister, Churchill said: 'I would say to the House, as I said to those who have joined this government: "I have nothing to offer but blood, toil, tears and sweat." '[57]

Churchill became the pre-eminent icon of the War, embodying traits that were to be the core of the new Britain: stoicism, heroism, determination, and also fighting for entirely the right cause, with no space for moral equivalence. No wonder that in 2002, when the BBC began a competition to elect the 'Greatest Briton', the winner was Winston Churchill. His iconic status in the formation of contemporary Britain wiped out the major failures of his life: his involvement in the deployment of troops in south Wales, the slaughter of the Gallipoli campaign, the economic disaster of the return to the Gold Standard, changing political parties not once, but twice …[58] And also forgotten was his continued and staunch advocacy of empire, including at the

[57] Sir Winston Churchill, 'Blood, Toil, Tears and Sweat', 13 May 1940, House of Commons, at www.winstonchurchill.org [accessed May 2008].
[58] In Germany's equivalent – *Unsere Besten* – the winner was also a product of the 1940s: Konrad Adenauer, who beat Martin Luther into second place.

time of Indian independence and beyond: an empire which, in 1940, he thought might last 'a thousand years', but which had evaporated by the time of his death in 1965.

If the speeches of Churchill came to embody the new Britain, it was the practice of the Blitz – or rather, of enduring the Blitz – that came to be seen as that which should show how the new Britain would operate. Churchill had himself commented in *The Second World War* that 'the power of enduring suffering in the ordinary people of the country, when their spirit is roused, seemed to have no bounds'.[59] The Blitz cost over 40,000 British lives, and continued night after night (fifty-seven consecutive nights in London, for example) from September 1940 until May 1941. Later, in 1944, over 8,000 more were killed in the V-weapons offensive. And the story that grew was that, despite the destruction and death, Britons carried on in the usual way and faced up to the challenges cheerfully and determinedly.

This 'Blitz spirit' has become a social truth that is frequently recounted. In a book of a child's diary during the Blitz, we learn from the editor that despite the 22,000 bombs that fell on Lewisham alone, and the 1,000 deaths in the Borough, 'the spirit of the British people in Lewisham and elsewhere wasn't crushed'.[60] Indeed, recovering the ordinary voices of those who endured the Blitz and created the 'Blitz spirit' is a recurring theme in the publishing world. One example is Gavin Mortimer's *The Longest Night: The Worst Night of the London Blitz*; another is M. J. Gaskin's *Blitz: The Story of 29th December 1940*; or voices of those who lived through it on the DVD *I Was There: True Stories of the Blitz*.[61] It is also possible to attempt to relive the Blitz, with *Home in the Blitz (What Happened Here)* by Marilyn Tolhurst and illustrated by Gillian Clements, which looks at artefacts of the time, or to follow a path through what were the bombed streets with Clive Harris's *Walking the London Blitz*.[62]

[59] Churchill, *The Second World War, 2: Their Finest Hour*, pp. 316–17.
[60] Vincent Cross, *My Story – Blitz: The Diary of Edie Benson, London, 1940–1*, London: Scholastic Children's Books, 2001, p. 144.
[61] Gavin Mortimer, *The Longest Night: The Worst Night of the London Blitz*, Phoenix Publishers, 2006; M. J. Gaskin, *Blitz: The Story of 29th December 1940*, London: Faber and Faber, 2005; *I Was There: True Stories of the Blitz*, Prism Studies DVD, 2004.
[62] Marilyn Tolhurst and illustrated by Gillian Clements, *Home in the Blitz (What Happened Here)*, London: A& C Black, 2000; Clive Harris, *Walking the London Blitz*, Barnsley: Pen and Sword, 2003.

The Blitz is a particular favourite in various museum exhibitions: in the Museum of London and The Churchill Museum and War Rooms in London, and in specific exhibitions in, for example, the Imperial War Museum (2007); the Coventry Transport Museum (2008); the Merseyside Maritime Museum (2007); and Hereford Museum (2004).

All of this commemoration is important not only historically, but also because it helps to inscribe the significance of the Blitz in the establishment of the new Britishness which, in turn, performed the function of contributing to the ontological security of some of the nation's citizens. It is not without controversy: Angus Calder's *The Myth of the Blitz* in part describes the way in which the 'Blitz spirit' was constructed by the propaganda of the state. Calder's father had, for example, published *Carry on London* at the height of the Blitz in 1941. Other examples of such work would include the photographs of, among others, Bill Brandt (notably his 'People Sheltering in the Tube, Elephant & Castle Tube Station', 1942) and of Ted Dearbeg, who shot a classic photograph of men looking on bookshelves in a bombed bookstore, with no roof – Britons carrying on. Philip Ziegler's *London and War 1939–1945* outlines examples of looting and other 'non-stoic' responses alongside accounts of heroism.[63] This was a theme of *Forgotten Voices of the Blitz and the Battle for Britain*.[64] Drawing on the Imperial War Museum's oral history work, the volume demonstrates just how complex the social reality of the Blitz was to those who lived through it; not just stoicism, but also, as Maev Kennedy put it, 'The slackers, the looters, the promiscuous and the just plain terrified men and women of the Blitz are finally being heard.'[65]

Yet in the retelling of the experience at the time and just after, the dominant narrative was one of British resolve. Symbols of previous ages became icons of the new struggle. One was St Paul's Cathedral in London. Tom Stothard, who served in the Auxiliary Fire Service, articulated this when he remembered:

---

[63] Angus Calder, *The Myth of the Blitz*, London: Pimlico, 1992; Philip Ziegler, *London and War 1939–1945*, London: Pimlico, 2002.

[64] Joshua Levine, *Forgotten Voices of the Blitz and the Battle for Britain*, London: Ebury Press, 2007.

[65] Maev Kennedy, 'Sex, Fear and Looting: Survivors Disclose Untold Stories of the Blitz', *The Guardian*, 5 October 2006.

The Guildhall was burnt out, but standing in its glory, towering over the wreck of the City, was St. Paul's. And do you know, I'm sure that if St. Paul's had ever suffered really great damage – it did suffer damage as you know, bad damage – but I think if St. Paul's had shown damage, I think the heart would have gone out of Londoners. But there it was, hope.[66]

St Paul's was chosen as the home for the Order of the British Empire because, as the Monarchy website puts it, 'St Paul's symbolised the victory of the British spirit during the war of 1939–45 in that, although badly damaged and shaken, it survived the ordeal by battle in an almost miraculous way.'[67] St Paul's became an emblem of and for the new Britain.

The essence of contemporary Britishness was not just the values and experiences exemplified by Churchill and the Blitz; it also includes the renewal of Britain under the Attlee government. The post-war period was 'Austerity Britain' – but also 'Tales of a New Jerusalem'.[68] The importance of that theme could not be overstated: William Blake's poem had been put to music by Hubert Parry in 1916 very deliberately as a means of improving morale during the First World War. The work was very English:

> And did those feet in ancient time,
> Walk upon England's mountains green:
> And was the holy Lamb of God,
> On England's pleasant pastures seen!
> And did the Countenance Divine,
> Shine forth upon our clouded hills?
> And was Jerusalem builded here,
> Among these dark Satanic Mills?[69]

'Those feet' were, of course, the feet of Jesus, calling into being the idea of England as the blessed land. It was not an idea that

---

[66] Tom Stothard, quoted in 'Keeping it Positive: Your Story', Museum of London website, undated, at www.museumoflondon.org.uk [accessed May 2008].

[67] 'Order of the British Empire', *The Monarchy Today*, undated, at www.royal.gov.uk [accessed May 2008].

[68] David Kynaston, *Austerity Britain 1945–51 (Tales of a New Jerusalem)*, London: Bloomsbury, 2007.

[69] Among many sources for the lyrics, see for example 'Jerusalem', on *Cyber Hymn*, at www.cyberhymnal.org [accessed May 2008].

specifically belonged to Blake, as from medieval times English writers had played with the idea that Jesus might actually (or metaphorically) have visited the country. But it was also subsequently to be overlaid by socialist interpretation, drawing on the reference to 'Satanic Mills', and the subsequent call to collective action to bring about a better country:

> Bring me my Bow of burning gold;
> Bring me my Arrows of desire:
> Bring me my Spear: O clouds unfold:
> Bring me my Chariot of fire!
> I will not cease from Mental Fight,
> Nor Shall my sword sleep in my hand:
> Till we have built Jerusalem,
> In England's green and pleasant Land.[70]

Indeed, the idea of building the new Jerusalem was used explicitly by the Labour Party in the 1945 general election. The idea of creating something new, in keeping with the new Britain, dominates in the literature on the period. Christopher Montague Woodhouse entitles his chapter on the period in his book *Post War Britain* 'The Land of Dreams'.[71] Post-war change in the interests of social justice were met with the pressures of austerity, as reflected in David Childs's *Britain Since 1945* ('Achievement and Austerity under Attlee') and Peter Dorey's *British Politics since 1945* ('Achievements to Atrophy under Attlee').[72]

And so the new Britain was (in retrospect) called into being: a Britain that was heroic and stoic whether in the face of evil, war or austerity; able to stand alone against tyranny; committed to social justice regardless of class, gender and (perhaps) colour; a Britain that was not morally conflicted. These were the values that were intersubjectively shared among the population; and these were the contributions offered by the national identity – with specific historical metaphors – to the ontological security of the citizens. These developed into five key commitments in the Britain of the 1990s and into

[70] *Ibid.*
[71] Christopher Montague Woodhouse, *Post War Britain*, London: Bodley Head, 1996.
[72] David Childs, *Britain Since 1945*, London: Routledge, 1997; Peter Dorey, *British Politics Since 1945*, Oxford: Blackwell, 2001 (first published 1995).

the new century: morality; exceptionalism; phlegmatism; meritocracy; and tolerance and inclusivity. All could be contested – the point is not to establish the objective veracity of each claim, but rather to see how these claims have come to be constructed as part of contemporary Britishness. They did not contribute to the ontological security of all; but were the best on offer to the individual from the national identity. They did so over three overlapping phases: the post-war period; the period of challenge over class of the 1960s to 1980s; and the developments of strategies and commitments to equality and inclusion (the new 'tolerance') from the late 1960s onwards.

Entrenching contemporary Britishness

These ideas did not, of course, emerge fully formed; and indeed what is important about them for this analysis is not their historical veracity, but rather the degree to which they are relevant in contemporary debates, what they therefore offer to the ontological security of individuals. Yet the ways in which these ideas and identities became entrenched in Britishness was through cultural, media and political calling. These inscriptions of Britishness were to come through and be reflected by book and film; through the lyrics of popular music; and through the power of television. Key values of the post-war experience were entrenched through book and film. Then the class division was (re-)exposed and re-expressed through the use of popular music. And finally the violence of Britishness was revealed through television and film, and the power of the television news. Of course, this did not happen in a clear and linear fashion; various inscriptions of Britishness occurred in different places, at different times, and in different ways – it has always been in motion. What is important for this book is the way in which elements of all the below have come to constitute the contemporary nature of Britishness in the early twenty-first century.

The post-war years: moral virtue, exceptionalism and phlegm

In the immediate post-war period, the key values that came to the fore were moral certainty in the use of force; heroism and uniqueness (what Americans might call exceptionalism) through 'standing alone' in

1940; and a combination of pragmatism and what became known as British 'phlegm'.[73] In cultural terms, these notions of Britishness were developed and reproduced by a variety of means. One of the most significant was through the work of an Australian, Paul Brickhill, who wrote a series of books in the 1950s, three of which were to be turned into iconic films, with stories (and film scores) that echo from the war years to the present: *The Dam Busters*, the epic tale of the bombing of dams in the Ruhr; *Reach for the Sky*, the tale of the great British hero, Douglas Bader; and Brickhill's first book, *The Great Escape*, that told of British ingenuity and bravery under imprisonment.

The Dam Busters, published in 1951, told the story of 617 Squadron's attack on dams in the Ruhr.[74] The attack famously used the 'bouncing bomb' designed by Barnes Wallis; but it was not originally made famous by the book, as the means of attack was still classified at the time of publication (although of course this crucial detail was added to later editions). What made the bouncing bomb famous was the subsequent film, also entitled *The Dam Busters*, although it was based not only on Brickhill's work, but also on that of Guy Gibson, wing commander and holder of the Victoria Cross, whose book *Enemy Coast Ahead* told of the raid that he himself had led.[75] It was, though, the film of *The Dam Busters*, frequently reshown, that did most to generate and reflect particular views of the war, and of the British. Released in 1955, the film is separated into two elements. In the first, we see British genius – Barnes Wallis – working feverishly and without the support of his Ministry in developing the bouncing bomb technology (Wallis denied in reality not getting support). The beginning of the film shows Wallis testing a bouncing device at home with his children, using home-made implements. This illustrates the claims to British pragmatism. But despite his successes at home, Wallis cannot get authorization; so he goes to the head of Bomber Command, Sir Arthur Harris, to make a direct plea; 'Bomber' Harris is convinced, and goes to persuade the Prime

[73] King cites football reports of Manchester United's successful run to the 1968 European Cup Final as being full of examples of 'British phlegm'. See King, *The European Ritual*, pp. 4–5.

[74] Paul Brickhill, *The Dam Busters*, London: Pan Books, 1999 (first published 1951). This is a later version than that discussed below.

[75] Guy Gibson, *Enemy Coast Ahead*, Manchester: Goodall Publications, 1998 (first published 1946).

Minister. It is a story about individualistic brilliance overcoming systemic conservatism; how the nature of (new) Britishness can overcome the (stifling) old ways. In the second section, Guy Gibson is recruited to build a squadron to deliver the bombs, and while he does so, Wallis struggles to perfect the technology. Just in time, he succeeds; but at a cost – whereas he had planned for the bombs to be dropped from 150 feet, they now need to be released from a near-suicidal 60 feet. But this does not deter the British crews, who with grit and determination carry out the raids, despite the loss of many aircraft. At the end of the film, Wallis turns to the exhausted Gibson in the early dawn after the raid, and suggests that he gets some sleep. Gibson declines: true to the British sense of duty, he says he cannot because he has letters to write – letters to the families of the aircrews that had died in the raid. Gibson made an interesting ironic reference to Britishness in *Enemy Coast Ahead*. Reflecting a period when constant flying had led the aircrews to exhaustion, he wrote: 'Many of the boys, especially old Jack Kynoch, would use one of the finest old British traditions to the full: that is, grumbling about everything: the weather, the aeroplanes, the bomb load, even the war.'[76] 'Even the war', indeed.

The Dam Busters continued to have resonance well beyond the 1950s: in 1989, an advert for Carling Black Label showed a group of Germans getting up early in a Mediterranean resort to seize the sun-loungers. Our hero, the Brit, greets them from his balcony, and then launches his Union Jack towel, which bounces on the swimming pool, gets ahead of the Germans, and unrolls successfully on the most desirable lounger. In another advert, as the Lancasters drop their bombs onto a lake, a German guard comes out and acts as a goalkeeper, saving bomb after bomb in increasingly balletic form. *The Dam Busters* translates easily into key channels of contemporary Britishness: hostility to Germans, and football. The music that accompanied the film, the 'Dambusters March' written by Eric Coates, was so popular in the 1950s that it entered the Top Ten, and stayed in the music charts for a year. The March is frequently sung at English football matches, connecting all in the crowd to that memory of this defining British film. The film is still popular in the 2000s: Jonathan Glancey referred to it in *The Guardian* in 2003 as 'the Dam Busters raid – an airborne,

[76] *Ibid.*, p. 84.

20th-century Agincourt or Waterloo'.[77] And the film itself was both digitally re-mastered and re-released in 2007, while a remake began in 2008.[78]

One aspect of the film that has been controversial, and undoubtedly will be the focus of a rewrite in the new version, concerns the name of Gibson's dog. The dog plays an important role, speaking to the British love of animals and reaching an emotional intensity when the dog is hit and killed by a car. The dog's name was also important as one of the code words for the aircrews, and the grave to the real dog is now a shrine at RAF Scampton.[79] But the dog was named 'Nigger', redubbed into 'Trigger' for the American release. It seems that naming the black Labrador 'Nigger' was a perfectly innocent move for the 1950s – indeed, from the 1940s, as Guy Gibson had written of his dog 'Nigger' in *Enemy Coast Ahead*. 'The parties in the Mess were prodigious,' Gibson wrote. 'No one even minded when Nigger, my new and lovely Labrador pup, would let himself go over the Mess carpet. A great flyer was Nigger; he used to go up on nearly every patrol.'[80] Of course, the word has become more controversial in the intervening decades. A survey ranked it the fifth most offensive swear word in Britain in 2000, up from eleventh in an equivalent survey in 1998.[81] But it cannot be said to have been a wholly innocent term in the 1940s; it may not have had the potency of the word in contemporary Britain, but it was certainly a derogatory term. The word was applied to those on the side of the British, and those against – people united by skin tone. For example, in the account by Private Frederick Hitch VC of the battle of Rorke's Drift in the Zulu War in 1879 we can find both such references. First, those on the side of the British: 'Just before the barricades had been

[77] Jonathan Glancey, 'Bombs Away', *The Guardian*, 6 May 2003, at http://arts. guardian.co.uk [accessed May 2008].
[78] See Alec Lom, 'The Dam Busters Return Sharper than Ever', *Daily Telegraph*, 29 August 2007, at www.telegraph.co.uk [accessed May 2008].
[79] An image can be found at 'Hangar, at RAF Scampton, showing Nigger's grave', at www.geograph.org.uk [accessed May 2008].
[80] Gibson, *Enemy Coast Ahead*, p. 135.
[81] Andrea Milwood-Hargrave, *Delete Expletives?*, research undertaken jointly by the Advertising Standards Authority, British Broadcasting Corporation, Broadcasting Standards Commission and the Independent Television Commission, December 2000, p. 52, at www.asa.org.uk [accessed May 2008].

completed the friendly niggers began to funk it, and as soon as they found out that the Zulus were really coming down upon us in great force they commenced to sneak away.'[82] And later, the same derogatory comment on the Zulu enemy: 'Each man in a businesslike manner singled out the nigger who was nearest him, and dealt out death if he could.'[83] Writing at the same time as Gibson, one of Agatha Christie's books was entitled *Ten Little Nigger Boys*, with the story matching the ditty of the same name, set on the fictional 'Nigger Island'.[84] Enid Blyton had written *The Three Golliwogs* in 1944, and one of the three characters was 'Nigger'; he and 'Woggie' apparently shared a liking for singing 'ten little nigger boys'. Unwittingly, Gibson, Christie and Blyton had produced an insight into the British confusion over race, a confusion that is still potent today. Lord Dixon-Smith was criticized for using the phrase 'nigger in the woodpile' in a parliamentary debate in 2008; the former football manager Ron Atkinson lost his television job in 2004 for describing a football player as 'a fucking lazy thick nigger'.[85]

Yet perhaps the most relevant and powerful insight on race in this regard comes from a wartime contemporary of Brickhill. Neil McCallum went to war in 1942 and, when it was over, he put together a book of his experiences drawn from his contemporary notebooks and letters that had been sent back to Britain. As his overfilled troop ship pulled alongside the port of Freetown, Africans rowed out to entertain the troops with songs and other performances, while some dived for pennies thrown from the ship. McCallum reported the call of one soldier: 'Hiya, Sambo. How does your mother know you're dirty?'[86] He commented: 'It was like the zoo. Oh, much better than the

[82] Account of Private Frederick Hitch VC, originally published in *Chum's Magazine* [for boys] 6(809), 11 March 1908, and now reproduced, at www.rorkesdriftvc.com [accessed May 2008].
[83] *Ibid.*
[84] Reprinted as *And Then There Were None*. The poem is published and illustrated in Stanley Cock, *Ten Little Nigger Boys*, London: Nelson, undated but Christopher Baron ('Chris Baron Books', Cheshire) dates it to 1895–1905.
[85] Rosa Prince, 'David Cameron Stands by "Nigger in the Woodpile" Peer', *Daily Telegraph*, 9 July 2008, at www.telegraph.co.uk; Ian Prior, 'TV Pundit Ron Atkinson Sacked for Racist Remark', *The Guardian* 22 April 2004, at www.guardian.co.uk [both accessed July 2008].
[86] Neil McCallum, *Journey with a Pistol: A Diary of War*, London: Victor Gollancz, 1959, p. 23. Thanks to Richard Aldrich for this source.

zoo. These negroes were not animals. They were human. Almost.'[87]
Later, the ship docked at Port Teufig, Suez, and, as McCallum put it,
'there was my introduction to the wog, a generic word covering every
person of swarthy colour in the Middle East ... Its usage indicates
that the wog is one of the lesser breeds, one of the naturally under-
privileged, who has had the misfortune not to be born a European,
and the particular bad luck not to be born British.'[88] McCallum
described the casual brutality of the imperial system: 'in Egypt the
casual servant works when he is beaten. It took some further days to
absorb the deeper truth, that the wog will not work without being
beaten or threatened, that otherwise nothing will be done, not out of
laziness but out of contempt.'[89]

The second iconic contribution from Paul Brickhill is *Reach for
the Sky*. The film was released in 1956, and won the BAFTA award
for the Best British Film for its portrayal of the life of Douglas
Bader. Without doubt, Bader's life was extraordinary; despite los-
ing his legs in an air crash in 1931, he persuaded the RAF to allow
him to join and fought in the Battle of Britain; shot down in 1941,
he was imprisoned in Colditz Castle. Heroic, defiant, cool under
pressure: as a prisoner of war, he was recaptured while trying to
escape, and during his interrogation by the angry Kommandant
the interpreter reports the Kommandant's view that 'you have
caused a great deal of trouble'. Brickhill has Bader reply: 'Tell the
Kommandant that it's my job to cause him trouble.'[90] Later, when
arguing about whether he should be charged with espionage (and
probably shot therefore), Brickhill reports Bader's 'inspiration', and
that the result of an exchange with his German interrogator was
that 'the prisoner (Bader) became too domineering, and the German
stood up and snapped: "That is enough." '[91] Brickhill also had some
of his Germans speaking English with the sort of accent beloved of
British comedy: 'Herr Ving Commander, ve haf found your leg.'[92]
And he told of German characters that could be ridiculed, such as
Hauptmann Harger. Bader would taunt him; once Bader refused to
come to roll call because it had snowed and 'my feet would get cold

---

[87] *Ibid.*   [88] *Ibid.*, p. 35.   [89] *Ibid.*
[90] Paul Brickhill, *Reach for the Sky*, London: Cassell, 2000 (first published
     1954), p. 334.
[91] *Ibid.*, p. 342.   [92] *Ibid.*, p. 286.

in the snow.'[93] Bader's struggle in Colditz connected to another element of the narration of the war: the heroism, determination, indefatigability and phlegm shown in films and television series about the prison castle. Adding to the interest in this was the 1954 film *The Colditz Castle*, and between 1972 and 1974 the BBC series entitled *Colditz*, which recounted the tales in twenty-five episodes.

Reach For the Sky is an important narrative for showing, of course, heroism and determination, but also the importance of British 'phlegm'; putting up with things, and getting on with it, without ever giving up. That was the essence of the Blitz spirit: ordinary Britons were said to continue with their lives as their homes burned and their children were kept awake night after night. Routine should be maintained, even in extreme circumstances, was the message; and in doing so, there was a chance that the ontological security of individuals could be maintained. In a similar fashion, Bader and his colleagues carried on despite it all – the loss of legs for Bader, and the loss of liberty for him and the others in German prisoner of war camps. David Thomas linked the two in an article in the *Daily Telegraph* on the difference between Americans and Britons in the 'war on terror'. While Americans seemed scared, 'we British … We've got that old Blitz spirit to stiffen our upper lips and keep us going through the grimmest crises with barely a second thought. We don't have blood running through our veins, we have phlegm, that mysterious substance that makes us, well … phlegmatic.'[94] However, as well as being a less endearing film than *The Dam Busters*, *Reach for the Sky* works less universally. The film is much more constructed in and through class. Of course, class is a defining aspect of *The Dam Busters*; but there, the sense that everyone is in it together is important. In *Reach for the Sky* it is the attitude of the public school that is to the fore, and it is very clear that there is a world of difference between the officers and the men. It contrasts significantly with the newer reading of Britain, at play in *Ice Cold in Alex* (director J. Lee Thompson, 1958), the key final scene of which shows the upper-class officer (a heroic, but deeply flawed individual), the working-class sergeant major and the female

[93] *Ibid.*, p. 319.
[94] David Thomas, 'British Phlegm Is an Excuse for Sheer Apathy', *Daily Telegraph*, 16 February 2003, at www.telegraph.co.uk [accessed May 2008].

nurse – two social classes, both genders – sharing a comradely beer together. This was the new Britain at work.[95]

The final work in the trilogy is *The Great Escape*, which was actually the earliest of the three volumes written by Brickhill, but was the last to be made into a film.[96] Brickhill's 1951 book was to a certain extent autobiographical, as he, himself, had been a prisoner in Stalag Luft III at the time of the escape. Again, we learn of British resolve and determination; but here the mix is different, for the action – particularly in the film version – is clearly Anglo-American. The 1950s film treatments of Brickhill's work have Britain centre stage; by the time of the release of *The Great Escape* by United Artists – this time an American production – in 1963, the Anglo-American nature of the film seemed much more in keeping with the geopolitical realities of the day. And to subsequent generations, it created a narrative of natural Anglo-American partnership. The iconic status of Steve McQueen's portrayal of the 'Cooler King' (Captain Virgil Hilts) only serves to underline the desirability of that relationship.

The final aspect of *The Great Escape* that has kept it in the public mind is the music. As with *The Dam Busters*, the music of *The Great Escape*, by Elmer Bernstein (an American), has long resonated in Britain. And again, in one of the recurring themes of the development of contemporary Britishness, it has been on the football terraces that, among other sites, the music has been kept alive, to be hummed whenever adversity is to be faced. The music featured in another British television advert for beer, with Griff Rhys Jones interspersed with footage of the 'Cooler King'. In 2003, a PlayStation game entitled 'The Great Escape', including the 'Cooler King', was released, again featuring the iconic music from the film. The MacDonald's 2008 Christmas television advert featured the music as a man digs for freedom from his boring and unintelligent family to escape, by motorbike, to the fast food store.[97]

There is no doubt in any of these books or films as to who is in the right; morality is clear and simple, and on the side of the British. This

---

[95] Of course the twist is that the three save the German spy from arrest as a spy as opposed to his being a prisoner of war, given his heroism in ensuring that the party survived in the desert: was this a metaphor for a new Europe?

[96] Paul Brickhill, *The Great Escape*, London: Cassell 2000 (first published 1951).

[97] Advert reproduced at www.brandrepublic.com [accessed December 2008].

powerful sense of moral certainty was crucially important in under-pinning the mass protest against the war in Suez in 1956, which was seen by many as precisely the opposite. The Prime Minister, Anthony Eden, shared the view that Colonel Nasser was a new Hitler.[98] However, many of the British citizenry saw the war as a betrayal of the morality of the Second World War. And the sense of moral certainty in what was and was not right in warfare was also a central part of the protests against nuclear weapons in the 1950s, when sometimes a third of the population expressed their opposition.[99]

Brickhill's works, in book form and when translated into film, played an important role in constructing and reflecting the nature of contemporary Britishness: resolute, united, individualistic, phlegmatic, humorous, detached, determined and – ultimately – the friend of America. These are, then, the elements on offer from the national identity to the ontological security of individuals at the time and, to an extent, subsequently. The British learned that they were collectively heroic and exceptional; that they were conditioned by the genius of common sense, and of getting on with it; and that they could be morally certain when they used force. These, too, could contribute to citizens' sense of ontological security. There are, however, key absences. Brickhill and the films did not deal with issues of race in ways that would be recognizable fifty years later; nor did they articulate a meritocratic Britishness, something that came to the fore in the 1960s and 1970s, not least through the social power of music.

The 1960s to the 1980s: the new 'meritocracy'

If the work of Brickhill and the associated films had done much to reflect and establish a new Britishness, they had nevertheless left a gap around class. The class system was, of course, one of the characteristics of Britain most known to those outside the country; and it

---

[98] Motti Golani argues that it was common in the Britain of the 1950s to see any leader who seemed to jeopardise British interests as a new Hitler or Mussolini, and that Eden's references to Nasser have to be understood in that context; that is, there was nothing exceptional about Eden calling the old enemy in the guise of the new. Golani, *Israel in Search of a War: Sinai Campaign, 1955–56*, Eastbourne: Sussex Academic Press, 1998, p. 55.

[99] See for example W. P. Snyder, *The Politics of British Defense Policy, 1945–1962*, Athens, OH: Ohio University Press, 1964, p. 59.

was something that framed the everyday life of all British citizens. In the 1960s, the 'class war' came even more powerfully to the fore than before, as strikes and trade union opposition were seen in the streets and in newspapers, and increasingly on television. It was to almost overwhelm the Labour government in reaction to the latter's *In Place of Strife* White Paper in 1969.[100] But perhaps an equal, or more powerful, expression of the refashioning of class came through music. The class war of the unions and the employers, which ultimately led to the downfall of a British government (that of Edward Heath in 1974), was by its nature divisive, and therefore hard to ascribe in terms of Britishness. But in music, dissatisfaction with the limits imposed by the class system could be shared by those across the class system, with the call for a more just and meritocratic Britishness. That is, while Britain's two major national political parties were constructed in and by the class system, social pressures grew for the overthrow of the limits of that class system.

The importance of pop music was first in the way in which it ascribed a new identity: that of the teenager. As Jon Savage has shown, the teenager did not emerge fully formed – it had significant antecedents.[101] But the teenager was trans-class; and the development of the commercialization of the teenager focused on fashion and pop music, which therefore were not constructed and sold in class terms, but rather in trans-class terms. In particular, through popular music working-class teenagers became spokespeople for their generation, and often became very rich in the process.

That sense of speaking for youth is, of course, the essence of The Who's 'My Generation', which reached number two in the charts when released in 1965, and the new energy of teenage youth is epitomized in the line: 'Yeah, I hope I die before I get old (talkin' 'bout my generation).'[102] The Who were held to be the quintessential British band, along with The Kinks, whose songs about British places (such as 'Waterloo Sunset') connected with their audience. But 'Waterloo Sunset' also evokes class; it tells the tale of the narrator, who is happy ('But I don't need no friends, As long as I gaze on Waterloo sunset,

---

[100] See Andrew Marr, *A History of Modern Britain*, London: Pan, 2008, pp. 308–11.
[101] Jon Savage, *Teenage*, London: Chatto and Windus, 2007.
[102] Lyrics at http://lyrics.doheth.co.uk [accessed June 2008].

I am in paradise') and who sees two happy working-class lovers ('Terry meets Julie, Waterloo Station, Every Friday night … But Terry and Julie cross over the river, Where they feel safe and sound, And they don't need no friends.').[103] They are content within themselves, with no need to aspire to reconstruct national social life.

Yet it is not these expressions of satisfaction with the generation and the (limited) possibilities of happiness within the working class that are important for understanding the contemporary nature of Britishness. It is the anger with the social order that became so powerful, and it is that which has underscored the need for change in the nature of Britishness, from the 'old' class system to the 'new' meritocracy. That sense of the stagnation of the class system was perfectly expressed in John Lennon's 'Working Class Hero':

> Keep you doped with religion and sex and TV
> And you think you're so clever and classless and free
> But you're still fucking peasants as far as I can see
> A working class hero is something to be
> A working class hero is something to be.[104]

Lennon's picture of a working class kept in its place – evoking Marx's reference to religion as the 'opium of the people' – was a widely shared common sense. That they were still 'peasants' evokes a longer history of the class system, not simply that born of the Industrial Revolution, but also that which animated British society throughout the preindustrial period. The temporality of that claim resonated strongly with the 'new' teenagers, who wanted to stay 'new' and not be ground into past roles. With such strong structural pressures, there was no escape; no matter how hard you worked or fought, there would be no social mobility, no chance to beat, or equal, your superiors. 'All that rugby puts hairs on your chest / What chance have you got against a tie and a crest?' as The Jam sang in 'Eton Rifles'.[105] If you were low down in the class system, true ontological security would be hard to find.

---

[103] Lyrics at http://lyrics.doheth.co.uk [accessed June 2008]. For a good analysis, see Tatu Henttonen, 'Something Else by the Kinks: British Society and Culture in Their Music', *British Society and Culture Paper*, 2005, at www.uta.fi [accessed June 2008].

[104] Lyrics at http://lyrics.doheth.co.uk [accessed June 2008].

[105] Lyrics at http://lyrics.doheth.co.uk [accessed June 2008].

In 1966, Marty Feldman and John Law had written a short sketch for *The Frost Report* in which the tall John Cleese played the upper-class man, Ronnie Barker the middle-class and, obviously far shorter than the others, dressed in a mac, flat cap and scarf, Ronnie Corbett played the lower class. Each man acted their class roles, dressed the part, and importantly also spoke the part, as the British class system had always had not only visual, but also aural markers. The middle class (Barker) says, 'I look up to him [Cleese] because he is upper class but I look down on him [Corbett] because he is lower class.' Corbett responds to this comment (and to others throughout the sketch) with, 'I know my place.'[106] It was the system that the lyricists attacked, often viciously, as did The Clash in 'Career Opportunities':

> They offered me the office, offered me the shop
> They said I better take anything they got
> Do you wanna make tea at the BBC?
> Do you wanna be, do you really wanna be a cop?
>   Career opportunities are the ones that never knock
>   Every job they offer you is to keep out the dock
>   Career opportunities, the ones that never knock.[107]

The middle class had the careers, the working class simply the jobs, and this division was passed on to the next generation, marked by where parents sat in the class system rather than for any meritocratic reasons. And as set out here in 'Career Opportunities', the focus was also for the upper classes to minimize social disorder in and by the working class ('Every job they offer you is to keep out the dock'). The lack of social mobility, as expressed in 'Career Opportunities', was laced with the depressing social reality of working-class life. As Sham 69 put it in their anthem 'Hersham Boys', 'Council estates or tower blocks / Wherever you live you get the knocks.'[108] Or, as Paul Weller put it far more eloquently in The Jam's 'That's Entertainment', for the working class:

> A police car and a screaming siren
> Pneumatic drill and ripped up concrete
> A baby wailing and a stray dog howling

[106] Quoted on *Television Heaven*, 'The Frost Report', at www.televisionheaven. co.uk [accessed June 2008].
[107] Lyrics at http://lyrics.doheth.co.uk [accessed June 2008].
[108] Lyrics at www.lyricsdownload.com [accessed June 2008].

The screech of brakes and lamplights blinking
That's entertainment, That's entertainment.[109]

This music reflected on a system that was now constructed as unfair, not valued as the traditional way of things; one that negatively affected the whole country rather than something that had made the country great. It was a working-class voice that was not matched by an upper-class or middle-class voice in popular music. And so regardless of personal class commitments, the only social position to hold was working class; for middle-class rockers from the 1960s, the only voice to have was a working-class voice.

By the middle of the 1970s, economic decline and social dissatisfaction with the class system were epitomized in the lyrics of the punk movement. In The Sex Pistols' 'God Save the Queen', Johnny Rotten growls:

God save the queen
Her fascist regime
They made you a moron
Potential h-bomb
God save the queen
She ain't no human being
There's no future
In England's dreaming.[110]

Clearly the point was to shock older generations as well as middle- and upper-class sensibilities with the anti-royalist sentiment, and the condemnation of the upper classes as 'fascist', the antithesis of Britishness to the wartime generation. Indeed, The Sex Pistols were so controversial precisely because they attacked these core elements in the ontological security of many British individuals. In short, staccato sentences, The Sex Pistols communicated other key elements of this anti-class system narrative. First, the class system prevents the working class from understanding their situation: here, Johnny Rotten sings 'They made you a moron', which earlier John Lennon had phrased 'Keep you doped with religion and sex and TV / And you think you're so clever and classless and free.' Second, the working class were kept ready for use by the upper classes in warfare: 'Potential h-bomb'.

---

[109] Lyrics at http://lyrics.doheth.co.uk [accessed June 2008].
[110] Lyrics at http://lyrics.doheth.co.uk [accessed June 2008].

Third, the system was epitomized as hierarchical and unfair by the queen – a systemic oppression, not personified, expressed in the line 'she ain't no human being'. And fourth, crucially, there is no way out, no meritocratic solution, for the working-class youth: 'There ain't no future / In England's dreaming.'

Life was therefore bleaker than it ought to have been for the working class, and the lives of the upper classes were, in contrast, luxurious. This narrative, of a social apartheid, was certainly much bleaker than for the working class of Ray Davies's 'Waterloo Sunset'. In fact, by the 1970s, working-class life was narrated as pretty unbearable: The Wildhearts sang 'Greetings from Shitsville', which is in 'London NW3'.[111] And although the young working class might enjoy themselves, and find happiness as in 'Waterloo Sunset', they are just fooling themselves, because ultimately the class system trap will close and that happiness will be limited, in a way that could also be read into Ray Davies's lyrics. For 'Waterloo Sunset', private happiness could be celebrated; for The Sex Pistols, The Jam and other bands, private happiness was not enough. Again, it was the class system that threatened ontological security. Pink Floyd's 'Another Brick in the Wall' echoed all these sentiments in their anthem against the class system:

We don't need no education
We don't need no thought control
No dark sarcasm in the classroom
Teachers leave them kids alone
Hey! Teachers! Leave them kids alone!
All in all it's just another brick in the wall.
All in all you're just another brick in the wall.[112]

It wasn't the case that working-class youth could even assume that they would at least have the chance of a happy few early years of adulthood. Perhaps that worked in the economic upturn of Ray Davies's late 1960s; but by the early 1980s, the working-class position was, for the lyricists, grimmer. The regular downturns of the economic cycle inevitably hit the working class much harder, and the working class would lose out in relation to their class betters. As Billy Bragg sang:

[111] Lyrics at http://lyrics.doheth.co.uk [accessed June 2008].
[112] Pink Floyd, 'Another Brick in the Wall, Part 2', 1979, lyrics at www.pink-floyd-lyrics.com [accessed July 2008].

Up in the morning and out to school
Mother says there'll be no work next year
Qualifications once the golden rule
Are now just pieces of paper …
If you look the part you'll get the job
In last year's trousers and your old school shoes
The truth is son, it's a buyer's market
They can afford to pick and choose.[113]

For much of the musical retelling of class limitations, there was a mutual constitution of the class system with the system of war, which somehow works in the interests of the higher classes. That is, the class system threatened both ontological *and* physical security. The Sex Pistols had sung of a 'Potential h-bomb', and Britain's class system meant that it was the upper classes who always ruled, and in so doing manipulated the working class. In Marillion's 'Forgotten Sons':

For I am but mortal and mortals can only die
Asking questions, pleading answers from the nameless faceless
    watchers
That parade the carpeted corridors of Whitehall
Who orders desecration, mutilation, verbal masturbation in the
    guarded
bureaucratic wombs
Minister, minister care for your children.[114]

During the 1970s, many lyricists wrote of the futility of war throughout the ages, and of the sad roles of various members of the working class caught up in and destroyed by it. Yet in the nuclear age, the fear of destruction was not only of armies of working-class youth, but of the whole of humanity, resulting in part from the class system. This was a much revisited theme during the 1980s, but perhaps the classic of this genre is The Clash's 'London Calling' from the 1970s:

London calling to the faraway towns
Now war is declared, and battle come down
London calling, now don't look to us

---

[113] Billy Bragg, 'To Have and to Have Not', lyrics at http://lyrics.doheth.co.uk [accessed June 2008].
[114] Lyrics at http://lyrics.doheth.co.uk [accessed June 2008].

Phoney Beatlemania has bitten the dust
London calling, see we ain't got no swing
'Cept for the reign of that truncheon thing.[115]

The centrality of the British state ('London calling to the faraway towns') is mixed with the aloofness of the government of the working class by the upper classes ('now war is declared'). As John Lennon had written of 'religion, sex and TV' as ways of assuaging the people, The Clash sang ironically of 'phoney Beatlemania' in the same vein. The 'swinging '60s' had gone, replaced by the swing of the police truncheon as more violent means were needed to keep order. The chorus, of nuclear destruction, represented another element of the revulsion of immoral wars. Most of the songwriters were not writing about pacifism (although John Lennon was a very important exception), but about unjust war bringing tragedy.

In their 1982 album *The Final Cut*, Pink Floyd echoed the moral indignation of war improperly fought, with 'Two Suns in the Sunset' similarly telling of the holocaust of nuclear war. That album illustrated another sub-theme, which was a return to the heroism of the 1940s. 'The Final Cut' included songs in the voice of the wartime generation, with 'The Gunner's Dream' and 'The Hero's Return'. In 'The Post War Dream' this is deployed to condemn the then contemporary Thatcher government:

What have we done Maggie what have we done
What have we done to England
Should we shout should we scream
'What happened to the post war dream?'
Oh Maggie Maggie what have we done?[116]

Invoking the voice of the heroic generation to condemn contemporary rulers was an important rhetorical move: no longer was it enough just to eulogize about 'My Generation': now there were the possibilities of trans-generational class solidarity. But it was a track by The Clash that brought together the class focus of the British pop movement. On the album *Sandinista*, in 'Something about England', a long narrative told the tale of an old man, discarded by society, whose working-class

---

[115] Lyrics at http://lyrics.doheth.co.uk [accessed June 2008].
[116] Pink Floyd, 'The Post War Dream' http://lyrics.doheth.co.uk [accessed June 2008].

life had been torn again and again by war and poverty. Because of the class system, he spent a life ontologically insecure, as illustrated by the homelessness and hopelessness of his old age. At the end, he tells the listener:

> But how could we know when I was young
> All the changes that were to come?
> From the photos in the wallets on the battlefield
> And now the terror of the scientific sun
> There was masters an' servants an' servants an' dogs
> They taught you how to touch your cap
> But through strikes an' famine an' war an' peace
> England never closed this gap.[117]

The line 'England never closed this gap' was key in this narration: of an ongoing class system. It was a trans-generational truth that the working class would be doomed to suffer in ontological insecurity. Those elements on offer from the nation to the working class – patriotism, monarchy – were actually elements of oppression, the singers told their audiences. Yet the sense of an ongoing class system was to change. One aspect of the power of these ideas was that it became socially important to demonstrate a working-class background: publications such as *The Face* attributed 'street cred' to just such factors.[118] To be from a working-class family, and to have 'made it' in the new Britain, was to show such personal drive that all would have to admire it. It would prove that success had been earned, and should therefore be lauded, as opposed to having been inherited, and thereby worthy of being despised. That is, by the 1990s a new idea had emerged: that Britain had become post class.[119]

Through much cultural work, with the newly enriched working-class pop musicians in the forefront, 'old' Britain's class system was condemned to the past, and in the process, the new myth of Britishness was generated – that Britain was increasingly meritocratic. Britain

---

[117] Lyrics at http://lyrics.doheth.co.uk [accessed June 2008].

[118] Toby Young, 'The Face No Longer Fits because We're More Meritocratic Now', *Daily Telegraph*, 24 March 2004, at www.telegraph.co.uk [accessed June 2008].

[119] For a theoretical discussion of meaning, see Jan Pakulski, 'Foundations of a Post-Class Analysis', in Erik Olin Wright, *Approaches to Class Analysis*, Cambridge University Press, 2005.

was now 'post class' – and that is an important element of contemporary Britishness. The wartime generation had suffered under the class system; the new Britain was beyond it. As the clearly middle-class band Blur sang in 'Sunday, Sunday':

> Sunday, Sunday here again a walk in the park
> You meet an old soldier and talk of the past
> He fought for us in two world wars and
> The England he knew is no more.[120]

Blur's 'Sunday, Sunday' was released in 1993, at the time that the 'post-class' world entered intellectual and political consciousness. As Pakulski and Waters put it, 'We believe not that class theory and analysis were a waste of intellectual effort but rather that their season and purpose have come to an end.'[121] And it was a 'reality' that Tony Blair sought to exploit, propounding a post-class politics on behalf of the Labour Party.[122] One cultural icon of this move was the knighting of The Rolling Stones' Mick Jagger in 2003. Criticized for accepting an honour from the 'establishment' by band colleagues, Jagger explained the new realities : 'I don't really think the establishment as we knew it exists any more.'[123]

None of this should be taken to mean that Britons no longer speak of class; rather, that there is a belief that the old class system has been changed so that it is possible to achieve social mobility (regardless of the evidence), that class identity is less important, and that therefore class identification has become more complex. This suggests that Britishness could offer more means to enhance the ontological security of all citizens. To further progress along these lines was a crucial driver for the 1990s Labour Party. An excellent example of this would be Andrew Adonis and Stephen Pollard's *A Class Act: The Myth of Britain's Classless Society*.[124] These two New Labour thinkers showed

---

[120] Lyrics at www.allthelyrics.com [accessed June 2008].
[121] Jan Pakulski and Malcolm Waters, *The Death of Class*, London: Sage, 1995, preface.
[122] See for example Bruce Anderson, 'Mr Blair Was Welcoming the Middle Classes and Hitting at the Toffs', *The Spectator*, 23 January 1999.
[123] Mick Jagger, quoted in Andrew Dansby, 'Mick Jagger Knighted', *Rolling Stone*, 12 December 2003, at www.rollingstone.com [accessed July 2008].
[124] Andrew Adonis and Stephen Pollard, *A Class Act: The Myth of Britain's Classless Society*, London. Hamish Hamilton, 1997.

how, in education and health, class still mattered in relation to out-comes; and that the health system had managed to create a cross-class reality, unlike the education system, which in their view was still divided by the privilege on offer from the private sector. They called for a stronger move to a more meritocratic country under a returning Labour government. There was some change; but the opportunity of much more to come. A truly classless society was attainable.

This changing sense of class was illustrated by a poll for the BBC *Today* programme in 1998 in which over 1,500 people were asked to identify their social class, in order to gain an impression of the contemporary class balance. In the ICM poll, a random sample of 1,178 adults aged over eighteen were asked, by telephone, over 4 and 5 September 1998 across the country, 'Which of the following social classes do you feel you belong to?' In response, the following division was presented:

Upper	1%
Middle	41%
Working	55%
Don't know	3%

The respondents were then asked to identify the nature of the social mobility that they believed they had managed to achieve themselves:

Q2. Which of those social classes do you feel your parents belong or belonged to?

Upper	2%
Middle	27%
Working	69%
Don't know	2%

Two aspects are immediately apparent.[125] First, Britons had a clear sense of their class position (note the low response in the 'don't know' categories). Second, fully 14 per cent claimed that they had moved

---

[125] The poll, conducted by ICM, is at www.icmresearch.co.uk [accessed June 2008].

'upwards' in social class in a single generation from working to middle class.

Partly in response to this new narrative of mobility, the 2001 census operated with significantly more categories of social class. Surrey County Council explained that as a consequence, 'it is not possible to compare the socio-economic profile of Surrey with the 1991 Census as the classification used has changed. The 2001 classification identifies 8 socio-economic classes.'[126] This makes surprising viewing, perhaps, for the citizen used to three classes. As an example of this phenomenon across the country, Leicestershire County Council's table headings were as follows: [127]

Large employers and higher managerial occupations	Higher professional occupations	Lower managerial and professional	Intermediate occupations	Small employers and own account	Lower supervisory and technical	Semi-routine occupations	Routine occupations

When the *Today* programme focused on the new class classification in March 2001, their website recorded a new record number of comments, some 50,000 in all. One police inspector, on learning that he would now be categorized alongside doctors and lawyers in Class I, responded: 'Does it mean now I have to wear tennis whites when I go out to do my gardening?'[128] Such an ironic question represented the change in the meaning of class. Tony Blair sought to continually emphasize this new reality. For example, in 2002 he had reiterated: 'I reject elitism because I believe that our country will only ever fulfil its true potential when **all** of our people fulfill **their** potential.'[129] Out with the old class system; in, apparently, with the new meritocratic one.

[126] Surrey County Council, '2001 Census: Socio-Economic Classification', update 8 May, 2008, at www.surreycc.gov.uk [accessed June 2008].
[127] Leicestershire County Council, 'Table KS14a National Statistics Socio-Economic Classification (NS SEC) – All people aged 16–74', www.leics.gov.uk [accessed June 2008].
[128] Cited in Erik Olin Wright, 'Introduction', in Wright, *Approaches*, p. 1.
[129] Tony Blair, 'Next Steps for New Labour', speech, at the London School of Economics, 12 March 2002, at www.lse.ac.uk [accessed June 2008]. Emphasis in the original transcript.

From the 1960s: the emergence of British 'tolerance'

Britishness, with all of the demands of the 1960s and 1970s to over-throw the class order, adding meritocracy to the values of heroism and exceptionalism, conditioned by pragmatism, and morally certain in the use of force, still seems very male and white in this reading. One other key value has been constructed in the post-war period that is important in contemporary Britishness: the focus on the twin related commitments to tolerance and inclusion.

Much of this was articulated through Discrimination Acts: the Sexual Offences Act 1967; the Equal Pay Act 1970 (amended 1984); the Sex Discrimination Act 1975 (amended 1986); the Race Relations Act 1976; and the Disability Discrimination Act 1995 (extended 2005). Other related Acts concerning social change would include the Abortion Act 1967, the Human Fertilisation and Embryology Act 1990, and the Civil Partnership Act 2004. Above all, much of the legal work was introduced with the Human Rights Act of 1998. Together, these rights are monitored and supported by the Equality and Human Rights Commission from 2007, which 'champions equal-ity and human rights for all, working to eliminate discrimination, reduce inequality, protect human rights and to build good relations, ensuring that everyone has a fair chance to participate in society'.[130]

This development of tolerance/inclusion has related to four forms of exclusion: gender, race, sexuality and disability. But the exclusion has historically not just meant exclusion from power structures and significant employment; it has also been connected with violence. Britain has seen outbreaks of violence, and it has seen significant lev-els of structural violence. In the 1950s and 1960s, groups of Teddy boys fought, as did mods and rockers. Racial violence broke out on Britain's streets in 1958, 1976, 1981, and again in 1995 and 2001. Strikers and their supporters fought with the police at Grunwick in the 1970s, throughout the miners' strike in the early 1980s, and again at Wapping over the move of News International's print works, in the late 1980s. On Bloody Sunday, 30 January 1972, members of the Parachute Regiment shot protestors in the streets. Two years later, IRA bombs killed 26 and injured 247 in Birmingham and Guildford.

---

[130] Equality and Human Rights Commission, 'Equality and Human Rights', at www.equalityhumanrights.com [accessed June 2008].

Violence was high profile, as in the above examples, but also everyday. More recently, second generation Britons would report the effect of racial violence as follows: 'Two of us went shopping together, always. Two of us had to be in the house to defend the others. We used to be scared going home. We used to phone mum and say "Mum I am coming round the corner. Please look out of the window." We always had to carry change for the phone in case something happened.'[131] Racial segregation was the norm; in cities such as Birmingham in the 1960s, rooms for rent would be advertised as follows: 'Rooms for Let – Sorry no Coloureds, no Irish, no Dogs.'[132] Domestic violence was a socially accepted norm at one level, and yet necessarily hidden from public view at another.[133] In the 1996 Stonewall 'Queer Bashing' Report, 34% of men and 23% of women reported that they had suffered violence because of their sexuality.[134] This was matched by a Gay London Police Monitoring Group (GALOP) study of London, with some 30% of those responding reporting that they had suffered attacks based on their sexuality.[135] Othering within, whether on the basis of class, nationality, race, gender or sexuality, has led to expressions of violence as the norm. Not fitting into dominant norms of Britishness could be a clear threat to both ontological and physical security. And for the violent men, performing violence against these 'un-British' people was a way of inscribing, of proving, their Britishness.

At all times, the threat of violence in general hung heavily around the country. Inevitably, this was reflected culturally. Genesis had sung a long narrative about rival gangland battles with the release of 'The Battle of Epping Forest' in 1973: 'it's the battle of Epping Forest /

---

[131] Eyewitness testimony quoted in Kusminder Chahal and Louis Julienne, 'The Experience of Racist Victimisation', *The Joseph Rowntree Foundation*, June 1999 – Ref 679, at www.jrf.org.uk [accessed June 2008].

[132] Quoted in 'Birmingham's Post War Black Immigrants: A Glimpse into Their Experiences', drawn from Peter L. Edmead, *The Divisive Decade*, and published by Birmingham City Council; see www.birmingham.gov.uk [accessed June 2008].

[133] See Gill Hague and Claudia Wilson, 'The Silenced Pain: Domestic Violence 1945–1970', *Journal of Gender Studies* 9(2), 2000: 157–69.

[134] Stonewall, 'Queer Bashing', 1996, at www.stonewall.org.uk [accessed June 2008].

[135] GALOP, 'Telling It Like It Is', 1998, at www.casweb.org p. 12 [accessed June 2008].

Right outside your door / You ain't seen nothing like it / No, you ain't seen nothing like it / Not since the civil war.'[136] Further evoking the Britishness of the exchange, they sang: 'With the umpire's shout, they all start to clout / There's no guns in this gentleman's bout.' In 1978, The Jam released 'Down in the Tube Station at Midnight', which told of the everyday nature of random violence:

I first felt a fist, and then a kick
I could now smell their breath
They smelt of pubs and Wormwood Scrubs
And too many right wing meetings.[137]

The last line – 'too many right wing meetings' – evoked a new type of violence, not just criminal or random, but connected with white on black attacks. The Clash had drawn attention to this in 'White Riot', released in 1977, after several members of the band had witnessed the Notting Hill Riots the previous year. As the black British population began to (literally) fight back, Joe Strummer had contrasted that with the unwillingness of the white working class to fight for a cause, given that 'All the power's in the hands / Of people rich enough to buy it.' The band sang: 'Black man gotta lot a problems / But they don't mind throwing a brick / White people go to school / Where they teach you how to be thick.'[138] The working class had been taught to be 'morons' in the Sex Pistols' 'God Save the Queen', and here the working class were accepting being taught to be 'thick'.

Perhaps the representation of British violence that made the strongest immediate impact, however, was *A Clockwork Orange*, Stanley Kubrick's film adaptation of Anthony Burgess's novel, released in 1971. Although set in a dystopian future, *A Clockwork Orange*, and the central role of Alex De Large, spoke to the contemporary audience very strongly. Mindless and brutal violence, including extreme sexual violence, dominate the film from start to finish.[139] The book had emphasized that this was a fable about Britain: while being beaten, an

[136] Lyrics at http://lyrics.doheth.co.uk [accessed June 2008].
[137] Lyrics at www.lyricsmode.com [accessed June 2008].
[138] Lyrics at http://lyrics.doheth.co.uk [accessed June 2008].
[139] For an analysis of the cultural impact at the time, see Christian Bugge, 'The Clockwork Controversy', *The Kubrick Site*, www.visual-memory.co.uk [accessed June 2008].

old man sings 'O dear dear land, I fought for thee, And brought thee peace and victory –' but the narrator continues:

So we cracked into him lovely, grinning all over our litsos, but he still went on singing. Then we tripped him so he laid down flat and heavy and a bucketload of beer-vomit came whooshing out. That was disgusting so we gave him the boot, one go each, and then it was blood, not song nor vomit, that came out of his filthy old rot.[140]

The imagery survives as a trope in contemporary British fears about youth and violence: in reporting on the conviction of a gang for violence in Lincolnshire in 2008, the *Daily Mail* reported that 'The attacks mirrored the ultra-violent 1971 film *A Clockwork Orange*, based on the Anthony Burgess novel, in which teenage misfit Alex and his gang of "droogs" roam the streets in search of victims.'[141] In 2010, the QC prosecuting a killing told the Court that 'one onlooker likened the level of violence to a scene from the film *A Clockwork Orange*.'[142]

Although the violence is incomparable, the gender dimension of *A Clockwork Orange* is reminiscent of *Alfie*, released in 1966, where the central character talks to the audience about the various women with whom he has relationships as if they were inanimate objects.

Creating a value of tolerance within Britishness was inevitably linked with the attack on the class system, but only in as much as it was in parallel with it. Class issues still tended to be white male issues; the broader drive for equal opportunities opened up access to Britishness to the majority of the country's citizens. Thus, initial representations of gendered issues were themselves contextualized by class and maleness: Ken Loach's *Up the Junction* caused a great controversy when it was shown on television in 1965 as part of the BBC's Wednesday Play series.[143] Although at the core was the

---

[140] Anthony Burgess, *A Clockwork Orange*, London: William Heinemann, 1962, republished by Paperview, p. 21.

[141] Andy Dolan, ' "Clockwork Orange" Schoolboys with "Insatiable Desire for Violence" Locked up Indefinitely', *Daily Mail*, 21 March 2008.

[142] Brian Altman, QC, quoted in Adam Fresco, 'Girls Accused of Killing Gay Man in Attack Like Clockwork Orange', *The Times*, 20 April 2010, at www.timesonline.co.uk [accessed June 2010].

[143] See for example Julian Petley, 'Fact Plus Fiction Equals Friction', *Media, Culture & Society* 18, January 1996: 11–25.

imbalance of risk and responsibility in the new sexual revolution, and the horror of the back-street abortion, the story still had to be grounded in a particular working-class context. In the film version, made in 1968, there is another twist in that the central character is middle or even upper class, attracted by the idea of 'slumming it' in a working-class area of south London. Similar themes were brought to the screen earlier in *The L-Shaped Room*: representative of the new British cinema wave's focus on reality, it showed a whole range of 'outsiders' – black, gay, prostitute – but kept at the core the pregnant woman and the class identity of her would-be lover/couldn't-be husband.

Conclusion

The contemporary narrations of Britishness therefore emerged in three mixed and overlapping waves. In the first post-war phase, Britons established themselves as a people that were concerned with the moral rightfulness of the use of force, as an exceptional state that could courageously stand alone against enemy might and was underpinned by a collective phlegmatic approach to life. In the second phase, from the 1960s through to the 1980s, the existing social order was challenged, leading to a notion of a post-class society by the 1990s. And from the late 1960s onwards, ideas of tolerance and inclusion were developed and implemented. Together, these values form what constitutes the parameters of contemporary Britishness: a search for moral certainty in the use of force; a belief in national exceptionalism; a valuing of the phlegmatic approach; the right to meritocratic outcomes; and a desire for tolerance and inclusivity of others.

Throughout, these narrations of Britishness have offered different resources to individuals in the construction of their ontological security. And indeed, sometimes these developments have threatened, or disempowered, individuals in their pursuit of ontological security. The elements of national identity have always been in motion, offering different resources to people at different times. Temporality has been very important; the identification of the 1940s for the foundational myth of contemporary national identity; the evocation of trans-generational class solidarity across the century and, in John Lennon's case, across the centuries. Spatiality has also been in flux, in differing relations with empire, commonwealth – and thereby race – Europe and America. But throughout there has been a contestation. How might Britishness be constructed to further ontological security: of whom, and when? And how might the denial of Britishness in those constructions inflict ontological insecurities on others?

4 | 'New Britishness' and the 'new terrorism'

Introduction

The key contributions to individuals' ontological security of the post-war construction of Britishness were all to the fore in the discourse of Tony Blair around the time of the millennium. In speeches in just a six-month period between December 1998 and May 1999 he spoke in favour of the just use of force; of the particular nature of the British; of the value of pragmatism; in favour of meritocracy; and in support of tolerance. Each of these values had become part of the political main-stream, that which represented the nature of the British Self, things that could be articulated safely in the knowledge that they would represent what in national discourse was the new common sense.

Famously, he had spoken in detail about the search for moral certainty in the use of force in his 'Doctrine of the International Community'. Initially speaking specifically about Kosovo, he had said: 'No one in the West who has seen what is happening in Kosovo can doubt that NATO's military action is justified ... This is a just war, based not on any territorial ambitions but on values.'[1] Later in that speech he developed five generic tests for the just use of force.[2] In terms of national exceptionalism, much of the case was made in terms of unique characteristics. As Blair said in a speech in December 1998:

I have said before that though Britain will never be the mightiest nation on earth, we can be pivotal. It means building on the strengths of our his-tory; it means building new alliances; developing new influence; charting

---

[1] Tony Blair, 'Doctrine of the International Community', Chicago, 24 April 1999, at www.number10.gov.uk [accessed July 2008].
[2] The five were certainty in the case; clarity that diplomacy was exhausted; agreement that military force could deliver a result; commitment to the long term; and the presence of national interests. *Ibid.*

a new course for British foreign policy. It means realising once and for all that Britain does not have to choose between being strong with the US, or strong with Europe; it means having the confidence to see that Britain can be both. Indeed, that Britain must be both; that we are stronger with the US because of our strength in Europe; that we are stronger in Europe because of our strength with the US.[3]

Emphasizing the phlegmatic and practical nature of Britishness, in a speech on Europe in 1999, Blair said:

I want to be very frank about my feelings about Britain and Europe. I am a patriot. I love my country. The British, at their best, have two great characteristics, creativity and common sense. As history shows, we have never lacked boldness, or courage. But our sense of adventure has always been tempered by practical realism. We are pragmatic visionaries, rather than utopians.[4]

And as is shown in this quote, this phlegmatism, this reification of common sense, was imagined as a temporal continuity, something as essentially always-British.

In relation to meritocracy, Blair gave voice to the importance of the New Britain in a speech in Birmingham to the International Convention on Sikhism following nail bomb attacks in Brixton and Soho:

We are defending what it means to be British. In the past, patriotism, national identity was defined by some by reference to those excluded. Nationalism in this sense can be dangerous: you have to come from one colour, one religion, one ethnic background as opposed to others. Today, we take pride in an identity, limited by the geography of the country, but within that country, open to all whatever their colour, religion or ethnic background. We celebrate our diversity, we recognise it brings us strength and teaches us a patriotism that enriches and unites our nation rather than divides it. And the true outcasts today, the true minorities, those truly excluded are not the different races and religions of Britain but the racists, the bombers, the violent criminals who hate that vision of Britain and try

[3] Tony Blair, 'Speech by the Prime Minister on Foreign Affairs', 15 December 1998, at www.number10.gov.uk [accessed July 2008].
[4] Tony Blair, 'Prime Minister's Speech: The New Challenge for Europe', 20 May 1999, at www.number10.gov.uk [accessed July 2008].

to destroy it. But they shall not win. The great decent majority of British people will not let them.[5]

On tolerance and inclusivity, one interesting example was the speech that Blair gave to the Muslim Council of Britain in 1999 concerning the role of government in supporting the ambitions and rights of minority communities, in which he said: 'We have a long way to go both at home and abroad to promote tolerance, conquer racism, and give all religions, faiths and cultures the chance to thrive. But if anything is worth fighting for it is a society of shared values and a belief in human dignity.'[6] Another example was the speech to the National Society for the Prevention of Cruelty to Children: 'We need to break the cycle of disadvantage so that children born into poverty, or let down by the education system, or abused, are not condemned to social exclusion and deprivation in adulthood. So throughout their childhood, children must get a better deal.'[7]

As the previous chapter has shown, Britishness has been an identity in motion for many years. At many points, the nature of Britishness became worthy of debate and contestation: when Margaret Thatcher sought to put the 'Great' back into 'Great Britain'; when New Labour was constructed, with the concern that Britishness had to be a key value; with the development of 'cool Britannia'.[8] By the millennium, it had been refashioned through successive waves of debate into particular meanings; those meanings were, in turn, to be subject to scrutiny in the light of the twenty-first-century demands for a new Britishness. But in so many ways, that new Britishness was to be constructed through fears of the new terrorism; in opposition to an Other. The Other here was not another nation, or a particular religion, but a group of 'new terrorists'.

[5] Tony Blair, 'Prime Minister's Speech to the International Convention on Sikhism', 2 May 1999, at www.number10.gov.uk [accessed July 2008].
[6] Tony Blair, 'Prime Minister's Speech to the Muslim Council of Britain', 5 May 1999, at www.number10.gov.uk [accessed July 2008].
[7] Tony Blair, speech at the NSPCC Full Stop Campaign launch, 23 March 1999, at www.number10.gov.uk [accessed July 2008].
[8] See respectively for example Philip Dodd, 'The Battle over Britain', *Demos*, London: Demos, 1995, at www.demos.co.uk; Mark Leonard, 'Cool Britannia', *New Statesman*, 1998, at http://markleonard.net [both accessed July 2008].

Walter Laquer has most often been given the credit for having first analysed the phenomenon of the 'new terrorism', about which he said that 'there has been a radical transformation, if not a revolution, in the character of terrorism, a fact we have been reluctant to accept.'[9] Small groups, committed to apocalyptic goals, prepared to use weapons of mass destruction, added a new twist to the ever present threat of terrorism.[10] Mark Juergensmeyer argued that these groups all tended to understand their objective as defending an elemental identity, in which defeat is unthinkable, and the struggle in which they are engaged is fixed, unwinnable according to normal rules.[11] Such groups may well be technologically sophisticated: as Ian Lesser put it, 'this new terrorism is increasingly networked; more diverse in terms of motivations, sponsorship, and security consequences; more global in reach; and more lethal.'[12] Each author added a new element: small groups, often religious in nature, committed to absolute ends, willing to use extreme violence, and able to take advantage of the modern networked world. Thus, as Bruce Hoffman argued, new terrorism 'represents a very different and potentially far more lethal threat than the more familiar "traditional" terrorist groups.'[13] This was all before the attacks on the United States of 11 September 2001; from that point on, the new terrorism was a potent and focused political reality: chapter 2 of the '9/11 Report', for example, was entitled 'The Foundations of the New Terrorism'.[14]

If there was a 'new terrorism' that had been called into existence, it was matched by the 'new Britishness'. The concept of Britishness had been in motion, and that was to continue during the early part of the twenty-first century. However, at this time there was also a very definite

[9] Walter Laquer, *The New Terrorism: Fanaticism and the Arms of Mass Destruction*, New York: Oxford University Press, 1999, p. 4.
[10] See for example Ashton Carter *et al.*, 'Catastrophic Terrorism', *Foreign Affairs* 77, November/December 1998: 80–94.
[11] Mark Jurgensmeyer, *Terror in the Mind of God: The Global Rise of Religious Violence*, London: University of California Press, 2001.
[12] Ian O. Lesser, 'Countering the New Terrorism: Implications for Strategy', in Ian O. Lesser *et al.*, *Countering the New Terrorism*, Santa Monica, CA: RAND, 1999, p. 87.
[13] Bruce Hoffman, *Inside Terrorism*, London: St Andrew's University Press, 1998, p. 200.
[14] National Commission on Terrorist Attacks on the United States, *The 9/11 Commission Report*, chapter 2, reproduced, at http://govinfo.library.unt.edu [accessed 2008].

and explicit political project of refashioning Britishness. Inevitably, the new Britishness was to meet the new terrorism – conceptually – head on. This chapter examines that process, first by analysing how two different conceptions of Britishness intersected, and then looking at how this 'new Britishness' began the process of becoming institution-alized. Finally, the chapter examines the impact of the threat of 'terror within': the crisis of the new, home-grown, terrorism.

Competing Britishnesses: Norman Tebbit and Gordon Brown

The Conservative politician Norman Tebbit prided himself on his ability to get to the essence of a situation. When faced with mass unemployment in the north and the creation of jobs in the south of the country, Tebbit called for the unemployed to 'get on their bikes' and travel to look for work. He was particularly provoked by riots during the 1980s in London and Liverpool by 'un-British' (and largely non-white) people. Whatever it took to get work, that was what the British did; that was what his father had done. Tebbit evoked one of his claims to Britishness: a commitment to hard work regardless of the social cost. To the Conservative Party Conference in 1981, Tebbit said: 'I grew up in the 1930s with an unemployed father. He did not riot. He got on his bike and looked for work, and he went on look-ing until he found it.'[15] In 1990, in a more direct call to Britishness, Tebbit spoke of the 'cricket test'; regardless of the country in which someone was born, the test of their Britishness now was whether they would support the English cricket team. This was once a deep issue: in the face of racism and exclusion, Britain's Caribbean population had shown great pride in the humiliation of the English team at the hands of the West Indies in the series of 1976, 1980 and 1984, each won by the West Indies, culminating in the 5–0 series win of 1984. That sense of pride was, in the 1980s, increasingly shared by Britons of South Asian origin when India or Pakistan toured the UK, espe-cially when India won the 1986 series against England.[16]

[15] Greg Philo, 'Television, Politics and the New Right', Glasgow University Media Group, p. 3, at www.gla.ac.uk [accessed August 2006].

[16] For an examination of English cricket's role in developing outsider roles see Steve Greenfield and Guy Osborn, 'Oh to Be in England? Mythology and Identity in English Cricket', *Social Identities* 2(2), June 1996: 271–92.

Speaking some twenty years after his 'on your bike' speech, the now Lord Tebbit set out the narrative into which the cricket test fitted:

Nobody used to talk about Britishness in the 1940s and 1950s, it is a phenomenon of large numbers of non-British people coming into the country ... The question is about foreigners and how foreigners are persuaded to adopt British customs and styles ... [about how to] persuade these people [the non-white populations] that Waterloo, Trafalgar and the Battle of Britain, is part of their heritage.'[17]

Some objected to Tebbit's cricket test on the grounds that their loyalty was being questioned; others that he looked at evidence of exclusion rather than ways of achieving inclusion. But there were other, equally fundamental problems with the cricket test. One would be hard pressed to find a Scot who would pass it. Although it is the England and Wales Cricket Board, it is not hard to find Welshmen and women who would not express support for *English* cricket. And in Northern Ireland, in the context of the Troubles of the 1970s and 1980s, the cricket test would be little more than bizarre.

There is a root dilemma in talking about 'Britishness': when is it Britishness, and when Englishness? Here again is the Tebbit narrative: 'My father's family came to Britain in the sixteenth century, but I regard the Anglo-Saxon period, King Alfred and William the Conqueror as part of my inheritance.'[18] Yet this narrative is an English construction, and one that comes quite late in the historical day. As Linda Colley records, in the eighteenth century Welsh speakers would refer to the English as 'saisons'.[19] Today, an English person may be referred to by a Scot as a Sassenach, and in the Welsh language today as Sais or Saeson: all are Gaelic words for 'Saxon'.[20] The Saxons were in those countries bringers of violence and destruction rather than democracy and inclusiveness. The Anglo-Saxons, Alfred, William are part of an English story that was grafted onto a British narrative

---

[17] Quoted in 'What Is Britishness Anyway?', *BBC News Online*, 10 December 2001, at http://news.bbc.co.uk [accessed August 2006].

[18] *Ibid.*

[19] Colley, *Britons: Forging the Nation 1707–1837*. Yale University Press, 2005; first published 1992, pp. 13–15.

[20] In Welsh as in 'twll tin pob Sais' ('down with the English'): see Heini Gruffudd and Elwyn Ioan, *Welsh Is Fun!*, Aberystwyth: Y Lolfa, 1971, p. 82.

with the Act of Union.[21] To many in the British and Irish islands, the English story was about the inhibition of their own national experiences. These were the contributions of the national identities to individuals' ontological security in terms of narrative and routine.

The essence of Tebbit's argument is that multiculturalism is not British; indeed, that a failure to develop Britishness is at the heart of contemporary dangers of terrorism. The attacks on the London transportation system of 7 July 2005 can be interpreted through this lens of a failure to entrench 'Britishness.' As Tebbit explained:

A society is defined by its culture. It is not defined by its race, it is not a matter of skin colour or ethnicity, it is a matter of culture. If you have two cultures in one society then you have two societies. If you have two societies in the same place then you are going to have problems, like the kind we saw on July 7, sooner or later.[22]

And it was not just some white Britons who objected in such terms to contemporary British identities. Sajid Mahmood, whose parents migrated to Britain from Pakistan in the 1970s, was subjected to verbal abuse loudly and frequently from some British Asians for being a 'traitor' as he played cricket for England against Pakistan in 2006.[23] Mahmood's cousin, the boxer Amir Khan, told the *Daily Mirror*, 'He's no traitor, he's our hero.'[24] But for some on the terraces, and in surrounding communities, Hassan Butt – a British citizen from Manchester – had more of the traits of the hero. Butt, who claimed to have helped recruit jihadists to fight in Afghanistan, said:

I feel absolutely nothing for this country. I have no problem with the British people ... but if someone attacks them, I have no problem with that either

[21] England produced a union with Wales through a series of Acts from 1536 to 1543; that 'England' joined with Scotland through the Act of Union of 1707; and that 'Great Britain' joined with Ireland through an Act of Union in 1800 to produce the 'United Kingdom of Great Britain and Ireland'. Of course, none of this can be understood without analyzing the wars and imperialism of the British and Irish islands.

[22] Quoted in 'Tebbit: "Cricket test" Could Have Stopped Bombings', *ePolitix*, 19 August 2005, at www.epolitix.com [accessed August 2006].

[23] See his comments in Jonathan Petre, 'Howzat for Integration as Pair Pass Tebbit Test', *Daily Telegraph*, 9 August 2006, at www.telegraph.co.uk [accessed August 2006].

[24] Quoted in David Anderson, 'Sajid Is Not a Traitor ...', *Daily Mirror*, 12 August 2006, at www.mirror.co.uk [accessed August 2006].

... I would agree to being called a radical and one day I may even be called a terrorist, if Allah permits me. That is something it would be an honour to be called.[25]

Tebbit continued to illustrate a particular narrative of Britishness beyond the 1980s into the new century. It was one that evoked an imagined simpler time, when people did not have to worry about their British identity as there were no other identities to choose from. Tebbit created a fixed temporal Self, with clear spatial imaginings. It was a time when there was a clear teleology of Britishness, from the fall of the Roman Empire to the modern period: a vision, or a myth, that had come to be compromised by difference, and one then threatened by violent terrorism. Such a concern with the dilution of the national 'essence' had, of course, a long history in British political life. Enoch Powell had said: 'Do I object to one coloured person in this country? No. To a hundred? No. To a million? A query. To five million? Definitely.'[26] As Andrew Marr commented in relation to this quote, in Britain '[t]here can be no serious doubt that most people in 1968 agreed with him'.[27]

When Gordon Brown began his discussion of 'Britishness', he did so by explicitly distinguishing his discourse from that of Tebbit. Brown sought to invoke a different vision from that of the 1980s; different in terms of its inclusiveness, as one would expect from a Scottish, as opposed to an English, politician. Brown said: 'As the Tebbit "cricket test" and the Stephen Lawrence case illustrate, there are those who would retreat from an expansive idea of Britishness into a constricted shell of right-wing English nationalism. My vision of Britain comes not from uniformity but from celebrating diversity, in other words a multi-ethnic and multinational Britain.'[28] Evoking the sense of rejection that the 'cricket test' had created among non-white Britons, and lacing that with reference to the racist murder of the black British schoolboy, Stephen Lawrence (a case in which the police had been found to be 'institutionally racist'), Brown argued

---

[25] Hassan Butt was interviewed by Aatish Taseer in 'A British Jihadist', *Prospect*, August 2005. Butt subsequently changed his views fundamentally.

[26] Enoch Powell in an interview with the *Daily Mail* in 1968, quoted in Andrew Marr, *A History of Modern Britain*, London: Pan., 2008, p. 305.

[27] *Ibid.*

[28] Gordon Brown, *The Guardian*, 12 November 1998.

that 'Britishness' actually has, at its heart, a commitment to inclusion and engagement and, in a claim to temporal continuity, that it always has done. It was, of course, important for a Scot who sought to be Prime Minister of a Britain in which five out of every six citizens live in England to make this 'inclusive' point. It was also important to a Labour Party that had traditionally secured support from immigrant populations, but whose popularity among a range of British Muslim opinions had collapsed following the invasion of Iraq. Over time, a 'Britishness' process may have been seen to hold important strengths for Brown and the Labour Party. But it also, of course, appealed to the political right. Matthew d'Ancona, editor of *The Spectator*, wrote in 2007 that '[t]here was a time when our sense of national identity was defined by our institutions: the monarchy, Parliament and more recently the NHS. But our society is now so diverse, so pulverized by modernity and so threatened by fundamentalist violence that we need a new national conversation about what draws us together as Britons, or rather what should.'[29] What is crucial here is that this 'traditional' sense of Britishness has been so 'threatened by fundamentalist violence' that it requires a 'new national conversation.' Terror, and specifically terror from 'within', meant that what we thought of as 'Britishness' needed significant adjustment. Six months after the 2005 London bombings, Gordon Brown delivered a speech calling for the Labour Party to embrace the Union flag, and for the country to have a national day. But in so doing, he evoked that which showed why such a commitment to Britishness was so immediately important. 'We have to face uncomfortable facts that while the British response to July 7th was remarkable, they were British citizens, British born, apparently integrated into our communities, who were prepared to maim and kill fellow British citizens irrespective of their religion.'[30] That is, Britishness had not prevented an enemy within from developing; it had not provided sufficient ontological and indeed physical security resources.

Central to these debates about Britishness has been an assertion of a particular narrative of British history, and an attempt to ascribe

[29] Matthew d'Ancona, 'And Season's Greetings to You, Ozymandias', *Daily Telegraph*, 23 December 2007, at www.telegraph.co.uk [accessed June 2008].
[30] Gordon Brown, quoted in 'Brown Speech Promotes Britishness', *BBC News*, 14 January 2006, at http://news.bbc.co.uk [accessed June 2008].

particular values to Britishness as a result. Lord Tebbit provides a series of prime examples of this project. In the foreword to Lindsay Jenkins's book *Disappearing Britain* (2005), he wrote:

England, and later the United Kingdom, has been the rock on which every attempt to create a European wide state has foundered since the collapse of the Roman Empire. The contemporary hostility of the European establishment towards the Anglo sphere has been built on the historic European ambition that powered Philip of Spain, Napoleon Bonaparte, the Kaiser and Hitler to create their European empires. Even today the would-be imperialists who dream of challenging America for world leadership know that until this Kingdom is subdued their ambition will not be achieved. That is at the heart of the plan, which Lindsay Jenkins exposes. With the enthusiastic backing of Prime Minister Blair 300 years of union with Scotland is being undone. Wales is being pushed away and IRA/Sinn Fein is not being so much appeased as treated like an ally in the destruction of the United Kingdom. Even so that is not enough. What New Labour pretends is devolution to the English regions, Lindsay Jenkins shows step by step is a plan from Brussels to take England back to its state before the time of Alfred the Great, divided and incapable of resisting foreign colonisation.[31]

It is a powerful, populist narrative, rooted in common-sense understandings of the nation that evoke a national interest in opposition to that of the manipulative elite. Trans-historic realism is at the heart of the analysis, including temporal and spatial imaginings of state identity. The Europeans – for here Britain is something outside, or beyond, Europe – have always sought to subjugate Britishness for its difference, whether the enemy be Spain, France, Germany or – at other times – Russia. Devolution is a form of national suicide, perpetrated by an elite that has been converted to the European cause. And so, the danger is one of truly millennial proportions. A divided Britain would fall prey to foreign aggression, a lesson learned by all leaders who had followed Alfred the Great. In the 790s, the Vikings had begun the process of conquering the kingdoms that then occupied what we now call Britain.[32] Evoking Britain's 'finest moment' in 1940, Alfred's

---

[31] Foreword by the Rt Hon. Lord Tebbit of Chingford to Lindsay Jenkins, *Disappearing Britain, the EU and the Death of Local Government*, Forest Hills, NY: Orange State Press, 2005.
[32] The Vikings raided, conquered and settled in large areas in England, Scotland and Ireland, but in Wales they merely raided and set up a few very small settlements.

Wessex stood alone against the powerful enemy; almost defeated, the king led a fightback that eventually led to the creation of the first Anglo-Saxon Kingdom (though it accounted for only roughly half of present-day England), and a process that led within three generations to a first recognizable all-English state. Stoicism and eventual victory against a European enemy: this was at the heart of the narration of Britishness/Englishness that Tebbit brought to the imagination.

Gordon Brown's spatial and temporal narrative of the national identity was deliberately different: it was one of rebirth. As such, it looked as it was meant to: radically different from the account that Tebbit had been developing over the previous twenty-five years. In a speech that contained many of his ideas on Britishness at the time, Brown said in 2004 that:

So deep rooted was the British problem – sometimes called the British disease – that as they said at the time:

- first in the fifties we had managed decline;
- then in the sixties we mismanaged decline;
- then in the seventies we declined to manage ...

we can speak of ... A Britain no longer looking backwards, its mindset one of managed decline ... a Britain no longer looking inwards but a Britain true to its tradition of global engagement, we can find a new confidence as a nation.[33]

Here the history is much more telescoped than in Tebbit's vision. No Alfred the Great in Brown's narration: rather, it is the story of a new post-war Britain. However, Brown has been careful not to suggest that this meant that there was an abrupt fissure with the past. His identification of certain British values – such as 'British enterprise, British creativity, the British openness to the world, the British adaptability to new ideas and our strong British sense of fair play and civic duty'[34] – would not have been out of place in descriptions of the Britain of the time of the Great Exhibition at the Crystal Palace in London in 1851. Indeed, later in the same speech Brown spoke of flexibility

[33] Gordon Brown, 'Mansion House Speech', 16 June 2004, at www.hm-treasury.gov.uk [accessed October 2006].
[34] *Ibid.*

and enterprise as 'historic British values', and also noted that 'British inventiveness is not just a feature of our industrial revolution past'.[35] But to lock in this imagination of Britishness, Brown turned immediately from his list of values to a reference to Winston Churchill, to re-evoke the foundational myth of a new Britain from the 1940s.[36]

In a later speech, at a seminar on Britishness in 2007, Brown moved back towards a Tebbit-style narrative in terms of the trans-historical dimension, but drew different conclusions.

One reason is that Britain has a unique history – and what has emerged from the long tidal flows of British history – from the 2,000 years of successive waves of invasion, immigration, assimilation and trading partnerships; from the uniquely rich, open and outward looking culture – is I believe a distinctive set of British values which influence British institutions. Indeed a multinational state, with England, Scotland, Wales and now Northern Ireland we are a country united not so much by race or ethnicity but by shared values that have shaped shared institutions.[37]

No mention of Alfred the Great standing alone against the European enemy, though still a dating of Britishness to the Roman period ('from the 2,000 years.'); but still embedded within the narrative was a teleology. If the claim of Britishness is not based on 'race or ethnicity, but … shared values', a great deal of importance must be placed on the nature and origin of those values. As to the nature of those values, they are 'British tolerance, the British belief in liberty and the British sense of fair play'.[38] Of course, these were the key themes in the Taking Liberties exhibition. And their origin? They are rooted in British history – specifically:

---

[35] *Ibid.*

[36] Brown quoted Churchill as follows: 'The ability to foretell what is going to happen tomorrow, next week, next month and next year. And to have the ability afterwards to explain why it didn't happen.' But in another remarkable phrase he warned his contemporaries that they must never be, as he put it: 'Resolved to be irresolute, adamant for drift, solid for fluidity and all powerful for impotence.' *Ibid.*

[37] Gordon Brown, 'Remarks by the Rt. Hon Gordon Brown MP, Chancellor of the Exchequer, at a seminar on Britishness, at the Commonwealth club, London', 27 February 2007, at www.hm-treasury.gov.uk [accessed July 2008].

[38] Brown speaks this in a third voice; that is, Britishness comprises what people say is Britishness, rather than what he himself is saying. *Ibid.*

- ... in Runnymede in 1215 when arbitrary power was fully challenged with the Magna Carta;
- on to the first Bill of Rights in 1689 where Britain became the first country where Parliament asserted power over the King;
- to the democratic reform acts [of the nineteenth and twentieth centuries] ...
- ... in the 1800s Britain led the world in abolishing the slave trade ...
- ... in the 1940s, in the name of liberty, Britain stood firm against fascism ...
- ... Britain's unique National Health service.[39]

So both Tebbit and Brown agreed that there was a historical narrative at the core of Britishness; that social interactions in a particular place (the British Isles) over a particular period of time (after the Roman invasion) had led to a unique and valuable product – Britishness. Where they sharply differed was over the importance of the new post-1940s national values, and over whether multiple identities associated with migration, national identity within the UK, and the future of integration with the European Union marked a continuity in British values and the continuation of the story of Britain, or threatened a radical discontinuity.

Institutionalizing the 'new Britishness'

Gordon Brown's work on British identity, while Chancellor of the Exchequer, and then as Prime Minister, has been highly influential, as is befitting for a holder of such important political positions. In the aftermath of the introduction of devolution for Scotland, Wales, Northern Ireland and London, Brown developed the 'tolerance and inclusion' theme, from equalities based on gender, ethnic minorities, sexuality and disabilities, to include the nations. He had claimed in 1999 that:

A Britain previously held back by what has been a disabling nostalgia for a story-book uniformity, for things that are lost and things that never were,

---

[39] *Ibid*. Inevitably, this list reflects the one that is on the government website which aims to provide information to potential citizens about the United Kingdom: see www.direct.gov.uk [accessed July 2008].

can and must yield to a Britain increasingly strengthened, not divided, by the reality of our diversity ... We can be proud of a Britain which becomes the first successful multi-cultural, multi-ethnic and multi-national country in the world.[40]

This is a clear attempt to communicate the resources provided by this reading of national identity to the ontological security of individuals. For many critics of Brown and New Labour, this attempt at refashioning Britishness was simply spin and hypocrisy. A *Daily Telegraph* editorial commented: 'It is not hard to see what Gordon Brown is up to, with all this talk of Britishness. He knows how awkward his position would be as a Prime Minister sitting for a Scottish constituency. There he would be, passing laws for 90 per cent of the British population from which his own constituents would be exempt.'[41] The politics could be read in many ways. But what were the *citizens* of Britain reporting about their attitudes to the country and to Britishness? Survey evidence has seemed to confirm the sense that if citizens are asked an 'either/or' question – 'do you feel British or Welsh', for example – there is a decline across the country in the numbers prepared to privilege the British element.[42] Even in England, those who feel primarily British seem to be less than 50%, with equivalent numbers under a third in Wales, and under a fifth in Scotland (see Table 4.1).[43]

The 24th British Social Attitudes Survey reported in January 2008 that:

- Few English or Scottish natives think of themselves as 'only' or 'mainly' British: 13% in England and 3% in Scotland.
- Nearly half of English natives (46%) say that they are 'equally English and British'. One in five (21%) Scottish natives describe themselves as 'equally Scottish and British'.

---

[40] Gordon Brown in a speech to the London School of Economics, quoted in 'Brown: Britishness is Booming', *BBC Online*, 15 April 1999, at http://news.bbc.co.uk [accessed June 2008].

[41] Editorial, 'Our Scottish PM in Waiting Goes British', *Daily Telegraph*, 14 January 2006, at www.telegraph.co.uk [accessed June 2008].

[42] 'Devolution, Public Attitudes and National Identity', *Devolution and Constitutional Change*, ESRC Research Programme, Final Report, March 2006, at www.devolution.ac.uk [accessed June 2008].

[43] National Centre for Social Research, *British Social Attitudes*, Press Release, 23 January 2008, p. 5, at www.natcen.ac.uk/natcen/pages/news_and_media_docs/BSA_24_report.pdf [accessed June 2008].

Table 4.1. *Trends in national identity in Great Britain*

	1974	1978–9	1991–2	1996–7	1999	2001	2003
England							
English			31	34	44	43	38
British			63	59	44	44	48
Scotland							
Scottish	65	56	72	72	77	77	72
British	31	38	25	20	17	16	20
Wales							
Welsh		59		63	57	57	60
British		34		26	31	31	

Sources: Election and Referendum Studies, British Social Attitudes, Scottish Social Attitudes, ESRC

- The most popular response from Scottish natives is to describe oneself as being 'only' or 'mainly' Scottish, chosen by nearly three-quarters (73%) of people. Far fewer – 37% – English natives describe themselves as being 'only' or 'mainly' English.[44]

That is, many British citizens find more resources for their ontological security in their Scottishness, Welshness or Englishness than they do purely in their Britishness.

These findings were mirrored by work undertaken by the Commission for Racial Equality (CRE), who following surveys in 2002 and 2006 reported that:

Britishness was felt by many participants in the discussion groups to be a more inclusive identity that could incorporate elements of ethnic minority culture, whereas Englishness, in particular, was felt to be equated with being white. However, the inclusiveness of the British identity was also felt to be part of its weakness. Britishness was felt to be vague and there was no clear consensus about the values, institutions or behaviours constituting it.[45]

---

[44] *Ibid.*
[45] Commission for Racial Equality, *Race Relations 2006: A Research Study*, London: CRE, 2007, p. 6, at www.equalityhumanrights.com [accessed July 2008]. For the 2002 Report, see CRE, *The Voice of Britain*, London: Mori/CRE, 2002, at www.equalityhumanrights.com [accessed July 2008].

For their 2006 survey:

very few of those surveyed (10%) thought people had to be white to be truly British, but nearly three quarters (73%) of the general population thought that ethnic minority people needed to demonstrate a real commitment to this country before they could be considered British. The feeling, regardless of country of birth, appears to be that 'you don't have to be white to be British, but it helps'.[46]

This led the CRE to argue that 'the debate about the nature of Britishness cannot be seen independently of a wider set of issues about race relations and integration'.[47] Thus, the resources on offer to individuals' ontological security from the various national identities of the country vary with racial identities. As the CRE Report put it, 'our qualitative and quantitative research reveals great complexity in the question of the relationship between cultural diversity, tolerance and Britishness. That is, diversity and tolerance are seen as at once characteristic of Britishness, the antithesis of Britishness and barriers to a common Britishness.'[48]

'Britishness', then, has become contested both nationally within the United Kingdom, and by minority communities within the state. Of course, there is nothing unique in such contestation, as in past times Britishness was able to exclude a whole series of people, whether Catholic, Irish or black. In common with other researchers in the first part of the twenty-first century, the CRE, working with a survey carried out by Ipsos/MORI, could find no clear consensus on that which constitutes Britishness. As the CRE Report argued:

Although there is widespread agreement that Britishness is not defined by ethnicity, our research shows that there is no consensus about what constitutes a sense of Britishness ... There are a number of potential bases for a unifying national identity: a common lifestyle, culture, or values; a shared history or founding myths; shared political institutions; a constitution. However, public opinion about Britishness does not seem to have coalesced around any of these.[49]

---

[46] *Ibid.*   [47] *Ibid.*, p. 32.
[48] *Ibid.*, p. 33.   [49] *Ibid.*, p. 32.

This is important because, of course, to provide resources to an individual's ontological security, values have to be capable of being clearly communicated and routinized. In the early twenty-first century, if the national identity is unable to do this on a widespread basis then inevitably many people will look elsewhere for resources for their ontological security.

This connects to a growing sense that Britishness is in some real and important way 'declining'. As an editorial in the *Daily Telegraph* in 2006 put it so clearly, people no longer understand what it is to be British. 'For a long time, they did. Ask any schoolboy in Banff or Bangor or Banbury what it meant to be British and he would have had a ready answer. It meant cheering for the underdog, seeing the other chap's point of view, standing up to bullies, bridling at injustice.'[50] However, the argument had been around for some time. In 1999, Linda Colley gave one of Downing Street's Millennium Lectures and began by asking rhetorically: 'For what can a new millennium do for British national identity except confirm and complete its disintegration?'[51] Trying to understand that sense of decline in all that Britishness is and meant was the focal point for an Ethnos study for the CRE in 2006. Entitled 'The Decline of Britishness', the research showed that for many white Britons 'a large proportion of the discussion focused on the decline of some idealized notion of Britishness that had existed in the past, rather than its contemporary reality.'[52] This reflected a new temporal imagining; a loss of an idealized past, when the national identity is imagined to be more potent in offering resources to ontological security structures.

This sense of decline, matched with an inability to describe that which was there before in any sense other than the 'idealized', draws on the idea that 'Britishness' is and always was a deliberate construction to manage political relations on the British and Irish isles. Linda Colley has described this historic process in relation to the Acts of Union.[53] David Starkey has given voice to the notion that Britishness

---

[50] Editorial, 'Our Scottish PM in Waiting Goes British'.

[51] Linda Colley, 'Britishness in the 21st Century', Millennial Lectures, 8 December 1999, at www.number10.gov.uk [accessed June 2008].

[52] Ethnos for the CRE, *The Decline of Britishness*, London: Commission for Racial Equality, 2006, p. 8, at www.equalityhumanrights.com [accessed July 2008].

[53] Colley, *Britons*.

is still just a combination of nations, in which, therefore, although there is a British state, a British *nation* as such cannot exist.[54] Alex Salmond inevitably agrees, arguing that Britishness 'went bust' long ago in Scotland.[55] To the contrary, in Northern Ireland the Democratic Unionist Party has created 'a British Cultural and Equality Unit to provide legal advice to the public on fighting the removal of British emblems from Northern Ireland society' in order to 'fight back against the erosion of Britishness'.[56] For Unionists in Northern Ireland the stakes are perhaps the highest, in needing the national identity to provide (along with Protestantism) a core foundation for their onto-logical security structures. They feel the need to protect the routine practices of identity. In Northern Ireland we see the intersubjective reality of the provision of ontological security by national resources; practised and routinized by the flying of flags, marching and Sunday services. And of course, for opposite reasons, resources are provided by Catholic Nationalist and Republican identities. Perhaps, then, this is one reason why church attendance in Northern Ireland – a routinized performance of identity – is so much higher than in the other countries of the United Kingdom, with 45% attending at least monthly as opposed to 18% in Scotland, 14% in England and 12% in Wales.[57]

Giving voice to this in a different – and English – context, Billy Bragg's 2002 release *England, Half English* contained the track 'Take Down the Union Jack', which included these lines:

> Britain isn't cool you know, its really not that great
> It's not a proper country, it doesn't even have a patron saint
> It's just an economic union that's passed its sell-by date[58]

---

[54] David Starkey is quoted in 'Can Pupils Learn Britishness?', *BBC News Online*, 12 October 2007, at http://news.bbc.co.uk [accessed May 2008].

[55] Alex Salmond, quoted in 'SNP Dismisses Brown's Flag Call', *BBC News Online*, 14 January 2006, at http://news.bbc.co.uk [accessed July 2008].

[56] Cited in 'DUP Fights Back against "Erosion of Britishness"', *Belfast Newsletter*, 22 July 2008, at www.newsletter.co.uk [accessed July 2008].

[57] See Jacinta Ashworth and Ian Farthing, 'Church Attendance in the United Kingdom', *Tearfund*, April 2007, at www.tearfund.org/ [accessed October 2009].

[58] Billy Bragg, 'Take Down the Union Jack', lyrics at www.billybragg.co.uk [accessed May 2008].

What is important about this is that the sense of Britishness has come to be understood not only by the political elite, but also more widely in society, as something in crisis. The political and cultural elite recognize that Britishness faces a moment of crisis; and that means that fewer resources are on offer to individuals should they have to face that which Giddens described as a critical situation. And that has been communicated to all, as previous national practices have declined and been replaced by new, contested ones. As a consequence, there have been projects to secure the recovery of Britishness. The Institute for Public Policy Research has worked on its 'Future of the Union' project, which has concentrated on the question of devolution.[59] The Smith Institute published a report that was focused very much on securing 'Britishness' as a key element of the New Labour/progressive project. Nick Johnson argued:

Britishness needs to be seen as an essential part of any progressive consensus. In part, this is due to our history as a nation of immigration and our openness to diversity ... entrenched in two of the founding traditions of the Labour movement – solidarity and mutuality ... Britishness must also be seen as not a threatening identity. It has always existed alongside both national and religious [identity] ... In stressing the importance of Britishness, we are not asking anyone to give up other loyalties or identities. We may, though, be asking for them to change their behaviour ... The process of change and the negotiation, tolerance and understanding involved are more important aspects of Britishness than either the end result or what went before.[60]

Britishness would, therefore, be a key focal point for the New Labour endeavour, creating a process within which various identities – national, regional, religious, secular – could be renegotiated towards a progressive political direction. Progressiveness as a core element of Britishness: again, in its trans-generational dimension, something imagined and communicated by Taking Liberties.

Notable among all this this work has been the activity of the Fabian Society, and their project 'Could a New Britishness Unite Us?'

[59] Details of which are at www.ippr.org.uk [accessed July 2008].
[60] Nick Johnson, 'Endnote: Towards a British Citizenship', in Nick Johnson, *Britishness*, London: The Smith Institute, 2007, p. 94, at www.youngfoundation.org.uk [accessed July 2008].

Inevitably, the answer is a qualified yes, placed in the context of the need to renew British identity. Deborah Mattinson explained:

Our poll found that 50% of people believe that we run the real risk of a divided society if we don't define what being British means. Britons feel we are at a turning point: that building our positive identity matters more than it has done in the past, and that it will matter more still in the future. There is an appetite for change: a new national sense of purpose.[61]

This wonderfully reflects the temporal imagining of something lost, while articulating a desire for a national identity to provide resources for ontological security (running the 'risk of a divided society'). This leads to a 'new Britishness', which involves understanding where we came from. As John Denham MP put it:

We need to learn to tell our history so that it explains why so many people have roots in other parts of the world. Telling the story of empire as fact rather than good or bad thing has an important role to play. A greater honesty about our migrant history would bring surprising unity among those who currently see themselves as divided between the naturally British and others.[62]

Denham was calling for a new temporal and spatial imagining as a way of providing shared resources for communicating a clear biography. Could it work? Perhaps. But as Andrew Marr put it, 'with new migrations from Eastern Europe, Iraq, Somalia and Ethiopia, it is now clear that this is a far bigger story than simply a tidying-up after Empire.'[63]

More than this – for the Fabians, the 'new Britishness' is a means for tying together the nations of the Union and the peoples of the state around the values of 'fairness, equality and social justice'.[64] And 'new Britishness' requires a series of new institutions, such as a written constitution, a multi-faith revision of national ceremony, a removal of empire from the honours system, developing a cohesive equality

---

[61] Deborah Mattinson, 'Britishness Voices', *Fabian Review*, Winter 2005, at http://fabians.org.uk / [accessed July 2008].

[62] John Denham MP, *ibid*.

[63] Marr, *A History of Modern Britain*, p. 324.

[64] Gordon Brown and Douglas Alexander, 'Stronger, Together: The 21st Century Case for Scotland and Britain', *Fabian Ideas 621*, London: Fabian Society, 2007.

agenda including white working-class youth, teaching Britain's global history, developing festivals of Britishness and so on.[65] Of course, much of this work was very clearly part of the government agenda; and to underline the new direction, Gordon Brown gave a speech on the subject at the Fabian Society. Here he announced a variety of initiatives, including one encouraging volunteering, which was henceforth to be inscribed as an important element in Britishness. Subsequently, there was debate on creating a 'Britain Day' – to the consternation of many in Scotland, Wales and Northern Ireland.[66]

The government introduced a Citizenship Test in 2005 to reflect a contractarian view of Britishness. As Brown had repeated in a 2007 speech, 'British citizenship is about more than a test, more than a ceremony – it is a kind of contract between the citizen and the country, involving rights and responsibilities that will protect and enhance the British way of life.'[67] The work to introduce the test was overseen by David Blunkett, when Home Secretary – a politician described by Norman Tebbit as being 'more in touch with the feelings of the average person in this country than his colleagues in the Labour Party'.[68] While Home Secretary, Blunkett began a process of developing a 'citizenship' test for immigrants to the United Kingdom. Professor Sir Bernard Crick was put in charge of the work in this area. Crick's understanding of Britishness is very illustrative: 'My own view is that Britishness is really a series of legal and political agreements between different nations.'[69] No claim here to values: Britishness on this view is essentially a matter of a social contract, the very sets of ideals that underpinned the formal construction of the British state some 300 years previously. This contractarian notion of citizenship was the reason that then-Immigration Minister Tony McNulty said: 'This is not a test of someone's ability to be British or a test of their Britishness.'[70]

---

[65] Sunder Katwala, 'Charter for a New Britain: "Progressive Integration" Agenda', *Fabian Review*, Winter 2005.

[66] See 'Ministers Proposing "Britain Day" ', *BBC News Online*, 5 June 2007, at http://news.bbc.co.uk; Guto Thomas, 'Poll Backs a St David's Day Holiday', 1 March 2006, at http://news.bbc.co.uk [both accessed July 2008].

[67] *Ibid.*

[68] Quoted in 'Blunkett Names "Britishness" Chief', *BBC News Online*, 10 September 2002 http://news.bbc.co.uk [accessed August 2006].

[69] Cited *ibid.*

[70] Tony McNulty, quoted in 'New UK Citizenship Testing Starts', *BBC News Online*, 1 November 2005, at http://news.bbc.co.uk [accessed July 2008].

What, then, would comprise a test of someone's ability to agree and then to perform to this contract?

A contractarian notion of citizenship would presumably require a formal or at least explicit contract to be produced, and the contractor would perhaps be expected to produce evidence as to his or her ability to fulfil contractual requirements. The latter, presumably, would be difficult, as a willingness to sign the British citizen contract carries with it in the vast majority of cases the determination to break a previous national citizen contract. But such nuances are irrelevant: the Citizenship Test may be described in contractarian terms, but it is actually about being able to perform knowledge of a variety of narratives. The 2007 Home Office guide is entitled *Life in the United Kingdom: A Journey to Citizenship.*[71] It comprises nine chapters, four of which describe how to perform everyday tasks in the country ('Everyday Needs', 'Employment', 'Knowing the Law' and 'Sources of Help and Information'). Four focus on the key elements of knowledge about state and society ('The Making of the United Kingdom', 'A Changing Society', 'UK Today: A Profile' and 'How the United Kingdom is Governed'). From this we learn that British history started with the Romans; that Alfred the Great, 1066, Robert the Bruce and the English conquest of Wales are important; and a variety of other events and processes are selected, over eighteen pages. Helpfully, the final chapter – 'Building Better Communities' – identifies some of the 'set of shared values with which everyone can agree'.[72] But beyond obeying the law, there is no list for the contractor to agree with. She or he is told that '[m]any of the values are mentioned in other parts of this book'.[73] The contractor is then presented with a list of values that are not explicitly endorsed, but rather come from a survey of public opinion. But this is a useful exercise if the purpose is to create a framework within which national identity offers resources for ontological security. It communicates a narrative into which the individual can fit his or her story. And it sets routines – 'Everyday Needs', 'Employment' – which the citizen can perform.

Study of this book leads the contractor to the position of being able to take a test. Prior to that, of course, she or he needs to be

[71] Home Office, *Life in the United Kingdom: A Journey to Citizenship*, 2nd edn, The Stationery Office, April 2007.
[72] *Ibid.*, p. 107.   [73] *Ibid.*

able to speak the language to a suitable standard. As the then-Home Secretary had said when introducing the system in 2002, 'we will ask that applicants for naturalization demonstrate a certain standard of English'.[74] Except, of course, that such a requirement cannot be enforced in 'diverse' Britain: as the official website puts it, 'however, if you are taking the test in a centre based in Wales you may request to take a test in the Welsh language, or if taking the test in Scotland you may request to take the test in Scottish Gaelic.'[75]

Tony McNulty had said: 'It is about looking forward, rather than an assessment of their ability to understand history.'[76] In the following example, the contractor would need to select one of the following descriptions as the correct representation of Britishness:

A: Respect laws, the elected political structures, traditional values of mutual tolerance and respect for rights and mutual concern
B: Share in the history and culture of an island nation with a character moulded by many different peoples over more than two thousand years.
C: Be part of a modern European democracy, one with a tradition of sharing our ways with the world – and allowing the world to bring its ways to us.

The correct answer, apparently, is A.[77]

One of the most significant means of institutionalizing the proposed ideas into concrete reforms came with the publication of Lord Goldsmith's *Citizenship Review*.[78] The report was full of ways of creating oaths and national days: for reinscribing Britishness in the school curriculum; for means of enhancing the 'national narrative'. It encapsulated the essence of the new Britishness: something important, declining

---

[74] David Blunkett, quoted in Matthew Tempest, 'Immigrants to Face Language and Citizenship Test', *The Guardian*, 7 February 2002, at www.guardian.co.uk [accessed July 2008].
[75] Home Office Border and Immigration Agency, 'Background to the Test', *Life in the UK*, at www.lifeintheuktest.gov.uk [accessed July 2008].
[76] McNulty, quoted in 'New UK Citizenship Testing Starts'.
[77] 'Can You Pass a citizenship Test?', *BBC News Online*, 16 June 2005, at http://newsvote.bbc.co.uk [accessed July 2008].
[78] Lord Goldsmith QC, *Citizenship: Our Common Bond*, at www.justice.gov.uk [accessed July 2008].

and in need of recovery; something shared with other identities; and something that needs to be performed. As Goldsmith put it:

People can feel British as well as feeling a strong sense of attachment to a local community, a faith, another nationality, or even to all of these ... Nevertheless these feelings [of Britishness] have fallen over time; they are less prevalent among younger people; and there is disaffection in parts of our communities. So the challenge is to renew our shared sense of belonging and take steps to engage those who do not share it. Especially in the light of social changes, we need a narrative of what we stand for together; and we may need to set out that narrative in more explicit terms than we have had to use before and using frameworks that are created for this purpose.[79]

It is a fairly clear statement about developing national resources for the ontological security of the citizens.

In September 2007, the Prime Minister's Office allowed the idea to emerge that a new national motto would be created.[80] In the *Christian Science Monitor*, Mark Rice-Oxley commented that 'Brown believes he has good reason to play the British card. Nationalism is rising in Wales, Scotland, and England, and disenchanted ethnic minorities are picking at the seams of British unity. Home-grown terrorism has added extra urgency.'[81] It was a telling insight. Britishness is being recast for all sorts of reasons, but a powerful urge emanates from that sense of domestic threat. As Gordon Brown put it, 'But, at another level, terrorism in our midst means that debates, which sometimes may be seen as dry, about Britishness and our model of integration clearly now have a new urgency.'[82] Or, as Lord Taylor of Warwick – described in *Ebony* magazine as 'the only black in England's House of Lords' – put it, 'The terrorists seek to rule by the law of force, not by the force of law, but we must build bridges, not walls, between racial and cultural groups in Britain. It is vital that people from different

[79] *Ibid.*, p. 88.
[80] See 'Brown Denies British Motto Plan', *BBC News Online*, 21 September 2007, at http://news.bbc.co.uk [accessed July 2008].
[81] Mark Rice-Oxley, '"Once Great" Britain Searches for a National Motto', *Christian Science Monitor*, 16 November 2007, at www.csmonitor.com [accessed July 2008].
[82] Gordon Brown, 'Speech by the Rt Hon. Gordon Brown MP, Chancellor of the Exchequer, at the Fabian New Year Conference, London', 14 January 2006, at www.hm-treasury.gov.uk [accessed July 2008].

communities feel a sense of being included in the British identity, alongside their other cultural identity.'[83]

The narrative of a collapse of traditional Britishness – although, as we have seen, viewing the national identity as being in constant motion is a better metaphor – and the emptiness that has followed is assumed to have contributed to physical insecurity. To put it another way, the lack of resources provided to individuals for their ontological security at the national level has led some to look elsewhere for that provision. And one source, for some, has been Islamic radicalization, as for others, in the past, it might have been Irish Republicanism, Anarchism, Fascism, Socialism, Communism, Suffragetism, Trade Unionism, Nationalism, Imperialism, Monarchicalism – value systems so important that, for some, self-integrity depends upon action in conformity, to the point of putting the physical security of the self at risk. And so, underpinning these concerns about the nature (and decline) of Britishness has been this concern, this fear, of a terrorist enemy growing within. It is a fear that has been powerfully communicated in Britain since, in particular, July 2005. New Britishness is being built in part as a response to the new terrorism.

Terrorism within

By the middle of 2005, a clear conventional wisdom had taken root that Britain has a 'home-grown' terrorist problem.[84] The greatest threat was from a community within, a group who opposed Britain's global role in the then 'war on terror', and who saw fellow British citizens as enemies, legitimate targets in the global war. In this, the archetypal figure is Mohammed Siddique Khan, the leader of the gang that bombed the London transport system on 7 July 2005 – Britain's '7/7'. In a broad Yorkshire accent, aurally making the point about the 'home-grown' dimension, Khan's 'martyr's testimony' included the following message for the British population.

---

[83] On Taylor and the 'only black in England's House of Lords', see Hans J. Massaquoi, 'The Lord John Taylor of Warwick', *Ebony*, May 1997, on Taylor's website, at www.lordtaylor.org; Lord Taylor of Warwick Speech on Britishness in the House of Lords, 19 June 2008, at www.theyworkforyou.com [both accessed July 2008].

[84] For an examination of this, and a critique, see Stuart Croft, 'British Jihadis and the British War on Terror', *Defence Studies* 7(3), 2007: 317–37.

Our religion is Islam – obedience to the one true God, Allah, and following the footsteps of the final prophet and messenger Muhammad ... Your democratically elected governments continuously perpetuate atrocities against my people all over the world. And your support of them makes you directly responsible, just as I am directly responsible for protecting and avenging my Muslim brothers and sisters. Until we feel security, you will be our targets. And until you stop the bombing, gassing, imprisonment and torture of my people we will not stop this fight. We are at war and I am a soldier. Now you too will taste the reality of this situation.[85]

For Mohammed Siddique Khan, the appropriate and acceptable way of acting in conformity with his sense of ontological security was to become a suicide bomber. The official report into the '7/7' attacks found that '[t]he backgrounds of the 4 men appear largely unexceptional. Little distinguishes their formative experiences from those of many others of the same generation, ethnic origin and social background.'[86] It was not their appearance or background that was important; it was their sense of ontological security.

Britons, attacked by Britons, who showed no outward markers of their Otherness: in such circumstances, the focus fell not on ideological or psychological factors, but rather on religious identity. If they were British and not foreign, if they were not clearly loners, then perhaps those attacks reflected that there was something wrong with the 'British Muslim community' itself? Such a perception was fed by opinion polls widely carried out in the aftermath of the '7/7 attacks'. One such poll 'showed' that some 24 per cent of the British Muslim population 'have some sympathy with the feelings and motives of those who carried [out the attacks]'.[87] Six per cent apparently said that the attacks were justified: as the *Daily Telegraph* put it, 'six per cent may seem a small proportion but in absolute numbers it amounts

---

[85] Quoted in 'London Bomber: Text in Full', *BBC News Online*, 1 September 2005, at http://news.bbc.co.uk [accessed February 2008].

[86] 'Report of the Official Account of the Bombings in London on 7th July 2005', London: The Stationery Office; Ordered by the House of Commons to be printed 11th May 2006, at www.official-documents.gov.uk [accessed January 2008]. The Report continues 'with the partial exception of Lindsay, who will be considered separately, at the end of this chapter'.

[87] Anthony King, 'One in Four Muslims Sympathises with Motives of Terrorists', *Daily Telegraph* 23 July 2005, at www.telegraph.co.uk [accessed February 2008].

to about 100,000 individuals who, if not prepared to carry out terrorist acts, are ready to support those who do.'[88] Such analysis could, of course, be critiqued: did this really reflect more than bravado on the part of the respondents? Was the survey in any scientific sense representative; or rather, of what was it representative? Yet such debates miss the social impact of the impression – which was one of a single 'British Muslim community' deeply alienated from the British 'mainstream'. That is, the work of the media and these polls was to construct a single category – British Muslim – and to ascribe to it a single value – alienation. An excellent example of this was published in the *Daily Telegraph*. In one graphic, respondents were asked: 'Whether or not you have any sympathy with the feelings of those who carried out the attacks, do you think you understand why some people behave in that way?' The graphic showed 56% reporting 'Yes, I think I can understand', 39% reporting 'No, I can't understand how anyone could behave like that' and 4% replying 'don't know'. Of course, what is evident here is that the message of the mass of respondents having an 'understanding' of how 'anyone could *behave* like that' was powerfully presented. Actually, behaviour was only part of the 'No' response, but could be imputed to the 'Yes' response by the way that the graphic was put together.[89]

This 'single' 'alienated' 'community' contained 56% that could 'understand' the bombers, which was clearly a shocking outcome. That 26% disagreed that the ideas behind '7/7' were 'perverted and poisonous' equally so. Shaping the questions in particular ways could therefore see the concern with the '6%' rise to a '25%'; or even a '56%'. A community had been called into being, and thereby subjected to particular scrutiny. It was a community – 'the' British Muslim 'community' – that did not map onto representations of Islamic communities abroad. For example, little was said about Iraq that did not discuss the importance of Sunni and Shi'a, or indeed often the tripartite distinction of Sunni, Shi'a and Kurd.[90] However, no such nuances

[88] *Ibid.*
[89] A fuller table of results is at www.telegraph.co.uk [accessed February 2008].
[90] See for example Tony Blair's statement in Parliament in which he said of the Iraqi election: 'It was expressly non-sectarian, including all the main elements of Iraqi society – Shia, Sunni and Kurdish.' Tony Blair, 'Statement on Iraq and the Middle East', House of Commons, 21 February 2007, at www.number10.gov.uk [accessed July 2008].

and distinctions were allowed in the construction of a 'single British Muslim community', imagined in a unitary fashion.

The idea that a 'single community' contained members willing to kill Britons has been reinforced since '7/7' by a whole series of terrorist plots that have been disrupted and have been the subject of extensive coverage. Two weeks after '7/7', another plot targeted against the London transport system took place, but the terrorists failed to detonate their bombs. But there had been plots before '7/7'. In January 2003 police discovered what they believed to be a 'ricin' factory in London. Four people were arrested in connection with this case and were charged with 'possession of articles of value to a terrorist'.[91] The news was reported dramatically, as in the *Daily Mirror*, whose front page was a skull and crossbones on a yellow British map, with the headline 'It's here' superimposed.[92] It powerfully and visually brought home the reality of the 'new terrorism' to the readership, spatially illustrating the threat to everyone everywhere, not just in London. In June 2004, Kamel Bourgass was convicted of the murder of a police officer at the time of his arrest, and in April 2005 he was found guilty of the ricin plot. Bourgass, convicted of being a terrorist and police killer, was also a failed asylum seeker who had continued living in Britain, 'having gone to ground'.[93] A foreigner able to get around Britain's immigration system with ease was an obvious political issue. The Conservative leader, Michael Howard, said:

The tragedy of what happened is that Kamel Bourgass, an al-Qaeda operative, should not have been in Britain at all. He was one of the quarter of a million failed asylum seekers living in Britain. If Mr Blair had delivered the firm but fair immigration controls promised eight years ago, Bourgass wouldn't have been in Britain. He wouldn't have been here free to plot a ricin attack.[94]

[91] 'The Ricin Case Timeline', *BBC News Online*, 13 April 2005, at http://news.bbc.co.uk [accessed February 2008].

[92] *Daily Mirror* front page, 8 January 2003, showing a skull and crossbones against a map of Britain with the headlines 'It's Here' and 'Deadly Terror Poison Found in Britain', reproduced at *Answers.com*, at www.answers.com [accessed February 2008].

[93] 'Mystery Still Surrounds Killer', *BBC News Online*, 13 April 2005, at http://news.bbc.co.uk [accessed July 2008].

[94] Michael Howard, quoted in 'Ricin Case Shows Asylum Chaos', *BBC News Online*, 14 April 2005, at http://news.bbc.co.uk [accessed July 2008].

In 2008, Hassan Tabbakh was convicted of making bombs for use by others in terrorist operations. He had materials and instructions for putting the bombs together, and on his MP3 player were a variety of 'jihadi' materials, including one with the chorus 'This is the meaning of terrorism'.[95] The judge, Frank Chapman, explained, 'provided you do not actively engage in terrorist activity, it's not a crime to hold those views.'[96] One of the key elements in the narration of Tabbakh's crime was his foreignness; a Syrian national, he arrived in Britain around 2000 to claim asylum, and was granted indefinite leave in 2005. A contributor to *The Sun*'s message board, Johann Schmitt, summed up popular feeling: 'Claimed he was tortured so the numpty squad let him stay indefinitely, then he abuses Us by waging war in this country against Us … Everyone else of the same ilk as him do the same to. You live here in peace, abide by OUR laws or **** of [*sic*].'[97] The foreigner taking advantage of our freedoms to attack us: a powerful trope. 'We' reinscribe our Self as fair, tolerant, free, democratic, good and peaceful by linking and differentiating signs with the Other. How ironic that the contributor to *The Sun*'s message board should be named Schmitt; were he to have been in Britain in the early or middle part of the twentieth century, as a British citizen he would not have been allowed to enjoy those national freedoms. With a Germanic name, national resources would have been denied to his search for ontological security. And the same would have been so for a someone named Croft during the Jacobite Uprisings of 1715 or 1745–6 in the major English cities.

More powerful than the 'foreigner as threat' trope was that of the home-grown terrorist. In March 2004, a police raid on a variety of suspects – which was termed 'Operation Crevice' – led to the conviction three years later of five men for planning to build and detonate nitrate bombs. The group had a variety of plans – including buying nuclear weapons, the fear of which attracted a lot of public

---

[95] Duncan Gardham, 'Terrorist Bomb Maker Hassan Tabbakh Jailed for Seven Years', *Daily Telegraph*, 30 July 2008, at www.telegraph.co.uk; and Joanna Sugden, 'Hassan Tabbakh Found Guilty of Making Homemade Bombs', *The Times*, 30 July 2008, at www.timesonline.co.uk [both accessed July 2008].

[96] Cited in Press Association, 'Man Jailed for Plot to Make Bombs', *Northern Echo*, 31 July 2008, at www.thenorthernecho.co.uk [accessed July 2008].

[97] Johann Schmitt, on *The Sun* message board, 31 July 2008, at www.thesun.co.uk [accessed July 2008].

attention – but key 'practical' targets were a London nightclub, and
the Bluewater shopping mall in Kent, the latter attack planned for a
busy Saturday afternoon.[98] One of their other 'ideas' was to poison
beer at a football stadium.[99] However, the idea of a group such as
this trying to purchase nuclear materials again reinforced the image
of the threat from the new terrorism. It was widely reported that the
group had connections with al-Qaeda, who had passed on information about whom to contact in Russian organized crime; those con-
tacts led to the possibility of purchasing a radio-isotope bomb from
one such organization in Belgium.[100] The high-profile trial – which
involved the longest ever consideration of a verdict by a jury at a criminal trial, twenty-seven days – brought home through the media the
message of danger to everyday life. Although '7/7' brought the threat
of 'home-grown terrorism' to the status of conventional wisdom, it
quickly became set into a narrative of terrorist plans emanating from
the 'British Muslim community' since the attacks of '9/11'. In another
example, Saajid Badat was convicted in 2005 of planning to be a shoe
bomber, following the failed attempt of the Briton Richard Reid in
2001. Indeed, it appeared that he was planning his attack to coin-
cide with that of Reid.[101] Badat lived with his parents in Gloucester –
another example of the home-grown phenomenon. In the imagining,
'Gloucester' was in many ways far more threatening spatially than
'London'; for 'Gloucester' could be taken to represent any city or
town of any size in the country, raising the issue of threat in the practice of everyday life in going to work, shops, or school.

'Home-grown' is a very particular phrase to describe this phenomenon. A New York City Police Department report defined it as
follows:

Terrorism is the ultimate consequence of the radicalization process. In the
example of the home-grown threat, local residents or citizens gradually

[98] Rosie Cowan, 'British Suspects Considered Blowing up London Club, Court
      Told', *The Guardian*, 23 March 2006 [accessed January 2008].
[99] Chris Summers and Dominic Casciani, 'Fertiliser Bomb Plot: The Story',
      BBC News Online, 30 April 2007 [accessed February 2008].
[100] See for example Jason Bennetto, 'UK Terror Cell's Plot "To Buy a Nuclear
      Bomb"', *The Independent*, 23 March 2006, at www.independent.ie
      [accessed July 2008].
[101] See 'Shoe Bomb Conspirator Admits Bomb Plot', *The Guardian*, 28
      February 2005, at www.guardian.co.uk [accessed July 2008].

adopt an extremist religious/political ideology hostile to the West, which legitimizes terrorism as a tool to affect societal change. This ideology is fed and nurtured with a variety of extremist influences. Internalizing this extreme belief system as one's own is radicalization.[102]

'Home-grown' has become the common sense shorthand for describing a national Muslim citizen who plans or carries out attacks against fellow citizens. The Parliamentary *Intelligence and Security Sub-Committee's* report on the '7/7' attacks stated:

We remain concerned that across the whole of the counter-terrorism community the development of the home-grown threat and the radicalization of British citizens were not fully understood or applied to strategic thinking. A common and better level of understanding of these things among all those closely involved in identifying and countering the threat against the UK, whether that be the Security Service, or the police, or other parts of government, is critical in order to be able to counter the threat effectively and prevent attacks.[103]

The 'home-grown' threat was more problematic precisely because it was from within. Indeed, within days of the '7/7' attacks, there was a consensus: 'Intelligence experts and Islamic leaders agree that Thursday July 7 marks the bloody emergence of home-grown Islamic terrorism in Britain rather than the arrival of Al-Qaeda's bombers on these shores.'[104] In political and cultural elite imaginings, the new threat could, just possibly, lead to the complete destruction of the nation.

In the *Daily Mail* Deborah Davies described the threat: 'No longer the battle-hardened veterans of the Afghan war. No more the diaspora of Arab nationals fired up by the persecution in their native countries. It's now our own home-grown kids who are the biggest threat to their fellow countrymen. We're now witnessing Al Qaeda's third

---

[102] Mitchell D. Silber and Arvin Bhatt, 'Radicalization in the West: The Homegrown Threat', New York City Police Department, 2007, p. 16.

[103] *Government Response to the Intelligence and Security Committee's Report into the London Terrorist Attacks on 7 July 2005*, with the original document cited within, CM6786, Norwich: HMSO, May 2006, p. 4.

[104] David Leppard and Nick Fielding, 'The Hate', *Sunday Times*, 10 July 2005, at www.timesonline.co.uk [accessed July 2008].

Table 4.2. *Lloyds quantification of the UK terrorism threat*

UK TERRORISM THREAT QUANTIFIED
Capabilities
• Significant, innovative and potentially unlimited
• Co-ordinated explosions, chemical, biological, radiological or nuclear (CBRN) aspirations
Known Scale
• 200 groups
• 2,000 identified individuals
• 30 or more plots to kill people and cause damage
Unknowns
Increasingly innovative, ambitious and resilient

generation in action.'[105] Here the meaning of home-grown is where those in a particular country are prepared not only to attack fellow nationals, but to do so using the 'new terrorism'. A report by Lloyds of London defined the nature of this new home-grown threat: 'multiple co-ordinated attacks against high profile iconic targets'; 'a consistent focus on mass transportation systems'; 'an emphasis on mass casualties'; 'a desire for high media impact'; 'a tendency for attacks to occur in late summer'.[106] They set out the nature of the threat as shown in Table 4.2.[107]

Again, importantly part of this new British terrorism is the focus on CBRN aspirations. As John Reid put it:

let's understand the magnitude of the challenge. The complexity of the threat environment we face underlines the degree to which today's terrorists have a different mindset and 'new' ways to cause harm. For the first time in history both of the orthodox elements of threat – intention and capability – are now almost completely unconstrained; terrorists embrace

[105] Deborah Davies, 'Home-grown Hatred is the Greatest Threat to Our Country', *Daily Mail*, 10 August 2006, at www.dailymail.co.uk [accessed July 2008].

[106] Lloyds and International Institute for Strategic Studies, 'Home-grown Terrorism: What Does It Mean for Business?', London: Lloyds, 2007, at www.lloyds.com [accessed July 2008], pp. 6–7.

[107] National Centre for Social Research, *British Social Attitudes*.

a willingness to kill millions and have available the destructive capacity to do so.[108]

And Reid wanted that translated into everyday routine behaviour with the demand that everyone be alert for terrorist activity.[109]

There have certainly been a large number of examples of this new home-grown phenomenon presented in the United Kingdom. In December 2005, Abu Bakr Mansha was convicted of possessing material likely to help terrorism. He had a gun that could fire blanks which was in the process of being altered so that it could fire live rounds, and he had information, and an address, for Corporal Mark Byles, a decorated British soldier, and the prosecution alleged that Mansha sought 'either to kill him [Byles] or to do him really serious injury to exact revenge for what the corporal had achieved in Iraq'.[110] In August 2006, twenty-four individuals were arrested on suspicion of planning to destroy as many as ten passenger aircraft while in the air. Gordon Brown, then still Chancellor of the Exchequer, described this as 'an alleged conspiracy more audacious and potentially more murderous than anything Britain has seen before'.[111] It made for dramatic reading and reporting, as can be seen from newspaper headlines. *The Sun*, for example, had as its main caption 'Bottle Bombers', but the secondary captions were: 'The Day Britain was Grounded', 'Plot to Blow up 9 Jets Foiled', '24 Brit Muslims Held in Raid' and '400,000 in Airport Chaos'.[112] The *Daily Express* pointed on its front page coverage of the story the key dimension – that the suspects were not foreign, but British: here was the home-grown phenomenon underlined: '24 Suspects **All** British' ran their headline.[113] Parviz Khan's Birmingham-based gang

---

[108] John Reid, 'We Must Be More Alert than Ever', *The Independent*, 9 September 2009, at www.independent.co.uk [accessed October 2009].

[109] On this, see Stuart Croft and Cerwyn Moore, 'Understanding Terrorist Threats in Britain', *International Affairs* 86(4), July 2010: 821–35.

[110] David Cocks QC, quoted from the court case in Duncan Gardham, 'Muslim Planned Revenge Attack on Hero Soldier', *Daily Telegraph*, 23 December 2005, at www.telegraph.co.uk [accessed July 2008].

[111] Speech by the Rt Hon. Gordon Brown MP, Chancellor of the Exchequer, on 'Meeting the Terrorist Challenge', given to Chatham House, 10 October 2006, at www.hm-treasury.gov.uk [accessed February 2008].

[112] The image can be found at www.septicisle.info [accessed February 2008].

[113] *Ibid.*; emphasis in the original.

were convicted of plotting to kidnap a British Muslim soldier on the streets of the city's entertainment district, and of planning between April 2006 and February 2007 to behead him on a film that would then be generally released.[114] The case proved again to be high profile in the court case that culminated in January 2008, particularly when the prosecuting lawyer, Nigel Rumfitt QC, described the plan as follows: 'He [the soldier] would be taken to a lock-up garage and there he would be murdered by having his head cut off like a pig.'[115] The description of the plan to kill the soldier – like killing a pig – resonated widely across the country. It spoke of the inhumanity of the enemy within, one prepared to treat heroes like animals. On 29 June 2007, two car bombs were discovered and dismantled outside the Tiger Tiger nightclub in London, and in a nearby street. The first car bomb contained explosives 'made up of 60 litres of petrol, several propane gas cylinders, nails and a detonation mechanism', with the second comprising something very similar.[116] The car bombs were clearly designed to mimic those in frequent use in Iraq: designed to kill and maim indiscriminately. The following day, a car filled with propane gas canisters was set on fire and crashed into the main terminal at Glasgow airport in another attempt to kill. Here, one of the two attackers – Kafeel Ahmed – died of burns.

In addition to this series of cases, there were those more directly associated with fears of weapons of mass destruction. Dhiren Barot was sentenced for planning a series of attacks in the United States; he had arrived in the country in 2000 to begin preparations. He and seven accomplices were convicted of a variety of plans, including clear elements of the new terrorism: 'planning to kill "hundreds if not thousands" of people using explosives-packed limousines and a "dirty" radiation bomb'.[117] In what was to become something of a pattern in

---

[114] 'Man Admits Plot to Behead Soldier', *BBC Online*, 29 January 2008, at http://news.bbc.co.uk [accessed January 2008].

[115] Quoted in 'Man "Plotted to Cut off Muslim Soldiers Head"', *The Independent*, 23 January 2008, at www.independent.co.uk [accessed February 2008].

[116] See Vikram Dodd and Richard Norton-Taylor, 'Car Bombs Come to London', *The Guardian*, 30 June 2007, at www.guardian.co.uk [accessed July 2008].

[117] '136 Years for "Dirty Bomb" Gang', *Daily Mirror*, 16 June 2007, at www.mirror.co.uk [accessed July 2008].

such cases, when confronted with the evidence Barot pleaded guilty.[118] Still more dramatic was the police raid that took place in East London in June 2006 in Forest Gate, where arrests were made over the construction of an alleged chemical weapon. The story was front-page news. Two brothers were – on the basis of intelligence – suspected of manufacturing, and planning to use, chemical weapons of mass destruction. The event was highly photogenic: police officers arrived wearing full chemical, biological, nuclear and radiological suits and respirators, and constructed a protective enclosure around the house. In the subsequent investigation of the police action, caused not least because one of the men was shot and injured in the raid, it was confirmed that police feared home-grown new terrorism: that 'a bomb with hazardous material (a "dirty bomb") was located in 46 or 48 Lansdown Road, Forest Gate'.[119]

Another dimension of the threat emerged with the arrest of Samina Malik, a twenty-three-year-old Londoner subsequently convicted under Section 58 of the Terrorism Act 2000.[120] Seemingly ordinary, working at W. H. Smith's – although at the airside shop at Heathrow Airport – she possessed a series of manuals that might be of assistance to terrorists, 'including the al-Qa'eda Manual, the Terrorist's Handbook, the Mujahideen Poisons Handbook and several military manuals'.[121] However, what drew her to wider attention were her attempts at glorifying terrorism through her poetry. Here is one of the most widely cited texts:

It's not as messy or as hard as some might think.
It's all about the flow of the wrist.
Sharpen the knife to its maximum.
And before you begin to cut the flesh.
Tilt the fool's head to its left.

[118] See 'Man Admits UK–US Terror Bomb Plot', *BBC News Online*, 12 October 2006, at http://news.bbc.co.uk [accessed July 2008].
[119] Independent Police Complaints Commission, 'Independent Investigation into the Shooting of Muhammad Abdulkahar in 46 Lansdown Road, Forest Gate on Friday 2 June, 2006', 3 August 2006, at www.ipcc.gov.uk [accessed July 2008], p. 2.
[120] 'Lyrical Terrorist Found Guilty', *BBC Online*, 8 November 2007, at http://news.bbc.co.uk [accessed December 2007].
[121] Sue Hemming, Crown Prosecution Service, quoted in Duncan Gardham, '"Lyrical Terrorist" Samina Malik Cleared on Appeal', *Daily Telegraph*, 17 June 2008, at www.telegraph.co.uk [accessed July 2008].

Saw the knife back and forth.
No doubt the punk will twitch and scream.
But ignore the donkey's ass.
And continue to slice back and forth.
You'll feel the knife hit the wind and food pipe.
But Don't Stop.
Continue with all your might.
And now you should feel the knife vibrate.
You can feel the warm heat being given off.
But this is due to the friction being caused.[122]

This example of her work she entitled 'How to Behead'. Malik was subsequently cleared on appeal: as Susan Hemming from the Crown Prosecution Service explained, 'Ms Malik was not prosecuted for her poetry. She was prosecuted for possessing documents that could provide practical assistance to terrorists.'[123] However, it was her poetry that resonated with the wider public, clarifying still further the Otherness of the home-grown terrorists.

British citizens have grown used to hearing representatives of the security apparatus explaining the scale of the home-grown threat. In May 2007, MI5 – Britain's Security Service, which is 'responsible for protecting the United Kingdom against threats to national security' – revealed that they and the police were following 2,000 individuals in the UK who they believed were 'actively supporting al-Qaeda'.[124] This was repeated by the MI5 head, Jonathan Evans, in November 2007 in a speech in which he said that the number had risen by 400 – that is, by 25 per cent – since the speech the previous year by his predecessor. Not only had the pool increased to 2,000, but Evans admitted that 'we suspect that there are as many again that we don't yet know of'.[125] That is, the actual number of individuals of concern was significantly more than 4,000. MI5 are responsible for setting and publishing the national threat level. This began on 1 August 2006, and

122 This and another poem – 'The Living Martyrs' – is reproduced in Arthur Martin, 'British Muslim Woman Convicted of Penning Poems about Beheadings', *Daily Mail*, 9 November 2007, at www.dailymail.co.uk [accessed February 2008].
123 *Ibid.*
124 Frank Gardner, 'MI5 Watch 2,000 Terror Suspects', *BBC Online*, 2 May 2007, at http://news.bbc.co.uk [accessed February 2008].
125 'MI5 Chief's Warning – Full Text', *The Guardian*, 5 November 2007, at www.guardian.co.uk [accessed January 2008].

was set at 'severe' – 'an attack is highly likely'. Ten days later, it was raised to 'critical' – 'an attack is expected imminently'. It was reduced to 'severe' four days later, where it remained until being raised again to 'critical' on 30 June 2007; it remained at severe from 4 July 2007 until 20 July 2009, when it was reduced to 'substantial' – an attack is a strong possibility'.[126] On 22 January 2010 it was raised again to 'severe'.

And so it is clear how this sense of the 'home-grown threat' has evolved from specific attacks, and from the impact of a series of police operations, over several years. First, the view was that 'they' were from without; 'they' once were able to kill only a few. Now 'they' are the citizen within, with such means that the existence of the whole country is at stake. And it is because Britishness has failed to bind society. At least, these are all widely shared perceptions; they have become the new common sense. The scale of the number of people under surveillance, the number of plots and the high-profile nature of the home-grown terrorism fears has led to a great deal of speculation. In the *Daily Mail*, Ruth Dudley Edwards asked: 'Will Britain one day be Muslim?' The core of her argument was this:

In my many conversations with like-minded people about the threat that radical Islam poses to the British way of life – and, indeed, to European civilisation – we frequently end by despairingly agreeing that the West seems intent on committing political and cultural suicide. When we look starkly at the demographic statistics, the wimpishness of our Establishment in the face of the threat, the perversions perpetrated by political correctness and our own passivity, it's hard to avoid the conclusion that within a couple of generations, Islam will be in control in Europe ... Yes, the vast majority of Muslims in Britain are tolerant and law-abiding but this is no time for timidity. The enemy may be a minority but he is within, armed and dangerous and we have to deal with him.[127]

The 'Muslim enemy' might be a minority, but it is so dangerous, the argument runs, that it requires fundamental changes in the way that Britain is governed.

---

[126] See the history on the MI5 website at www.mi5.gov.uk [accessed October 2009].

[127] Ruth Dudley Edwards, 'Will Britain One Day Be Muslim?', *Daily Mail*, 5 May 2007, at www.dailymail.co.uk [accessed March 2008].

Such concerns affect everyday life, and as a consequence, everyday perceptions and understandings. In February 2008 the Archbishop of Canterbury, Dr Rowan Williams, gave a highly academic lecture on civil and religious law in England.[128] In the course of interviews with the media, particularly with BBC Radio's *World at One* programme, he was reported to have commented on an approach to law in which 'there's one law for everybody and that's all there is to be said, and anything else that commands your loyalty or allegiance is completely irrelevant in the processes of the courts – I think that's a bit of a danger ... There's a place for finding what would be a constructive accommodation with some aspects of Muslim law, as we already do with some other aspects of religious law.'[129] The Archbishop had, it was said, argued that the introduction of sharia law was 'inevitable.' Whatever he actually meant – and he seems to have been referring to the work of religious courts in family and financial matters, where agreed by the participants[130] – the reaction was overwhelming, hostile and negative. Gordon Brown's spokesperson told the media: 'Our general position is that sharia law cannot be used as a justification for committing breaches of English law.'[131] Of course, what was being heard was 'sharia' and was what being understood by that was 'jihadi'. Damian Thompson in the *Daily Telegraph* wrote that 'Williams is lending his support to the establishment of a non-Christian theocracy in Britain.'[132] On the BBC television *Ten O'Clock News*, the Home Affairs correspondent, Mark Easton, reported the story not with images from the Archbishop, but rather three 'images' of sharia law: the first a man being whipped, a second man showing an amputated hand, and the third an only slightly out-of-shot summary execution. Popular opinion – such as it can be judged through online responses – was particularly interesting. The BBC – having 'broken' the story – received a large number of such responses. Declan Maguire wrote

---

[128] The full text is at www.archbishopofcanterbury.org [accessed March 2008].
[129] Quoted in 'Sharia Law in the UK is "Unavoidable"', *BBC News Online*, 7 February 2008, at http://news.bbc.co.uk [accessed March 2008].
[130] The Archbishop's defence is at www.archbishopofcanterbury.org [accessed March 2008].
[131] Quoted in Riazat Butt, 'Archbishop Backs Sharia Law for British Muslims', *The Guardian*, 7 February 2008, at www.guardian.co.uk [accessed March 2008].
[132] Damian Thompson, 'Holy Smoke', *Daily Telegraph*, 7 February 2008, at http://blogs.telegraph.co.uk [accessed March 2008].

'Live in Britain work in Britain, live by British laws and standards! The rules are the rules and in such respect one size does fit all!' For Ian Knowles, '"this is how it works in England". If this isn't what you want, then no one forces you to stay here.' Or as Umm Muhammad – a self-identified British Muslim – put it, 'To me this has only achieved one thing: reinforce the idea in the English commoner that all what Muslims are after is changing their country's law, habits etc.'[133]

The Archbishop had clumsily reinforced a key point about contemporary Britain: in public discourse, Islam is frequently referred to in relation to terrorism. Thus, in January 2007, Sir Cyril Taylor, Chair of the government's Specialist Schools and Academies Trust, argued for the closure of faith schools, as they presented a 'strategic security problem'. Muslim children – although not mentioned explicitly, the groups that were spoken of by Taylor were 'Pakistanis' and 'Bangladeshis' – failed to mix if they went to faith schools (i.e. Islamic), and '[t]hey would be much more likely to collaborate with the police and tell them people within their own community are doing things they shouldn't be doing if they were better integrated'.[134] This was needed, Taylor argued, in twenty urban areas in the country.

In these ways, the nature of the 'home-grown' terrorist has been called into existence. S/he is a member of the 'single Muslim community' in Britain, British and yet a traitor to the citizens of the country. As Sir Michael Astill, the judge in the so-called 'Crevice', plot told Omar Khyam and his colleagues, 'you have betrayed this country that has given you every opportunity.'[135] They may take their ideology from al-Qaeda, may even have visited training camps in South Asia, but are fundamentally self-starters, self-radicalized, individuals who look at ways for 'protecting and avenging my Muslim brothers and sisters', as Mohammed Siddique Khan had said in his martyr's testimony. Committed to the new terrorism, they use the Internet to create networks and to learn techniques, and are interested in perpetrating attacks using weapons of mass destruction. A new, violent, potent, enemy within has been called into being.

[133] All reactions on the BBC website, at www.bbc.co.uk [accessed March 2008].
[134] Quoted in Jon Boone, '"Multi-faith" Academies Set to Force Integration', *Financial Times*, 22 January 2007, at www.ft.com [accessed March 2008].
[135] Astill quoted in 'Five Get Life over UK Bomb Plot', *BBC News Online*, 30 April 2007, at http://news.bbc.co.uk [accessed July 2008].

Conclusion

'New Britishness' has been developed in part because of the 'new terrorism'; the new Britishness Self is being constructed against those who support home-grown terrorism, those who are the internal Others. This discourse has led to the creation and adaptation of institutions to further this new Britishness. Through this, a new identity has been constructed – that of the 'single British Muslim community' – which has become the focus of so much debate about the interplay of identities in the building of the new Britishness. But that 'single Muslim community' has two functions in this identity construction: that of Radical Other, to be feared, demonized and destroyed; but also that of Orientalized Other, to be engaged, patronized and led.

In these ways, the new terrorism has been constructed not just as a threat to the lives and property of those in the United Kingdom, but as something far more sinister, far more dangerous: as an existential threat. Charles Clarke, when Home Secretary, spoke frequently of the way in which 'al-Qaida and their related organisations are about destroying democracy. Some ride a particular issue on the back of it, such as Iraq, but that is not actually what it is about. It is about a fundamental attack on the values of our society.'[136] Clarke's successor, John Reid, argued 'Sometimes we may have to modify some of our own freedoms in the short term in order to prevent their misuse and abuse by those who oppose our fundamental values and would destroy all of our freedoms in the modern world.'[137] For Reid, Britain was facing 'probably the most sustained period of severe threat since the end of the second world war' in the face of 'unconstrained international terrorists'.[138] Echoing the theme, the MP Frank Field wrote:

Much of the war on terrorism has to be planned for the long term. It is best to see it as an evolving programme of measures spanning a period perhaps as long as the four decades of the cold war. Such a judgment is not given

---

[136] Charles Clarke MP, quoted in Mark Day and Jennifer Gerber, 'Who Are the "No-Hopers" on Labour's Backbenches?', *Progress Online*, 15 December 2005, at www.progress.squareeye.com [accessed July 2008].

[137] Alan Travis, 'Anti-terror Critics Just Don't Get It, Says Reid', *The Guardian* 10 August 2006, at www.guardian.co.uk [accessed July 2008].

[138] *Ibid.*

to chill the reader's blood. We have entered a new political age; the threat to the safety of large numbers of citizens is now an everyday reality. The Islamist bombers differ from those of the IRA.[139]

Such ideas are replicated in the media: Gerard Baker, for example, argues that 'September 11, 2001, gave birth to a radical and dangerous new world … It provided a terrifying harbinger of much larger atrocities to come, when terrorists and their state supporters get hold of weapons with which they can kill millions, not thousands. This new enemy is not like old enemies. It is fundamentalist and suicidal and apocalyptic.'[140] And it led to new practices. By 2005, powers to stop and search under the 2000 Prevention of Terrorism Act, Section 44, had been used on 35,776 people, leading to 455 arrests.[141]

The final chapter of this book examines the ways in which the political and cultural elite has securitized this 'single Muslim community' through a variety of genres. And it explores how this securitization is performed and routinized in many aspects of everyday life. In so doing, it explores how the evolution of identity, while offering resources for the ontological security of the majority, can undermine the ontological security of the minority.

[139] Frank Field, 'Without Security, Liberty Dies', *The Guardian*, 31 August 2005, at www.guardian.co.uk [accessed July 2008].

[140] Gerard Baker, 'The First Step towards Defeating the Terrorists: Stop Blaming Ourselves', *The Times*, 11 August 2006, at www.timesonline.co.uk [accessed July 2008].

[141] Ben Russell, 'Police Stop and Search 100 People a Day under New Antiterror Laws', *The Independent*, 25 January 2006, at www.independent.co.uk [accessed July 2008].

5 | The construction of ontological insecurity

Introduction

This book began by examining the ways in which the national identity, socially transmitted, can provide means of support for the ontological security of individuals. Having examined contributions by figures such as Cruikshank, Grierson and Colley it is clear that there is nothing new in this; that such processes of linking the national identity to the ontological security of citizens and subjects has a long lineage. Indeed, in the sense in which Giddens has reconstructed ontological security from Laing's work, it is clear that for the majority of individuals, security cannot be achieved without understanding the social, and here national, dimension. Much of this connection is through the imagery and tokens that come to represent that permanent and fixed sense of nation that thereby contributes to the ontological security of individuals. This can be seen in three, interrelated dimensions: shared topics for conversation (and thereby social norms that are accepted as common sense); shared social practices (of appropriate and acceptable ways of behaving); and a shared recognition of the meaning of images. This understanding of the way in which ontological security can link the national identity with individuals' struggles to keep dread at bay was overlaid in Chapter 2 with a post-Copenhagen securitization theory, developed to understand the construction of contemporary security threats in the United Kingdom. Through particular means, two socially constructed crises – '9/11' and '7/7' – have come to be the social mechanisms through which the British Self has come to securitize the Radical Other – Islamic/ Islamist/ international terrorism – and has come to (re)construct an Orientalized Other, here being the 'British Muslim community'. The claim is that these processes of constructing the Radical and Orientalized Other have taken place through language and imagery, and the securitizing actor has been not just the government but also a range of other social agents, including the media, religious figures and academics/public intellectuals.

Throughout, as argued in Chapter 3, these narrations of Britishness offered different resources to individuals in the construction of their ontological security. The elements of national identity have always been in motion, offering different resources to people at different times. Temporality has been a key element, seen for example in the identification of the 1940s for the foundational myth of contemporary national identity, or the trans-generational class solidarity that from the 1960s was evoked by looking back across the century. Further, spatiality has also been in flux, in relation to differing relations with empire, commonwealth and race, and in relation to Europe and America. But throughout there has been a contestation, and sometimes developments have threatened, or disempowered, individuals in their pursuit of ontological security. Chapter 4 examined how Britishness has been constructed to further ontological security, and how the denial of Britishness in those constructions inflicts ontological insecurities on others. The 'New Britishness' that developed from the 1990s has been constructed in part because of the invocation of the 'new terrorism'. That is, the new British Self has in part been constructed against those who are deemed to support home-grown terrorism, those who are thereby called into being as the internal Others. To institutionalize this discourse, a new identity has been constructed – that of the 'single British Muslim community' – which has become the focus of so much debate about the interplay of identities in the building of the new Britishness. But that 'single Muslim community' has two functions in this identity construction: that of Radical Other, to be feared, demonized and destroyed; and also that of Orientalized Other, one that might be engaged, patronized and led. The Radical Other has been constructed through the fear of the new terrorism, and it has become entrenched not just as a threat to the lives and property of those in the United Kingdom, but as something far more dangerous: as an existential threat.

The argument now requires substantiation with particular evidence, and that is the purpose of this chapter. I have argued that ontological security is structured around four claims. First, that self-identity is based on a sense of biographical coherence, comprehended by the individual and communicable to others; that it allows for a sense of agency, that is the subject of reflexivity, of self-monitoring; and that this self-identity is performed in, through and by an everyday routine. Second, this self-identity, and the actions that it leads to, is produced in a cocoon of trust structures, notably in the role of social tokens and in confidence in professional experts, that nevertheless require constant regrounding. Third, the ontologically secure agent is able to act in conformity with his/her sense of self-integrity; the ontologically secure agent has a firm sense of the appropriate and the acceptable. Finally, no matter how ontologically secure the agent may be, there is always a fragility as well as a robustness to that position; there is always an awareness of the polar opposite, ontological insecurity, in which dread is dominant. The ontologically secure individual can never be always secure in that position. Further, a post-Copenhagen securitization theory might also be described through four claims. First, that it would focus not only on speech but also on the intertextuality of images and silences. Second, it would explicitly examine the securitizing moves not only of governments, but also of other elite social agents in society. Third, such a theory would analyse the ways in which securitizing moves reconstruct audiences into in-groups and out-groups, and into those who accept the new securitization, and those who seek to resist. And fourth, that it would focus on the ways in which extraordinary measures take place not only at the level of the state but also at the level of the everyday, by focusing on the performances of the securitization both in embedding that securitization by making the securitizing move every day, and in maintaining it subsequently in the everyday.

In order to develop the empirical element of the argument, I will draw on Lene Hansen's routes for such a study.[1] However, these will be reconstructed to focus on the core social actors. The first section examines the way in which the political and especially the governmental elite has developed constructions of Radical and Orientalized Others. The second focuses on media work to securitize those communities. The third examines the way in which performances in everyday life securitize communities. Whereas the second section looks at securitizing moves in media outlets, the fourth focuses on the role of individuals, by illustrating the ways in which securitizations have been developed and performed by particular public intellectuals, with the examples of a bishop, a novelist, an academic and a journalist.

---

[1] Hansen, *Security as Practice: Discourse Analysis and the Bosnian War,* London: Routledge, 2006, pp. 59–64.

Elite constructions of Radical and Orientalized Others

The most obvious place to begin the examination of the constructions of Otherness is with those who have the most social power to develop such constructions, which is the political elite. Those arguments that became understood as appropriate and acceptable, the common sense upon which all else – discussion, policy, performance – were constructed through the political legitimacy achieved by successful securitizing moves. But it is not only the Prime Minister, of course, who has agency in such securitizations of identity; the role is also performed by other ministers and, given the 'internal' as well as 'external' nature of the new terrorist threat, a succession of Home Secretaries also played their role. This section examines public speeches by Tony Blair and Gordon Brown, and also by three Home Secretaries – Charles Clarke, John Reid and Jacqui Smith – that were individually and collectively clear securitizing moves.[2] These speeches took place in 2001, when the new narrative of the challenge to Britishness by the new terrorism, and the consequent re-ascription of identity to 'British Muslims', developed – and in 2005, 2006, 2007, 2008 and 2009. They were connected around three propositions. First, that a 'new Britain' had been called into existence; second, that this 'new Britain' was challenged and threatened by a 'new terrorism'; and third, that in this situation, the focus had to be on the (singular) Muslim community, which could be understood as a dichotomy between a Radical Other and an Orientalized Other.

In relation to the call to a 'new Britain', these securitizing actors noted particular temporal points that could be contrasted with the happier present state. For Gordon Brown, 'in the new Britain of this generation, we must unlock all the talents of all of the people.' He emphasized the struggle for betterment in the country – 'past generations

---

[2] The speeches are: Tony Blair, 'Speech by Prime Minister, Tony Blair, at the Labour Party Conference', 2 October 2001, at www.guardian.co.uk; Gordon Brown, 'Gordon Brown's Labour Conference Speech in Full', 24 September 2007, at www.24dash.com; Charles Clarke, 'Contesting the Threat of Terrorism', to the Heritage Foundation, published 21 October 2005 by Heritage, at www.heritage.org; John Reid, 'Full Text of the Speech from Home Secretary John Reid to the Labour Party Conference', 28 September 2006, at http://news.bbc.co.uk; and Jacqui Smith, 'Home Secretary's Oral Statement to Parliament on 24 March 2009', at http://press.homeoffice.gov.uk [all accessed February 2010].

unlocked just some of the talents of some of the people' – and spoke of 'the next chapter in our progress. The next stage of our country's long journey to build the strong and fair society.' In this speech, the temporal other was oblique: 'And in Britain where once there were three million unemployed, there are today more men and women in jobs than ever in our history – for the first time over 29 million people in work.' This – to his audience – would have been taken as a reference to the Thatcher years of the 1980s. Charles Clarke's temporal other was earlier: 'Compare the United Kingdom of the 1950s – before significant migration took place – with the United Kingdom of today. In so many key fields of life and endeavour – design, literature, food; there are too many to name – the vibrancy of diversity has powered creativity and economic success, but always within the framework of our common values.'

The nature of the new terrorism was particularly clear in Tony Blair's speech given to the Labour Party at the time of the 9/11 attacks. 'In retrospect, the Millennium marked only a moment in time. It was the events of September 11 that marked a turning point in history, where we confront the dangers of the future and assess the choices facing humankind.' He argued: 'They have no moral inhibition on the slaughter of the innocent. If they could have murdered not 7,000 but 70,000 does anyone doubt they would have done so and rejoiced in it?' John Reid was characteristically clear that there was an appropriate and acceptable way to look at the new realities: 'This is not a clash of civilisations. It's not Muslims versus the rest of us. It's evil terrorists on one side against all civilised people on the other. There can be no compromise, no appeasement with terrorism.' Charles Clarke marked the period of the new terrorism very precisely: 'my own view is that the 1945–89 Cold War was succeeded by the period to 9/11 in 2001, when democracy became better entrenched, and now, after 2001, all that democratic progress is under attack from al-Qaeda and their allies'. And the nature of the new terrorism was different, as Clarke argued: 'Because they recognize no common bonds with people who have different beliefs, they are prepared to kill indiscriminately. Indeed, mass murder is their explicit objective, their measure of success in their terms, and their methods of recruitment bear more comparison with self-destructive cults than political movements.' Jacqui Smith confirmed that 'we know that this new form of terrorism is different in scale and nature from the terrorist threats we have had to deal with in recent decades'. And she was concerned with 'the specific threat posed by terrorist use of chemical, biological, radio-logical or nuclear weapons and explosives'.

Such analyses required a third move: the identification of 'British Muslims' as a 'group' worthy of focus, and the consequent subdiv-ision within that 'group' into the acceptable and mainstream on the one hand, and the deviant and alien on the other. John Reid made the strength of the British self-evident: 'We will go where we please, we will discuss what we like and we will never be brow-beaten by bullies. That's what it means to be British.' But the 'British Muslim' mainstream was not fully part of the British Self. As Tony Blair put it: 'We're standing up for the people we represent, who play by the rules and have a right to expect others to do the same. And espe-cially at this time let us say: we celebrate the diversity in our country, get strength from the cultures and races that go to make up Britain today; and racist abuse and racist attacks have no place in the Britain we believe in.' That is, 'we' the British are duty bound, as part of our Britishness, to 'stand up' for the British Muslim who acts legitim-ately by 'playing by the rules'. John Reid developed this theme: 'And Muslims are our friends as well as our fellow citizens. They are owed our support ... Because if we, in this movement, are going to ask the decent, silent majority of Muslim men – and women – to have the courage to face down the extremist bullies, then we need to have the courage and character to stand shoulder to shoulder with them in doing it.' Again, the 'decent, silent, majority of Muslims' are a separ-able group, connected with the Self, but not a constitutive part of it. The Self has to protect this group; but that group is at the core still separable from that Self. And the Radical Other is a total threat, one with whom there is no space for compromise, for as Reid put it, 'And let's be clear. It cannot be right that the rights of an individual sus-pected terrorist be placed above the rights, life and limb of the British people. It's wrong. Full stop. No ifs. No buts. It's just plain wrong.' As Charles Clarke argued, 'there can be no negotiation about the re-cre-ation of the Caliphate; there can be no negotiation about the impos-ition of sharia law; there can be no negotiation about the suppression of equality between the sexes; there can be no negotiation about the ending of free speech. These values are fundamental to our civiliza-tion and are simply not up for negotiation.' Indeed, in this sense, the Radical Other was an existential threat: 'Their nihilism means that our societies would only cease to be a target if we were to renounce all those values of freedom and liberty which we have fought to extend over so many years.'

Of course, such securitizing moves carried alongside a determination to perform emergency measures. As Tony Blair put it, 'whatever the dangers of the action we take, the dangers of inaction are far, far greater'. He went on: 'Every reasonable measure of internal security is being undertaken. Our way of life is a great deal stronger and will last a great deal longer than the actions of fanatics, small in number and now facing a unified world against them.' From Charles Clark, the suggestion was 'that the best way to contest this threat is by building and strengthening the democracy of our society, by isolating extremism in its various manifestations, by strengthening the legal framework within which we contest terrorism, and by developing more effective means to protect our democracy'. John Reid commented: 'To counter radicalization as a nation, we need not only to tackle the immediate dangers but put in place the concept, doctrine, laws and capabilities for a challenge we expect will last a generation.' And in terms of specificities, Jacqui Smith outlined a series of developments: 'In recent years, the number of police dedicated to counter-terrorism work has grown by from 1,700 to 3,000. The Security Service has doubled in size. We have trained tens of thousands of people throughout the country in how to prepare for, and protect against, a terrorist attack. And we are working with communities to prevent the spread of violent extremism. We currently spend £2.5bn on countering terrorism. By 2011, this will rise to £3.5bn – the majority of it on the main focus of work – pursuing terrorists wherever they are and stopping their attacks.'

These three themes, and the implications for Britain and Britishness, were to be brought together by Blair in the series of lectures that he produced while Prime Minister, entitled *Our Nation's Future*. Lecture Five was the 'speech on multiculturalism and integration' given on 8 December 2006 with the heading 'The Duty to Integrate: Shared British Values'.[3] Although this speech was wide-ranging across a number of themes, the three main elements discussed above were brought to the fore.

[3] All references from this speech are drawn from the transcript, at http://webarchive.nationalarchives.gov.uk [accessed March 2010].

First, Blair was able to emphasize that there was a 'New Britain'; Blair repeated this theme, in particular in connection with race relations. Much of what he was to say was based on this call to a new nation. In this context, he said: 'When we won the Olympic bid to host the 2012 Games, we presented a compelling, modern vision of Britain: a country at ease with different races, religions and cultures'. This was a moment that could mark the move from the temporal other: 'This was not the stuffy old Britain that used to be sent up in the comedy sketches of the 1970s but a nation proud, willing and able to go out and compete on its merits'. And to underline this point of transformation: 'The ethos of this country is completely different from thirty years ago'. In specifying what that difference was, Blair suggested that it was common sense to realize that 'Our public culture is also completely different. We now have more ethnic minority MPs, peers, and ministers though not enough ... The media are generally more sensitive, and include ethnic minority reporters and columnists. Racism has, for the most part, been kicked out of sport. Offensive remarks and stupid stereotypes have been driven out of public conversation.' Crucially, though, this was a product that was not natural or organic; it was the product of struggle. 'It didn't happen easily. Most of us grew up in an era when action against discrimination was condemned as political correctness.' So, in the presentation of the world by the Prime Minister, there had been struggle against reactionary forces ('It is a matter of some pride to me that it has only been Labour governments that have introduced anti-discrimination legislation'), but by the middle of the first decade of the twenty-first century the new Britain was clear for all to see ('The basic courtesies, in other words, have been extended to all people'). There could not be a contrast with the 1940s, as that would have seemed odd and out of place; instead, the counter point was the 1970s, a period after which there had been renewal (and to which, presumably, given the dates, the Thatcher governments of the 1980s were therefore in some way contributors).

Second, this new nation was threatened by a new terrorism. The new terrorism was at the heart of the speech – a new reality to be faced. In this context, he said:

The day after we won the Olympic bid came the terrorist attacks in London. These murders were carried out by British-born suicide bombers who had lived and been brought up in this country, who had received all its many advantages and yet who ultimately took their own lives and the lives of the wholly innocent, in the name of an ideology alien to everything this country stands for.

Several important moves were made here. First, contrasting the success of the Olympic bid – just constructed as a marker for the progress and change in Britain compared with the past – and the direct challenge of the 7/7 attacks. That is, those terrorist attacks were deliberately aimed at the new Britain. Those involved within the country – the 'British-born suicide bombers' – were traitors to this new British reality; they had 'received its [the new Britain's] many advantages'. But they were instead motivated by the 'alien ideology'. As he went on to say, 'This ideology is not, of course, confined to Britain. It is a global phenomenon, long in the making and taking a long time to unmake.' To emphasize the point about the terrorist threat being 'new', Blair repeated his often made contrast with the violence in Northern Ireland's past:

Others warned me against putting the issue in the context of 7/7, of terrorism, of our Muslim community. After all, extremism is not confined to Muslims, as we know from Northern Ireland and fringe elements in many ethnic groups ... But the reason we are having this debate is not generalised extremism. It is a new and virulent form of ideology associated with a minority of our Muslim community.

The new terrorism was carried out by those with 'alien' ideology, capable of causing great harm to Britain, and rooted very specifically within the (singular) Muslim community.

Third, there was a distinction between legitimate and illegitimate Islamic practice. The legitimate were unradicalized: 'Nor is it a problem with the majority of the Muslim community. Most Muslims are proud to be British and Muslim and are thoroughly decent law-abiding citizens.' However, there was an enemy within that group: 'But it is a problem with a minority of that community, particularly originating from certain countries ... Their emphasis was not on shared values but separate ones, values based on a warped distortion of the faith of Islam.' And the majority Other were Orientalized, in their failure to control the Radical Other: 'integrating people whilst preserving their distinctive cultures, is not impossible. It is the norm. The failure of one part of one community to do so, is not a function of a flawed theory of a multicultural society. It is a function of a particular ideology that arises within one religion at this one time.' Thus, Blair's main claim was:

> Integration ... is not about culture or lifestyle. It is about values. It is about integrating at the point of shared, common unifying British values ... But when it comes to our essential values – belief in democracy, the rule of law, tolerance, equal treatment for all, respect for this country and its shared heritage – then that is where we come together, it is what we hold in common; it is what gives us the right to call ourselves British. At that point no distinctive culture or religion supersedes our duty to be part of an integrated United Kingdom.

At one key part of the speech, Blair brought the British identity and the challenge of the Radical Other together in a call to action: 'I always thought after 7/7 our first reaction would be very British: we stick together; but that our second reaction, in time, would also be very British: we're not going to be taken for a ride.' Through the speech acts of these various post-holders, a new security terrain was constructed, in which a new Britishness was challenged by a new terrorist threat; and in seeking to confront that threat, the British Self was constructed in contrast to both a Radical British Muslim Other, and an Orientalized one.

Media (re)securitizations

It is, however, important not to focus solely on the securitizing moves of the political elite post holders, as other social agents can and do also participate in securitizing moves in their own right. One of the central social actors in this sense is the media – which is to say, those organizations that impact upon the understanding of issues and problems for large numbers of citizens, and do so both by constructing stories in particular ways, and by the power of their editorials. This may occur when a story is generated essentially as part of the process of securitization; and the example examined here is a speech by the Archbishop of Canterbury in February 2007, mentioned in the previous chapter. In addition, a media organization may look to take a variety of opportunities to continually engage in securitizing moves, and the example of this form is taken from the *Evening Standard.*

Media organizations might conduct a securitizing move through the development of a story that can then be used to securitize. The example that illustrates this powerfully is the reaction to a speech given by the Archbishop of Canterbury, Dr Rowan Williams, on 7 February 2008. The Archbishop spoke of the value of 'an increased legal recognition of communal religious identities', and in a highly theoretical lecture concluded that 'if we are to think intelligently about the relations between Islam and British law, we need a fair amount of "deconstruction" of crude oppositions and mythologies, whether of the nature of sharia or the nature of the Enlightenment. But as I have hinted, I do not believe this can be done without some thinking also about the very nature of law.'[4] The speech – and the briefings that went to support it – was subjected to a torrent of highly critical comment which, while criticizing Dr Williams personally, were focused on the threat that sharia law posed to the United Kingdom.

The Sun reported the speech on its front page, under the heading 'What a Burkha'.[5] The linguistic play – 'burkha' for 'burke' – was designed to indicate that the Archbishop was an 'idiot'. The imagery chosen to support this heading was of 'burkha'-clad women raising two fingers in the direction of the reader in the left-hand corner of the page, and a picture of Dr Williams on the right – clearly indicating that the latter supported the former. Williams's comments were deemed to be 'an explosive outburst', and he was said to be calling for 'one set of rules for Muslims – and another for everyone else'. More importantly, though, the comments were placed immediately within the context of security. Those called upon for comment had both been involved in the violence of 7/7.

Paul Dadge, famously pictured helping masked 7/7 victim Davina Turrell, 24, was left stunned. The 31-year-old former fireman, of Cannock, Staffs,

---

[4] Rowan Williams, 'Archbishop's Lecture – Civil and Religious Law in England: a Religious Perspective', *The Archbishop of Canterbury*, 07 February 2008, at www.archbishopofcanterbury.org [accessed December 2009].

[5] 'What a Burkha' and 'Williams: Victory for Terrorism', *The Sun*, 8 February 2008, at www.thesun.co.uk [accessed December 2009]. All subsequent quotes in this paragraph are from this source.

said: 'The Archbishop's remarks are unhelpful. I am proud to be British and find the idea that Sharia law would ever become part of British law incredible.' Mary Burke, 50 – who survived the King's Cross bomb on July 7 2005 – said: 'Britain is a Christian country and should stay a Christian country. I don't want Islamic law here and I believe most of the British public agree with me.'

The story inside was under the title 'Williams: Victory for Terrorism', and was followed by a report on the 'practice' of sharia law:

The medieval punishments meted out to offenders – who can have their hands cut off or face the lash – have appalled the West. Many British Muslims share the horror felt about the barbarity of sentences handed out to offenders. But they stress that these punishments – known as hadd penalties – are the extreme end of a religious legal system that covers virtually every aspect of life in many Muslim countries.

Of course, the work here was to define a particular view of sharia law; to set it in contradistinction with, and as a (terrorist) threat to, Britishness; and then in that dichotomy, to find that British Muslims – albeit 'many' might be reluctant – are not on the side of Britishness.

The Sun's leader column was unambiguous: 'He also gives heart to Muslim terrorists plotting our destruction. They will see his foolish ramblings as a sign that our resolve against extremism is weakening.'[6] But although particularly forthright, *The Sun* was not alone in these constructions. In the *Daily Express*, the headline was 'Muslim Laws Must Come to Britain'.[7] On the front page, the headline was framed by an image of Abu Hamza (purportedly a different story), and on the inside pages, *The Express* used the same image of the 'burkha'-clad women raising two fingers to the reader, and reminded all that 'Sharia law has been used to justify stoning, beheadings and other brutal punishments in many Muslim countries. In extreme cases, Islamic courts have even put people to death for converting to Christianity.'[8] In a similar vein, in *The Independent*, Yasmin Alibhai-Brown spoke

[6] *Ibid.*
[7] Macer Hall, 'Muslim Laws Must Come to Britain', *Daily Express*, 8 February 2008, at www.express.co.uk [accessed December 2009].
[8] *Ibid.*

with the authority of the believer: 'I write here as a modern Muslim woman'. She explained:

What Rowan Williams wishes upon us is an abomination ... Many will be sent back to bastard husbands or flinty-eyed mullahs will take their children away. In Bradford and Halifax, they may be forbidden to drive or work where men are employed. Adultery will be punished. I don't think we will have public stonings but violence of some sort will be meted out (it already is) with lawmakers' backing.[9]

Alibhai-Brown's rhetoric and condemnation of sharia law was given powerful backing in the *Daily Telegraph*, which chose this moment to report on Sandy Mitchell, who

has terrifying first-hand experience of being on the wrong side of sharia law. Mr Mitchell, 52, was falsely accused of being involved in a car bombing in Saudi Arabia in 2000 when he was working there as an anaesthetic technician. He was held in prison for three years and tortured until he eventually signed a confession, which he later had to read out on Saudi television. A sharia court sentenced him to having his head partially severed, followed by public crucifixion. The sentence was later reduced to beheading, before the Saudi authorities finally conceded that al-Qa'eda terrorists had planted the bomb and let Mr Mitchell return home to Halifax, West Yorks. Yesterday he accused the Archbishop of Canterbury of 'betraying' Christians with his comments on Islamic law.[10]

In this story again, the Islamic Other was pitted against a Christian Self, although the latter would not stand up to empirical scrutiny in contemporary British practice.

Whether Williams's views were persuasive or not – and there are certainly plenty of problems with a speech that, although very theoretical, did not focus on important matters of definition – the point here is that the speech was taken as a cue for a series of securitizing moves from powerful social actors, major media organizations. It was a moment for connecting Islam and terrorism; sharia law and

---

[9] Yasmin Alibhai-Brown, 'What He Wishes on Us Is an Abomination', *The Independent*, 9 February 2008, at www.independent.co.uk [accessed December 2009].

[10] 'My Sentence Was Reduced to Beheading', *Daily Telegraph*, 9 February 2008, at www.telegraph.co.uk [accessed December 2009].

barbarism; sharia law, Islam and a threat to British values. The 'story' was not about security; it was the securitizing moves that emanated from the media (not the government, who were forced to respond) that created the security discourse.

The second type is a different form of securitizing move – not one following a security incident, nor an incident which is itself securitized. Instead, it is a long-term process of securitization, when a common theme becomes that of an identity frequently reported in security terms. The *Evening Standard*, London's daily newspaper, engaged in such actions, and this can be illustrated by focusing on the front-page coverage in September 2006 and by looking in detail at reporting over a ten-day period in November 2007.

In September 2006, the *Evening Standard* published a poll investigating Londoners' attitudes to British Muslims. A year and a summer after the attacks of 7/7, the poll showed that '[m]ore than a third of all Londoners – and more than a quarter of non-white Londoners – say they have felt uncomfortable near people of Asian or North African appearance on public transport. One-sixth of all Londoners surveyed have felt unhappy enough to move seats in such a situation.'[11] The leader argued that this was, apparently, the responsibility of the British Muslim community: 'London's tolerance and openness has held up amazingly well to date. It would be a tragedy if it were damaged by one community's reluctance to face up to the threat.' This was an excellent example of the securitizing process, whereby identities are separated, and the Self is demonstrated to be responsible and restrained, in the face of the failure of the Other – and here not just the Radical Other, but the 'mainstream' which was being Orientalized: 'The response of organisations such as the Muslim Council of Britain to terror raids and tougher laws has almost invariably been to cast Muslims as the victims, effectively playing down the anxieties of the majority of Londoners, whites and non-whites alike.' As part of this process, the newspaper would also provide a platform for individuals with strong views: Patrick Sookhdeo, for example, would argue that Islam is a different entity from other religions, and that a part of its

---

[11] Editorial comment, *Evening Standard*, 5 September 2006. A report on the survey is, at Nicholas Cecil, 'Londoners Who Want a Ban on Religious Schools', *Evening Standard*, 6 September 2006, www.thisislondon.co.uk [accessed December 2009].

difference is its inherently threatening nature. 'Christian denomin-
ational schools as well as Jewish schools continue to play an important role in community cohesion. Whether Islamic schools can fill such
a role is highly questionable.'[12] Later that same month, the newspaper
came out against plans to build a new mosque in east London, with
implicit concerns about both the Muslim cultural threat to Britishness,
and the security danger of having such a mosque close to the site of
the London Olympics. Its leader warned: 'Britain is not a Muslim
country. There are already ample places for its Muslim population
to gather and pray. What can possibly justify the creation of such a
huge new mosque on the doorstep of the 2012 Olympics? ... London
does not need this mosque.'[13] Here, the newspaper made a clear identity stand: Britain is not – and is therefore separate from – a Muslim
country, while also being clear that Muslims had to be content with
existing religious provision.

November 2007 is an interesting month to examine the publication
of materials in the *Evening Standard*, as in that month the newspaper
organized a debate entitled 'Is Islam good for London?' That such
an event could be organized illustrated the degree to which the identity of the British Muslim had already been securitized. But to make
the point clear, the introduction, by Anne McElvoy and Katharine
Barney, stressed the identity/security link: 'In a city with a Muslim
population of well over half a million and growing and against a
background of the terror threat that affects us all, the question of
how a modern diverse city can live with Islam – and vice versa – has
a fresh salience'.[14] However, the salience of the question ran through
the newspaper's coverage of news stories during the month. On
2 November, for example, it ran a story on a bomb-proof bin: 'It is
a bin unlike any other ... The Renew bin, which costs £15,000 to
produce and £3,000 to install, has been designed to withstand the
force of a bomb blast so it can be used in sensitive areas such as Tube
stations and airports.' Entrepreneur Brian James said: 'We recognised
that in a post-7/7 world we needed to deliver a sustainable and secure

---

[12] Patrick Sookhdeo, 'The Schools that Divide the Nation', *Evening Standard*,
5 September 2006.
[13] Editorial in *Evening Standard*, 27 September 2006.
[14] Anne McElvoy and Katharine Barney, 'Is Islam Good for London?', 15
November 2007, at www.thisislondon.co.uk [accessed December 2009].

solution.'[15] Discussion of the introduction of an anti-terrorist public bin was part of the normalization of the everyday reality of a capital city facing terrorist threats from Muslims. In another story on the same day, columnist David Sexton wrote: 'The conviction and sentencing of the Madrid train bombers has been reported here as though it were strictly foreign news'.[16] Here, Sexton was to remind the reader that the Islamic threat was global, and that the attack in Madrid was directly relevant to the lives of Londoners.

On Wednesday 5 November, the newspaper ran a story under the title 'Animal rights activists attack ASDA for stocking "cruel" Halal meat', which again marked Islamic practices as Other.[17] The same day, in reporting a speech by Jonathan Evans, the head of MI5, the newspaper ran the title 'Al Qaeda grooming British children to carry out terror attacks in UK', with images of Shehzad Tanweer, the 7/7 bomber, in school uniform and in a singlet, looking relaxed and ever-British.[18] The message was that there was a susceptibility in the British Muslim identity that made children (Evan's speech had said 'even' as young as fifteen) capable of terrorist attacks. On 6 November, alongside a report of Adel Yahya for possession of information helpful to the 21/7 London bombers, the newspaper reported on a YouTube video under the title 'Opponent of "mega-mosque" receives chilling death threat on YouTube'.[19] That the threat was 'chilling' was again to mark out the barbaric nature of the Other.[20]

[15] Ross Lydall, 'The £18,000 Bomb-Proof Litter Bins', *Evening Standard*, 2 November 2007, at www.thisislondon.co.uk [accessed October 2009].

[16] David Sexton, 'We Show Pity for Islamic Extremists at Our Peril', *Evening Standard*, 2 November 2007, at www.thisislondon.co.uk [accessed October 2009].

[17] 'Animal Rights Activists Attack ASDA for Stocking "Cruel" Halal Meat', *Evening Standard*, 5 November 2007, at www.thisislondon.co.uk [accessed October 2009].

[18] 'Al Qaeda Grooming British Children to Carry out Terror Attacks in UK', *Evening Standard*, 5 November 2007, at www.thisislondon.co.uk [accessed October 2009].

[19] 'Opponent of "Mega-Mosque" Receives Chilling Death Threat on YouTube', *Evening Standard*, 6 November 2007, at www.thisislondon.co.uk [accessed October 2009].

[20] The Councillor concerned, Alan Craig, himself had made use of *YouTube* to argue against the development of the new mosque in east London, arguing that the impact on the community would include dangers of violence and terrorism; see for example www.youtube.com [accessed October 2009].

On 7 November, the newspaper published columnist Nirpal Dhaliwal's article entitled 'Young Muslims aren't oppressed – just lucky'. Dhaliwal argued that '[r]ather than fixate on the Middle East and perceived slights at home, British Muslims should consider the whole world and their fortunate position in it. It might cure those suffering from the hysteria and hypocrisy that extremists exploit – and help them realise that being British is something to feel grateful for.'[21] Again, the work of this piece was to isolate British Muslims in their new identity position, offering them a route into the 'British' mainstream through Orientalism. On 8 November, the newspaper reported on the investigation into the shooting of Jean Charles de Menezes after the July 2005 attacks, and on a hairdresser suing her employer over whether she could wear a headscarf. On 9 November, a report about criticism of Chief Constable Richard Brunstrom, who had shown an image of a dead motorcyclist at a road safety talk, was headlined: ' "Mad Mullah" police chief caused "profound distress" by showing photo of headless crash victim'.[22] There was no aspect of the story that had any connection with Islam; the term 'mad mullah' was simply to demonstrate the unacceptability of the Chief Constable's behaviour. But it connected across the newspaper, as on the same day there was a report about the conviction of Samina Malik, the so-called Lyrical Terrorist; readers could make the connection between what was acceptable and appropriate to the Self, and that which spoke to the nature of the Other.

On 10 November, the newspaper contained three pieces connecting Islam and terror. One examined claims that those arrested for the 'airline plot' had been charged at the end of the legal limit, twenty-eight days, when there was enough evidence to charge them earlier. A second covered the interview of 'Leader of the Muslim Council of Britain Muhammad Abdul Bari' in another newspaper, with images of the bus attacked on 7/7. And a third, entitled 'The surprising truth about Rage Boy, America's hated poster-boy of Islamic radicalism', produced an interview with a man identified as representing

[21] Nirpal Dhaliwal, 'Young Muslims Aren't Oppressed – Just Lucky', *Evening Standard*, 7 November 2007, at www.thisislondon.co.uk [accessed October 2009].

[22] ' "Mad Mullah" Police Chief Caused "Profound Distress" by Showing Photo of Headless Crash Victim', *Evening Standard*, 9 November 2007, at www.thisislondon.co.uk [accessed October 2009].

the implacability of the enemy; someone with whom it would be impossible to negotiate. However, 'Rage Boy' emerged as thoughtful, uneducated and immersed in poverty in Kashmir. The article ended with the view that:

The terrorist threat we face in Britain comes from the spread of Al Qaeda ideology, combined with the failed multicultural project that led successive governments to refuse to promote the active integration of immigrant communities. This calculated lack of loyalty led directly to the obscenity of the 7/7 bombings, when men who were born and bred in England blew up themselves and their fellow citizens, since their only allegiance was to a synthetic external identity. That is true rage.[23]

Both by taking an issue and subjecting it through a securitized lens, and by continually reading local and global events in a securitized fashion, media organizations are able to conduct securitizing moves, regardless of the views of government. Here, the focus has been on media organizations. However, there are a variety of securitizing moves that take place every day, involving everyday people, and it is to these actions that the analysis now turns.

Securitized performances in everyday life

One of the most powerful ways of communicating the nature of Otherness and of threat is through the medium of jokes. Jokes take a variety of different forms, but in the ones to be examined here what is central is the distinction between the British Self and the (British) Muslim Other; this Other is both to be feared (that is, it is a Radical Other) and to be patronized (an Orientalized Other). It is not that everyone knows of these jokes, or tells them to fellow citizens; but there is sufficient traffic for such practices to be important in the process of social securitization.

Message boards are a powerful contemporary means of communicating securitizing jokes, partly because they reach a wider audience, and partly also because, of course, the teller is able to hide behind some anonymity, allowing a greater boldness. Sometimes there is

---

[23] Patrick French, 'The Surprising Truth about Rage Boy, America's Hated Poster-Boy of Islamic Radicalism', *Evening Standard*, 10 September 2007, at www.thisislondon.co.uk [accessed October 2009].

organization behind the joke-telling, deliberately creating (and reflecting) that sense of violent otherness, reinscribing narratives about Muslims. The British National Party work hard to collect such jokes and transmit them. On their website, Home of the Green Arrow, there was a specific call for such jokes. Taking the most simple form (statement, response), many focused on the use of illegitimate violence. Thus, for example, 'Q: What do you call a first-time offender in Saudi Arabia? A: Lefty!', 'reminding' the readership of violent, impulsive 'Islamic justice'. Others of the genre were, predictably, gender specific, thus: 'Q: What do you ask a man who's just converted to Islam? A: Have you started beating your wife?'; and 'Q: What do you say to a Muslim woman with two black eyes? A: Nothing! You told her twice already!'; and even 'Q: How do you get a Muslim woman pregnant? A: Dress her up as a goat.' Another set of contributions focused on the lack of rationality constructed in the Islamic world: 'Q: How many Muslims does it take to change a lightbulb? A: None, they prefer to sit in the dark and blame it on the Jews'; and Q: Did you hear the one about the Muslim who won a Nobel Prize in Mathematics? A: Neither did I.' And finally, again a classic for the genre, connecting the Other with unhygenic practices: 'Q: How many Muslims does it take to change a roll of toilet paper? A: What's toilet paper?'[24]

However, it is not sufficient to simply see the hand of right-wing political movements behind the use of the joke as a means of securitizing. What can be gathered from message boards is the sense of individual agency that a number of British citizens take upon themselves to clearly mark one section of the citizenry as Other. Message boards such as those supported by major organizations – for example, *The Sun* and Yahoo! – can be mined for evidence of the Othering of British Muslims. And such Othering takes three clear forms, as will be clear from the following examples: of course, a focus on violence and terrorism, with an attempt to declare the nature of acceptable consequences; an emphasis on the 'dirty' nature of the Other; and a clear normative declaration that the Self must purge the Other.

There are many examples of the trope of the Muslim terrorist, but carrying a message about the acceptability of certain consequences.

---

[24] 'Muslim Jokes – Lets Have Them Please', *Home of the Green Arrow*, 2 November 2006, at BNP website, at http://isupporttheresistance.blogspot. com [accessed May 2008].

So, for example, on a Yahoo! message board we read: 'A Muslim on our street doused himself in petrol, set himself on fire. Poor sod died. We've been having a collection for his wife and kids … we've got 80 litres so far.'[25] Such a narrative is hate-ridden; the Other is both irrational ('dousing himself in petrol') and to be feared so much that the punchline is about the murder of children. The key theme in such jokes is the willingness of the Radical Other to destroy themselves in the pursuit of attacking the British Self. On Yahoo! again:

2 muslim mothers walking down the road when one asks 'hows your son el rab?' the other replies 'oh he went to spain and got on a train and it blew up' so the other asks 'hows your daughter injeeta?' oh she went to the gazza strip and went in a club and it blew up' aww said the other one 'the problem these days is that our kids blow up so quickly'.[26]

Or, from the same website, NobleJohn's contribution: 'ADVERT … Suicide bomber wanted (no experience needed).'[27] And on *The Sun* message boards, 'Pistoffman' contributed: 'Two muslims in a Vauxhall Zafira have driven off a cliff in Wales. Officers at the scene said "it's an appalling tragedy, as this car is capable of seating 7"'.[28] Again, the unacceptability of the Other and their violence is seen, in these jokes, to legitimate violent responses by the Self. The violence of the Other is such that it is acceptable for us to wish for violence to be done to that Other. A particularly popular joke is: 'Guy goes in an adult store and asks for an inflatable doll. Guy behind the counter says, "Male or female?" Customer says, "Female." Counter guy asks, "Black or white?" Customer says, "White." Counter guy asks, "Christian or Muslim?" Customer says, "What the hell does religion have to do with it?" Counter guy says, "The Muslim one blows itself up".' This particular rendition is from the social networking site for Triumph

[25] Contributor: 'shutyerface' on the Yahoo! Answers board, July 2007, at http://uk.answers.yahoo.com [accessed May 2008].

[26] Contributor: 'Ploppy Pants' on the Yahoo! Answers board, at http://uk.answers.yahoo.com [accessed May 2008, though available during 2007].

[27] Contributor: 'Noble John' on the Yahoo! Answers board, at http://uk.answers.yahoo.com [accessed May 2008, though again available during 2007].

[28] Contributor: 'Pistoffman', male, married, three children, no location entered, profile viewed 4,440 times, contribution on 11 September 2009, 19:46:24, at www.thesun.co.uk [accessed October 2009].

motorcycle owners.[29] In the first four months of 2010, it could also be found on the websites of Blackpool Football Club Supporters (April), on MSN under Britain, Politics (January), on the Liverpool Football Club supporters' website (February) and on the *Daily Telegraph* message board (February), as well as on at least another half-dozen message boards over the previous two years (including, for example, on Cycle Net chat, the IT-focused website Nerdsville, and eLert Gadget). Such jokes have currency across different fields, spread from one to another by individuals whose interests connect fields together.

The second form of the genre is to be expected; it has long been the norm to declare the Other to be 'dirty'. A classic historical example is a cartoon from the magazine *Punch*, in 1851. Rather than celebrate the Self directly with the ongoing Great Exhibition, the cartoonist instead shows a Briton displaying jugs and bowls for washing, to the astonishment of visiting Frenchmen. Under the title 'Puzzled Visitors', one Frenchman asks the other what this is called, and is told by his colleague that he does not know.[30] In the 1850s, it was the French who were Other and therefore dirty. In the first decade of the twenty-first century, on the website Sickipedia, we can read that: 'Dr. Who lands the TARDIS on planet Earth way back in the Dark Ages, in a faraway land we now call Bangladesh. "Where the bleedin' hell are we?" asks his companion Donna. "Well" replies the Doctor, leaving the tardis and walking around. "Judging by that disgusting smell and the fact that we appear to be surrounded by towelheads (little sheet heads) with no significant intelligence living in caves and mud huts ..." "This is Bradford 2008!"'[31] And on *The Sun* message board, 'Expatriot' contributed a comment which is clearly deemed to be ludicrous and impossible: 'a muslim goes into a store and buys some deodorant'.[32]

A third form is action-oriented. For whatever reason – terrorism, unhygienic practices – this form of joke is about what the British Self wants: to be rid of that Other.

[29] Contributor: Baldbloke, Moray, Scotland, 22 April 2010, 10:25, at www.triumphtorque.com [accessed April 2010].
[30] The image of 'Puzzled Visitors' drawn by John Leech in 1851 is reproduced from *Punch*, at www.john-leech-archive.org.uk [accessed April 2010].
[31] Contributor: 'Boogaloo' early 2008, at www.sickipedia.org [accessed May 2008].
[32] Contributor: 'Expatriot', male lives in the US, supports Everton, 3,920 views, 1 September 2009, 22:51:04, at www.thesun.co.uk [accessed October 2009].

Iqbal and Habib are beggars. They beg in different areas of London. Habib begs just as long as Iqbal but only collects £2 to £3 a day. Iqbal brings home a suitcase FULL of £10 notes, drives a Mercedes, lives in a mortgage-free house and has a lot of money to spend. Habib says to Iqbal 'I work just as long and hard as you do but how do you bring home a suitcase full of £10 notes every day?' Iqbal says, 'Look at your sign, what does it say?' Habib's sign reads 'I have no work, a wife and 6 kids to support.' Iqbal says 'No wonder you only get £2–£3. Habib says … 'So what does your sign say'? Iqbal shows Habib his sign … It reads, 'I only need another £10 to move back to Pakistan!'[33]

This contributor, 'Numptie', is a male from Staffordshire, whose profile on *The Sun* message board had been viewed 2,080 times by 22 October 2009, which implies a readership for such contributions significantly higher, given that it would not be the case that each reader would view the profile each time a contribution was read. 'Rachel05' was a thirty-one-year-old from the West Midlands, with a profile viewed 777 times, when she contributed this:

Did you know – That the words race car spelled backward says race car. That eat is the only word that if you take the 1st letter and move it to the last, it spells it's past tense ate. And Have you noticed that if you rearrange the letters in 'illegal immigrants' and add just a few more letters it spells … F*** off and go home you free loading, benefit grabbing, kid producing, violent, non- English speaking **** suckers and take those hairy faced, sandal wearing, bomb making, goat f******, smelly rag head b******* with you. How weird is that.[34]

Such hostility, aggression and fear is summed up by a joke on *The Sun* message board by 'Manxkitten', a woman living in Brighton, who wrote – under the heading 'Could you be a Muslim?' – the following:

1. Do you have more wives than teeth?
2. Do you own a £25,000 rocket launcher but can't afford shoes?
3. Do you cultivate Heroin but have a moral objection to Beer?

[33] Contributor: 'Numptie', 'Art of Begging', 11 September 2009, 17:29:52, at www.thesun.co.uk [accessed October 2009].
[34] Contributor: 'Rachel05', 11 September 2009, 09:58:13, at www.thesun.co.uk [accessed October 2009].

4. Do you think vests come in 2 styles? Bullit-proof & suicide! and most significantly
5. Do you scrape shít off your sweaty arse with your bare hand but consider bacon unclean?[35]

The tropes of violent terrorism, lack of hygiene and unacceptability are all brought together.

Again, this is not to ascribe all agency to individuals; there are other ways in which such securitizations take place. As Michael Bywater noted in the *New Statesman*:

Did you hear the one about the suicide bomber? You will, if you go to the Edinburgh Fringe: roughly 1,800 acts, and sometimes it seems as if they are all comedians, all of whom want to talk about terrorism. Carry your own rucksack, then if some dodgy-looking Asian tries to get on you just point at it and say, 'It's OK, mate, I've got this one'.[36]

Shazia Mirza, Birmingham-born 'Muslim comedienne', said that 'when 9/11 happened, I thought I'm never going be able to do stand-up comedy ever again. Nobody's going to want to hear comedy from a Muslim woman after 9/11 … There was so much hatred towards Muslims that I just thought, I was scared to go on stage.' However, it took her only three weeks to be able to capitalize on the new discourses: 'I went on stage and said, "hello, my name's Shazia Mirza, at least that's what it says on my pilot's license." '[37]

Yet although humour is important in the everyday communication of such identity reconstructions, there are also other elements of communication that reveal dominant discursive patterns. One way of looking at those elements is to focus on a moment of drama. In 2007 there were terrorist attacks in London (at the Tiger Tiger nightclub) and at Glasgow airport. In response to a report on the latter, linking the attack to what had happened in London, the BBC opened a 'have your say' response site on their website. The tropes that dominated there were very illuminating about the other side of the argument, the

---

[35] Contributor: 'Manxkitten', Female, Brighton 'Could You Be a Muslim?' 12 September 2009, 10:27:52, at www.thesun.co.uk [accessed October 2009].

[36] Michael Bywater, 'Have You Heard the One about …', *New Statesman*, 22 August 2005, at www.newstatesman.com [accessed May 2008].

[37] 'Female Muslim Comic Shazia Mirza Talks to Ed Bradley', *60 Minutes*, 2 May 2004, at www.shaziamirza.org [accessed May 2008].

British Self. One element was the superior character of the British: unable to be intimidated. Andrew, in Bognor, wrote: 'despite the continuous efforts of the media (perticulary [*sic*] this one) the British people will as always carry on regardless, well done Fellow Brits you do your forebarers [*sic*] proud :)'.[38] Such a trope does important relative work: relative in temporal terms ('doing forebarers proud'), and also implicitly in relative contemporary terms, to other nationalities and to those committing the violence. Princessnewshound, from Manchester, made the contrast with the Other more directly: 'I don't feel that London or any of our major cities are safe. We have an enemy that may live next door that does not want the democracy that we have had for hundreds of years. They want us to be scared of them and they do not want to comply with our laws.'[39] Again, the temporal dimension is important: 'we' have lived our way of life for 'hundreds of years', and now we face a major, domestic enemy ('that may live next door'). Ginzy, in Halifax, made the temporal comparison explicit: 'As my 90-year-old mother said ... they've made more fuss about a couple of bombs that didn't go off than they made of all the ones that did go off in London during the war!'[40] 'We' must live up to the standards set by those who created contemporary Britain's foundational moment, in the Second World War.

If it is possible for individuals in everyday life to engage in securitizing moves, thereby reconstructing identities and naming Others as threats, it is also the case for individual social agents given prominence by their social positions; and it is to the role of public intellectuals – securitization entrepreneurs, if you will – that the analysis now turns.

The public intellectual as securitizing actor

Public intellectuals, by virtue of their social position and thereby influence, may have real impact upon the process of securitization.

[38] Andrew, Bognor, added Saturday, 30 June 2007, 21:22 GMT 22:22 UK, BBC News article 'Car Crashes into Glasgow Airport with Fuel Bombs', 30 June 2007, followed by a 'have your say' forum, all at http://newsforums.bbc.co.uk [accessed June 2007, now no longer available].
[39] Princessnewshound, Manchester, added: Saturday, 30 June 2007, 11:07 GMT 12:07 UK, *ibid.*
[40] Ginzy, Halifax, added Saturday, 30 June 2007, 20:09 GMT 21:09 UK, *ibid.*

This section will examine the role of four individuals, from different fields: the bishop, the author, the academic and the journalist. All have played important roles, from different fields, in the process of identifying and securitizing the British Muslim identity. The purpose of this section is not to critique these moves but, rather, to examine the nature of those moves.

The bishop

Michael Nazir-Ali was Bishop of Rochester in the Church of England, which led to his holding a position in the House of Lords as one of the 'Lords Spiritual' from 1999. He was born in Pakistan, the son of a Muslim convert to Christianity, and his work for the church led to his life being at risk. As a consequence, he was invited by the then Archbishop of Canterbury to move to, and work in, the UK. Nazir-Ali was a very senior member of the Anglican Church; he was one of two candidates, though the unsuccessful one, for the position of Archbishop of Canterbury, which led to Rowan Williams's enthronement in 2003.

The bishop delivered a long-term set of securitizing moves in constructing Islam as a threat to Britishness, but a depth to the analysis can be attained by focusing in particular on his public statements in 2008–10. In May and June 2008 he spoke of the danger to Britishness of the collapse of Christianity in the United Kingdom, in an article in *Standpoint* and a series of interviews in the media.[41] The article was evocatively titled 'Breaking Faith with Britain'. He argued that collective values were being replaced by a destructive individualism, and that the whole was being threatened by an external Other. 'Radical Islamism, for example, will emphasise the solidarity of the umma (worldwide community of the Muslim faithful) against the freedom of the individual. Instead of the Christian virtues of humility, service and sacrifice, there may be honour, piety and the importance of "saving face".'[42] This was a theme to which he returned in a series of

[41] Michael Nazir-Ali, 'Breaking Faith with Britain', *Standpoint*, June 2008, at www.standpointmag.co.uk [accessed January 2010].
[42] Michael Nazir-Ali, 'Radical Islam Is Filling Void Left by Collapse of Christianity in UK', *Daily Telegraph*, 28 May 2008, at www.telegraph.co.uk [accessed January 2010].

interviews connected with his resignation in 2009, when he made his view very clear:

I think there's a double jeopardy – on the one hand an aggressive secularism that seeks to undermine the traditional principles because it has its own project to foster. On the other is the extremist ideology of radical Islam, which moderate Muslims are also concerned about. This is why there must be a clear recognition of where Britain has come from, what the basis is for our society and how that can contribute to the common good.[43]

The connection of Britishness with values, and with a focus on the threats to those values, was a key element of Nazir-Ali's public discourse. In his book *Islam, Christianity and World Order* he had argued that 'for whatever reason, a sizeable number of young Muslim males feel alienated from wider society … Only a small proportion of these men, however, are drawn to religious extremism, though more may be involved in moderate Islamist activity.'[44] Echoing Melanie Philips, he called for security measures against those who might be seen as a threat in other countries, though now residing in the UK: 'In the past, foreign governments have been in despair that such people have been able to continue with their activities in this country, both to our detriment and to that of others'.[45] And he argued that all 'ministers of religion' should be able to demonstrate training at a 'recognised institution' that included command of English language and 'sufficient cultural awareness'.[46]

That elements of Islam were a threat to Britishness was made clear when Nazir-Ali spoke of 'a worldwide resurgence of the ideology of Islamic extremism … One of the results of this has been to further alienate the young from the nation in which they were growing up and also to turn already separate communities into "no-go" areas where adherence to this ideology has become a mark of acceptability.'[47] In

[43] Quoted in Martin Beckford, 'The Bishop of Rochester Farewell Interview', *Daily Telegraph*, 2 September 2009, at www.telegraph.co.uk [accessed January 2010].

[44] Michael Nazir-Ali, *Conviction and Conflict: Islam, Christianity and World Order*, London: Continuum, 2006, pp. 163–4.

[45] *Ibid.*   [46] *Ibid.*

[47] Quoted in 'Islamic Extremism Creating "No-Go" Areas for Non-Muslims in Britain, says Bishop of Rochester', *Evening Standard*, 1 August 2008, at www.thisislondon.co.uk [accessed January 2010].

the coverage in the *Evening Standard*, the report was framed by a picture of six veiled women. But it also came through, for example, his comments on sharia law:

The question is whether any aspect of Sharia ought to be recognised in public law. My own view is that it shouldn't be – Sharia is basically a totally different background to the Judeo-Christian tradition. You start off straight away with the question of will bigamy remain a crime and for whom, then there's the question of divorce and equality in divorce law. There are a huge number of questions that arise.[48]

And, in calling for the Church of England to 'recover' its 'nerve' in relation to a commitment to convert individuals from other religions – but particularly British Muslims – the bishop argued that by 'allowing the rise of another religion in our country, all that Britain stands for is up for grabs'.[49] Perhaps he was clearest in a piece on Afghanistan in January 2010:

Not since the demise of Marxism has the world been faced with a comprehensive political, social and economic ideology determined, by force if necessary, to achieve hegemony over large parts of the world. I mean, of course, the rise of radical Islam, in its various manifestations, with its claim to be the only authentic interpretation of the religion. I am aware that there are many Muslims who reject such an interpretation of their faith and, indeed, there are secular forces in the Muslim world prepared to resist such programmatic extremism. We should not, however, underestimate Islamism's capacity for disruption and destruction and its desire to remake the world in its own image.[50]

What was crucial in this quote and this article was the connection of Radical Islam to national and global threat; the apocalyptic nature of that threat; and the link between Radical Islam and Islamism, which

---

[48] Quoted in Beckford, 'The Bishop of Rochester Farewell Interview'.
[49] Jonathan Petre, 'Church Is Not Doing Enough to Convert UK Muslims, says Bishop', *Daily Mail*, 25 May 2008, at www.dailymail.co.uk [accessed January 2010].
[50] Michael Nazir-Ali, 'We Must Not Leave Afghanistan Yet', *Standpoint*, January/February 2010, at www.standpointmag.co.uk [accessed January 2010].

was to say that Muslims with political views about Islam having a role in society were all, in some way, linked to that apocalyptical threat.

As for the bishop, in a seminal article published in 2009 that brought many of his ideas together, he wanted to see an active reconstruction of Britishness: 'Simply extolling "Britishness" or "British values" is not enough. It is not enough even to remind ourselves of the importance of Christian faith for Britain.'[51] This would be an inclusive project, facing the problems of past policy:

What we got was a multiculturalism built on amnesia. On the grounds of tolerance, it consigned newer arrivals to ghettoes where, it was imagined, they would be happier with their own kind. The housing, education and social policies of the elite … reinforced the separation, fostering, as we have seen, ignorance rather than engagement, fear rather than neighbourliness and resentment rather than generosity. It has led to extremism, of different kinds, flourishing because of the lack of a vision of a just, compassionate and neighbourly society based on a meta-narrative which provided the grounding for adequate social capital.

The processes of communicating a Britishness – and yes, with a commitment to Christian values at the core – would be the solution to contemporary threats. He wrote:

We certainly need a recovery of memory: regarding the basis of our national life, a tradition of civil liberties set in train by the Magna Carta, the Reformation's insistence on direct access to the sources of the authority (the Scriptures) for everyone, the Counter-Reformation's missionary zeal, the Christian origins of 'natural rights' language, campaigns to abolish the slave trade and slavery, to restrict working hours and to improve working conditions for men, women and children, universal education, the emergence of nursing as a profession, the hospice movement and much else besides.

In evoking these elements of Britain's past, and in elevating them to the heights of representing the 'best' of the nation, the work was to root contemporary debates about values that were connected to history

---

[51] All quotes in this paragraph are from Michael Nazir-Ali, 'Only God Can Save Us from Ourselves', *Standpoint*, July/August 2009, at www.standpointmag.co.uk [accessed January 2010].

and tradition, and thereby could be called into contrast with 'foreign' elements, whether that be Islam as a whole, or elements of Islamic practice – sharia, divorce – about which he had previously spoken. This, for the bishop, needed a process of institutionalization:

Such a recovery of memory in our schools and other educational institutions, for instance, would not be for the sake of nostalgia or to foster national pride but to provide the basis for an engagement with contemporary issues whether these have to do with fundamental liberties, the inclusion of the marginalised, the care of the sick or concern for the poor, whether in this country or abroad.

The use of the term 'recovery' was particularly powerful: it pointed to an objective reality to which all people could reach, an objective reality simply covered by mistakes over the past forty years.

The author

Martin Amis has had a long career in English literature; and according to *The Times* in 2008, ranks as one of the top twenty postwar authors.[52] Amis's career has involved engagement with a large number of subjects; but in the first decade of the twenty-first century he became embroiled in criticisms of his views, deemed by some to be racist and Islamophobic.[53] Such normative evaluations are not the purpose of this section; rather, what is of importance is the work of Amis in carrying out securitizing moves.

In the context of the August 2006 airliner plot, Amis asked:

What can we do to raise the price of them doing this? There's a definite urge – don't you have it? – to say, 'The Muslim community will have to suffer until it gets its house in order.' What sort of suffering? Not letting them travel. Deportation – further down the road. Curtailing of freedoms. Strip-searching people who look like they're from the Middle East or from Pakistan … Discriminatory stuff, until it hurts the whole community and they start getting tough with their children. They hate us for letting our

---

[52] 'The 50 Greatest British Writers Since 1945', *The Times* 5 January 2008, at http://entertainment.timesonline.co.uk [accessed January 2010].

[53] Most notably, Terry Eagleton in the introduction to the revised edn of *Ideology: An Introduction*, London: Verso, 2007.

children have sex and take drugs – well, they've got to stop their children killing people. It's a huge dereliction on their part. I suppose they justify it on the grounds that they have suffered from state terrorism in the past, but I don't think that's wholly irrational. It's their own past they're pissed off about; their great decline. It's also masculinity, isn't it?[54]

It was this statement that led to arguments with Terry Eagleton and others.[55] But what is the securitizing move here? The whole argument is about extraordinary measures: that 'a' community should be held responsible for the acts of individuals, treated in a particular and by definition discriminatory way, and required to act as 'a' community to 'stop their children killing people'. Amis was attacked for racism, but not for the process of securitizing that went along with his comments. That seemed more acceptable and appropriate. Later, in 2008, when responding to critics such as Eagleton and others, he argued: 'It seems on actuarial, evidential grounds they [Muslims] are more likely to be interested in that [terrorism]. I'm assuming that 95 per cent at least of Muslims are longing to get their house in order, and hate this extremism. I said this to [the former Islamist] Ed Husain and he said yeah, about 95 per cent.'[56] The 'actuarial' grounds are, of course, spurious: the figure of 95 per cent has no statistical validity. Understanding this, Amis grasped for an authentic voice to back him up, and settled on Ed Husain, a founder of Quiliam – but still without an evidential basis for the claim.

   The 2006 statement was followed with a piece entitled 'The Age of Horrorism'.[57] Amis argued that a clear distinction could be drawn between Islam and moderate Muslims on the one hand, and Islamism on the other. 'Naturally we respect Muhammad. But we do not respect Muhammad Atta.' However, we should not spend much time on the importance of moderate Islam, because that is a faction that has lost the 'Muslim civil war', and now 'moderate Islam, is always

---

[54] Martin Amis quoted in Ginny Dougary, 'The Voice of Experience', *The Times*, 9 September 2006, at www.ginnydougary.co.uk [accessed January 2010].

[55] Eagleton, *Ideology*.

[56] Martin Amis quoted in Johann Hari, 'The Two Faces of Martin Amis', *The Independent*, 29 January 2008, at www.independent.co.uk [accessed January 2010].

[57] Martin Amis, 'The Age of Horrorism', *The Guardian*, 10 September 2006, at www.guardian.co.uk [accessed January 2010].

deceptively well-represented on the level of the op-ed page and the public debate; elsewhere, it is supine and inaudible. We are not hearing from moderate Islam.' On the other hand, '... Islamism? No, we can hardly be asked to respect a creedal wave that calls for our own elimination. More, we regard the Great Leap Backwards as a tragic development in Islam's story, and now in ours.' The majority – the 95 per cent in the above reading – are now Orientalized; and instead, the focus is kept on the Radical Other. The latter, again, is guilty of unacceptable behaviour: 'It is difficult to exaggerate the sexualisation of Islamist governance, even among the figures we think of as moderate.' The threat is new and terrible: 'Suicide-mass murder is more than terrorism: it is horrorism. It is a maximum malevolence. The suicide-mass murderer asks his prospective victims to contemplate their fellow human being with a completely new order of execration.' He raised the threat stakes in a letter to *The Guardian* some months later, in response to a piece accusing him of racism: 'jihadism ... is irrationalist, misogynist, homophobic, inquisitional, totalitarian and imperialist. And it isn't merely "racist". It is genocidal.'[58]

In 2008, Amis published *The Second Plane: September 11, 2001–2007*, a collection of non-fiction and short stories that he had published since 9/11, focusing on terrorism, radicalization and the war on terror.[59] By examining one of these texts, we can understand the various strands of Amis's securitizing move. 'The Last Days of Muhammad Atta' had originally been published in the *New Yorker*, in April 2006. It was republished in *The Observer* on 3 September 2006, and has also been made available electronically.[60] By examining the architect of the 9/11 attacks, and by mixing imagination with fact, Amis was able to construct particular images of the enemy. One aspect was misogyny: 'the attitude to women: the blend of extreme hostility and extreme wariness he found highly congenial ... Adultery punished by whipping, sodomy by burial alive: this seemed about right to Muhammad Atta.' Second, the power of lust within Islam to

---

[58] Martin Amis, 'No, I Am Not a Racist', *The Guardian*, 1 December 2007, at www.guardian.co.uk [accessed January 2010].

[59] Martin Amis, *The Second Plane: September 11, 2001–2007*, London: Jonathan Cape, 2008.

[60] The texts are available on the Martin Amis website, from which the quotes below are taken: 'The Last Days of Muhammad Atta', *Martin Amis Web*, at www.martinamisweb.com [accessed January 2010].

motivate men to violence: 'Ah yes, the virgins: six dozen of them, half a gross'. But third, what, to him, could be portrayed as the ludicrous nature of the Koran:

He had read in a news magazine that virgins, in the holy book, was a mistranslation from the Aramaic. It should be raisins. He idly wondered whether the quibble might have something to do with sultana, which meant a) a small seedless raisin, and b) the wife or concubine of a sultan. Abdulaziz, Marwan, Ziad, and the others: they would not be best pleased, on their arrival in the Garden, to find a little black packet of Sunmaid Sultanas (average contents 72).

Fourth, ridicule of the religion could be focused also onto disgust of Atta himself:

Now, emitting a sigh of unqualified grimness, he crouched on the bowl … he had not moved his bowels since May. In general his upper body was impressively lean, from all the hours in the gym with the 'muscle' Saudis; but now there was a solemn mound where his abdominals used to be, as taut and proud as a first trimester pregnancy … Every few minutes he was required to wait out an interlude of nausea, while disused gastric juices bubbled up in the sump of his throat. His breath smelled like a blighted river.

The revolting nature of Atta embodied the attitude of disgust towards the Radical Other. Fifth was the willingness of Atta, and hence the core of the Radical Other, to consider untrammelled violence, far beyond the destruction of 9/11. What of

the nuclear power plant that Muhammad Atta had seen on one of his training flights near New York. Puzzlingly, the Sheikh withheld his blessing despite the presumably attractive possibility of turning large swathes of the eastern seaboard into a plutonium cemetery for the next 70 millennia (that is, until the year 72001). The Sheikh gave his reasons (restricted airspace, no 'symbolic' value). But Muhammad Atta sensed a moral qualm, a silent suggestion that such a move could be considered exorbitant. It was the first and only indication that, in their cosmic war against God's enemies, there was any kind of upper limit.

And finally, there was the sense that there was some justice to be seen in the attack after all – that Atta *suffered*:

American 11 struck at 8.46.40. Muhammad Atta's body was beyond all healing by 8.46.41; but his mind, his presence, needed time to shut itself down. The physical torment a panic attack in every nerve, a riot of the atoms merely italicised the last shinings of his brain. They weren't thoughts; they were more like a series of unignorable conclusions, imposed from without … Yes, how gravely he had underestimated it. How very gravely he had underestimated life. His own he had hated, and had wished away; but see how long it was taking to absent itself and with what helpless grief was he watching it go, imperturbable in its beauty and its power. Even as his flesh fried and his blood boiled, there was life, kissing its fingertips. Then it echoed out, and ended.

The pleasure of this grief and pain, the almost luxurious description of Atta suffering, when conventionally the death was seen in terms of instant vaporization, worked to deny to Atta, and to Radical Islam, any sense of victory even at their most potent moment.

Amis's work in 'The Last Days of Muhammad Atta' thereby both securitized and reassured. It securitized because it showed how religious identity (far more than religious faith) could lead to mass murder, how that sensibility was powerful among Muslims, how women in particular had much to fear, and how such a threat was capable of still more murderous acts. And it reassured in being able to show disgust for Atta, to ridicule the Koranic-inspired belief of 'virgins in Paradise', and in being able to feel the suffering of the guilty Atta at his end.

Whatever normative judgements may be made about the Islamophobic and racist content of Amis's speech and writing, what is clear is that he has acted as a securitizing norm entrepreneur, identifying a group as problematic. 'Moderate' Muslims are deemed to be inadequate in facing up to the problems within 'the' community – condemned for not controlling Radical Islam, and for representing societies that are less 'evolved' – this grouping has been Orientalized.[61] The Radical Other has been presented as alien (above

---

[61] See for example Martin Amis quoted in Laura Clark and Tahira Yaqoob, 'Martin Amis Launches Fresh Attack on Muslim Faith Saying Islamic States Are "Less Evolved"', *Daily Mail*, 18 October 2007, at www.dailymail.co.uk [accessed January 2010].

all, the continued resort to violence, and in gender relations) and inherently threatening. And Amis has encouraged measures beyond the law to be taken, to meet the emergency that he has been describing and calling into existence.

The academic

Anthony Glees spent thirty years at Brunel University, working on intelligence and on German politics and history. He obtained a wider public profile in his work on communist intelligence and security agencies, including the East German Stasi, through which he made several accusations about individuals working for those organizations. He obtained a media profile in discussions of terrorism in and through the London bombings of 2005, and his published work shows a move into that field from that time. In 2008, he moved to take up a position at the University of Buckingham as full professor.

Glees's first significant move into the field of contemporary terrorism was with the publication, with Chris Pope, of *When Students Turn to Terror: Terrorist and Extremist Activity on British Campuses* in the autumn of 2005.[62] The report was for the Social Affairs Unit, and through that agency achieved a high level of media profile, being the subject of coverage on *Channel Four News*, the *Today* programme on the BBC, in the *Sunday Times*, *The Scotsman*, *The Times* and the *Financial Times*. The report asserted that terrorist or subversive groups operated at some thirty UK higher education institutions. And as he subsequently wrote, this means that 'universities are a problem'.[63] In the report, and in the interviews given to the press, Glees claimed that there were two main dimensions to this threat. First, that British universities simply had no grasp on what was going on across their campuses: 'UK universities and colleges have dropped their guard for so long that there is every reason to believe such groups constitute a real security threat.'[64] And again, Glees said: 'We have discovered a

[62] Anthony Glees and Chris Pope, *When Students Turn to Terror: Terrorist and Extremist Activity on British Campuses*, London: Social Affairs Unit, 2005.

[63] Anthony Glees, 'Beacons of Truth or Crucibles of Terror?', *Times Higher Education Supplement*, 23 September 2005, at www.timeshighereducation. co.uk [accessed January 2010].

[64] Glees, 'Beacons of Truth or Crucibles of Terror?'.

number of universities where subversive activities are taking place, often without the knowledge of the university authorities'.[65] Second, though, not only were terrorist and subversive organizations operating freely, but universities were also complicit in the process of 'softening up' candidates for radicalization and recruitment into these organizations, as 'universities may be teaching them subjects or theoretical tools for understanding the world – Marxism for example – which could encourage them to believe Britain and other Western states are in terminal decline. Moving from campus to mosque, students convinced by their dons might gain further inspiration from radical mullahs ...'[66]

When Students Turn to Terror – a particularly evocative title in the tense post-7/7 months – did not simply focus on 'jihadi' terrorism, but it was the dominant theme. Of the fourteen named individuals who had attended British universities (or colleges) before committing acts of violence (or being accused of such acts), thirteen were 'Islamists' (the other being Nick Griffin, the leader of the BNP). Chapters 1 and 2 are largely on the 'Islamist' threat, and the specific chapter on 'Islamists on UK Campuses' has 10,179 words, whereas that on the BNP is 2,456 words long and that on animal liberation violence 918 words. The fear of students turning to terror was presented as overwhelmingly a problem associated with Islam, and a problem that universities should have resolved:

In particular, university administrators and academics have failed, or have not been instructed, to do some fairly basic and straightforward things which have allowed radical terrorists to emerge from our campuses. Individuals who went on to put British security at risk could certainly have been identified whilst still undergraduate students had certain safeguards been put in place by universities. What is more, many if not most could probably have been turned away from terrorism by effective control, containment and careful teaching.[67]

---

[65] Anthony Glees, quoted in Matthew Taylor and Rebecca Smithers, 'Extremist Groups Active inside UK Universities, Report Claims', *The Guardian*, 16 September 2005, at www.guardian.co.uk [accessed January 2010].
[66] Glees and Pope, *When Students Turn to Terror*, p. 15.
[67] *Ibid.*, p. 17.

The authors end the report by focusing on policy recommendations. They have identitfied a threat; called attention to it; and logically, the final element of the securitizing move is the call for extraordinary measures. In this case, the measures were to be:

- Institute proper screening to exclude dangerous students.
- Interview all students to test them for their commitment to higher education.
- Abolish 'clearing'.
- Establish direct links between university registrars and immigration officers at ports of entry.
- Deny a university place to any applicant, home or overseas, who cannot provide proof of identity.
- Maintain a friendly community police presence on campuses. Communities with populations measured in the tens of thousands need a regular police presence.
- Ensure that the ethnic composition of any single university reflects, broadly, the ethnic mix of the UK as a whole.
- Give serious thought to the content of courses currently being taught on UK campuses to test whether they are conducive to a culture of security in British campuses; reviewing all courses which appear to extol or glorify violent revolution.
- Establish comprehensive lists of all student societies to check membership, aims and objectives and provide monitoring of activities. Include dons on all student society and club committees.
- Maintain accurate student records based on clear proof of identity.
- More actively promote liberal democratic aims and citizenship requirements courses for all students.
- Teach students how to become part of an academic community, based on trust and shared values, regardless of race, religion and gender, whilst stamping out activities such as plagiarism which undermine the concept of a community of scholars.[68]

The resources required for such measures would be enormous: university resources to interview all applicants, or at least, all those who might qualify, would lead to annual conversations with millions;

[68] *Ibid.*, p. 123.

campus police presences would require hundreds of officers; reviewing all courses would demand a new level of regulation.[69] All was justified, for Glees, by the level of threat.

This theme, of campus radicalization, was one to which Glees returned again and again. In November 2006, he said: 'From my research I would say this issue probably affects more than 25 universities, not the small handful they talk of. The fighting in Iraq and Afghanistan has radicalized many young men and I think an opportunity has been missed to take serious action against a very real threat.'[70] By March 2007, he claimed that the number of universities affected had grown to forty-eight, and he was invited to speak to the Association of University Chief Security Officers.[71] He told that meeting: 'We must accept this problem is widespread and underestimated ... Unless decisive action against campus extremism is taken, the security situation in the UK can only deteriorate.'[72] In April 2008, he widened his critique to suggesting that those who ran universities were culpable for putting the nation's security at risk. He argued that since 1995, eight British universities had accepted over £233.5 million from what he described as 'Saudi and Muslim' sources. This meant that policy was to 'push the wrong sort of education by the wrong sort of people, funded by the wrong sorts of donor'. He went on to suggest that 'Britain's universities will have to generate two national cultures: one non-Muslim and largely secular, the other Muslim ... We will have two identities, two sets of allegiance and two legal and political systems. This must, by the Government's own logic, hugely increase the risk of terrorism.'[73]

[69] There were 2,396,055 students in UK higher education establishments in 2008–9; see www.hesa.ac.uk [accessed January 2010].
[70] Anthony Glees, quoted in Graeme Paton, 'Islamic Fanatics "Grooming Students, at 25 Universities"', *Daily Telegraph*, 18 November 2006, at www.telegraph.co.uk [accessed January 2010].
[71] Roya Nikkhah, 'Islamic Extremists "Infiltrate Oxbridge"', *Daily Telegraph*, 11 March 2007, at www.telegraph.co.uk [accessed January 2010].
[72] Anthony Glees, quoted in Philip Johnston, 'Universities "Targeted" by Islamic Extremists', *Daily Telegraph*, 17 April 2007, at www.telegraph.co.uk/news/uknews/1548853/Universities-targeted-by-Islamic-extremists.html [accessed January 2010].
[73] Anthony Glees, quoted in Ben Leach, '"Extremism" Fear over Islam Studies Donations', *Daily Telegraph*, 13 April 2008, at www.telegraph.co.uk [accessed January 2010].

In these ways, the marking of the Islamic Other was carried through over a period of time. The Radical Other was deemed to be among 'us' in terms of university students; leaders, in government and of universities, were at best appeasing that Radical Other; and there was no space for compromise, with any inward investment to the UK from 'Muslim' sources inevitably connected to threat. But there was throughout a very important sub-theme: of 'our' complicity. 'Our' weakness made it easier for the Radical Other, whether because of the greed of universities, inadequate security on campus, poor teaching – or just irresponsibility on the part of those teaching in universities: 'The tutors of these students have to look out for signs of radicalisation ... People do not become terrorists at the flick of a switch. It's a process of brainwashing and it should be detectable.'[74]

However, this terrain – the specific dangers created by university management, student recruitment, dangerous teaching and lack of control – proved to be too narrow for the sets of arguments that Glees was making. He stepped beyond this field in calling for the introduction of internment. He argued that '[t]he legal profession has taken the European Convention far too far in a way that is inappropriate in a country that's at war'. And then, that

Internment needs to be talked about. There shouldn't be things that shouldn't be considered – if they can help ... Liberal democracy will be easily destroyed if we do not act against extremism. We give our enemies the weapons they need to destroy us. We need to be more mindful that there is a threshold that should not be crossed. Not everything is permissible. Wearing the niqab is saying we don't want to be British. Forty per cent of British Muslims say they want to live under sharia law. That is unacceptable. They should go to a country with sharia law.[75]

Clearly, extraordinary measures were to be used to distinguish between the Radical Other – to be interned, even if only for wearing the niqab, or holding views favourable to sharia law, even if in relation only to consenting Muslims within family law, as the Archbishop

[74] Anthony Glees, quoted in 'Brit Unis "Hotbed"', *News of the World*, 27 December 2009, at www.newsoftheworld.co.uk [accessed January 2010].

[75] Anthony Glees, 'Anthony Glees: Internment Should Be a Policy Option', *The Independent*, 19 October 2006, at www.independent.co.uk [accessed January 2010].

would discuss – and the Orientalized Other, to be rendered invisible in the British whole.

Although Anthony Glees has mostly engaged in securitizing moves around one sector of the country – higher education – his work over a number of years has clearly been influential in public debate, securing a profile in the media and in government. And it is work that has contributed to the securitization of the British Muslim identity.

The journalist

Melanie Philips is a journalist and author, winning the Orwell Prize for journalism in 1996 and writing frequently in the *Daily Mail* and *The Spectator*. She achieved best-selling status with the publication of her book *Londonistan: How Britain Is Creating a Terror State Within*.[76] It communicates much through its changing front cover over time, as various editions have been printed: from a (South Asian) man with large sunglasses peering out from a monochrome background; to a split image of a man with a headscarf looking fierce and apparently chanting above a baby with 'I [heart] Al-Qaida' on his/her hat below; and then to an image of three women wearing veils, gesturing with two fingers, pushing a baby in a pushchair; to an image of a burning car from the attack on Glasgow airport. The central concern of a changed, weak and threatened Britain emerges at the very beginning, with the first lines of chapter 1 reading as follows:

London, Britain's capital city, has become the human entrepôt of the world. Walk its streets, travel on its buses or Underground trains or sit in a hospital casualty department and you will hear dozens of languages being spoken, testimony to the waves of immigration that have transformed the face of London and much of southeast England as people from around the world have arrived in search of work. But you will also notice something else. The urban landscape is punctuated by women wearing not just the hijab, the Islamic headscarf, but burkas and niqabs, garments that cover their entire bodies from head to toe – with the exception, in the case of the niqab, of a slit for the eyes – in conformity with strict Islamic codes of female modesty.

---

[76] The book was fourth in the politics section of *The Times* bestseller list for 2007: see Peter Riddell, 'The Times Christmas Choice: Politics', *The Times*, 7 December 2007, at http://entertainment.timesonline.co.uk [accessed January 2010].

In general, religious dress, even of an outlandish kind, makes a welcome contribution to the variety of the nation. But in this case, one wonders whether such attire really is a religious requirement commanding respect, or a political statement of antagonism towards the British state. The effect is to create a niggling sense of insecurity and unease, as the open nature of London's society is vitiated by such public acts of deliberate concealment, with faces and expressions – not to mention the rest of the body – hidden from sight. In the wake of the London bombings in July 2005, such concealment appears to be a security issue too.[77]

This opening paragraph perfectly expresses the core messages of Melanie Philips's securitizing moves. The first problem is immigration, indicated with the choice of description of London as an 'entrepôt', a place of holding, from which goods are then sent. London has ceased to be a centre in its own right, as migration has 'transformed' its face. The second problem is that, within this newly transformed city, there are those who conceal themselves, and in so doing profoundly challenge 'the British state'. And this is linked, thirdly, to the use of direct violence – 'the London bombings in July 2005' – with which a woman wearing a burka or niqab is, in this narrative, complicit.

However, the analysis is more pointed than that. Britain had failed to realize that there was a threat in its midst. And the conclusion condemns national weakness – or, indeed, betrayal by the political and managerial classes – as follows:

Britain is in denial. Having allowed the country to be turned into a global hub of the Islamic jihad without apparently giving it a second thought the British establishment is still failing even now – despite the wake up calls of both 9/11 and the London bomb attacks of 2005 – to acknowledge what it is actually facing and take the appropriate action.[78]

The need for emergency measures is overwhelming; it is not just that emergency measures are called for by Philips, but that there is a vital temporal dimension – they are late. She continues, 'instead, it is deep into a policy of appeasement of the phenomenon that threatens it, throwing sops to both radical Islamism, and the Muslim community'.[79] And thus the distinction between the Radical Other – 'radical

[77] Melanie Philips, *Londonistan*, New York: Encounter Books, 2006, p. 1.
[78] *Ibid.*, p. 182.   [79] *Ibid.*

Islamism' – and the Orientalized Other – 'the Muslim community' – is made clear.

These themes, crystallized in *Londonistan*, have been at the core of her journalism in the subsequent years. Radical Islam is a fundamental threat to Britishness. As she wrote in 2009, 'the Islamists, or jihadis, are intent upon snuffing out individual freedom and imposing a totalitarian regime of submission to religious dogma which erodes and then replaces British and Western values'.[80] Her calling is to the nation to understand both the profundity of the threat faced and its novelty:

> Britain thinks of a national threat only in terms of a total war waged by one nation against others. But we now face a very different kind of threat from a different kind of war: an intricate, global network of terrorists and rogue states who want to cripple the west and re-establish the medieval Islamic empire by conquest, and who intend to use weapons of mass destruction to do so.[81]

These statements are classic securitizing moves: the identification of a threat of such scale that the existence of the Self is at stake; and here, that threat is connected directly to the 'use of weapons of mass destruction'. Philips's role in the securitizing move is, to her, urgent, as 'the pragmatic British simply don't grasp that what they are facing is totally irrational and non-negotiable'.[82]

There is, however, also an acknowledgement of the Orientalized Other, a grouping who are not radically threatening:

> But many in Britain simply refuse to acknowledge that the root cause of the threat that Britain faces is Islam. This does not mean that all Muslims sign up to these evil ideas. Hundreds of thousands of British Muslims do not, while across the world Muslims are among the most numerous of its victims. But an insupportable number do subscribe to extremist ideas.[83]

---

[80] Melanie Philips, 'The Clash of Uncivilisations', *The Spectator*, 24 October 2009, at www.spectator.co.uk [accessed January 2010].

[81] Melanie Philips, 'D-Day for Defeatism', *Daily Mail*, 7 June 2004, at www.melaniephillips.com [accessed January 2010].

[82] Melanie Philips, 'A Terror So Great We Forgot it at Once', *The Spectator*, 6 December 2006, at www.spectator.co.uk [accessed January 2010].

[83] Melanie Philips, 'Suicide of the West', *National Review*, 18 August 2006, at http://article.nationalreview.com [accessed January 2010].

So the Radical Other is far more numerous than many suspect – here Philips takes upon herself the role of expert, and of far-sighted strategist. But there is a space for 'hundreds of thousands of British Muslims' who are not Radical, although there must be a sense for her readers that this is a minority; after all, 'indigenous Brits have been forced to become strangers in their own country – and are then vilified as racists if they dare protest'.[84] Yet in her writing, there is a repeated conflation of identities, which leads to an emphasis on the totalizing nature of 'Islamic identity'. Although there is a distinction in her writing between the Radical Other and the Orientalized Other, on many different occasions the two are conflated. Thus, for example, she wrote that 'the alliances forging the Islamic world's war against the west are immensely complicated. And the truth is that whatever the west does to defend itself against such aggression is used as a pretext for more such aggression.'[85] There seems little space here for an Orientalized Other – given that here the 'Islamic world' is at 'war' with the West. At greater length, she argued that:

Muslims not only despise Western secular values as decadent, materialistic, corrupt and immoral. They do not accept the distinction between the spiritual and the temporal, the division which in Christian societies confines religion to the margins of everyday life. Instead, for Muslims, the whole of human life must represent a submission to God. This means that they feel a duty to Islamicise the values of the surrounding culture. Since most of the mass immigration now convulsing Europe is composed of Muslims, it is therefore hardly surprising that anti-immigrant feeling is largely anti-Muslim feeling. The sheer weight of numbers, plus the refusal to assimilate to Western values, makes this an unprecedented crisis for Western liberalism. The crisis is forcing it to confront the fundamental questions of what constitutes a country, national identity and the very nature of a liberal society.[86]

Thus even the Orientalized Other is a threatening other, by the very nature of their belief system, incapable of being part of a British whole.

---

[84] Melanie Philips, 'Britain's Broken Heart', *Daily Mail*, 10 March 2008, at www.melaniephillips.com [accessed January 2010].

[85] Melanie Philips, 'Talking Ourselves to Death', *Daily Mail*, 23 October, 2006, at www.melaniephillips.com [accessed January 2010].

[86] Melanie Philips, 'How the West Was Lost', *The Spectator*, 11 May 2002, at www.spectator.co.uk [accessed January 2010].

Part of the power of Philips's securitizing move is the emphasis on the betrayal of the nation by its leaders in the context of this new threat. Time and again, a recurring theme is the failure of 'government', 'political elite', sometimes of the police, to face the nature of the threat. She is therefore a voice in the wilderness, implicitly evoking the role of Churchill during the 1930s in speaking about the threat before the leaderships recognized that threat. But the danger is primarily a self-imposed one: she repeatedly writes about a crisis in civilizational values. 'The source of this confusion is a profound loss of national, cultural and religious nerve. The Christian values that once defined national identity have simply collapsed, creating a cultural vacuum which Islam – Britain's fastest-growing and most assertive religion – is busily filling.'[87] So 'Islam' – and thereby all othered Muslims – are filling a space left by the Self, and in so doing, are profoundly threatening that Self.

In her latest book, Philips argues that 'virtues such as equality, freedom and justice are defined strictly on the basis of submission to Allah. Therefore they embody the precise *opposite* of equality, freedom and justice as understood in the Western world. Servitude is freedom and freedom servitude.'[88] In such a way, she is clear that Islamic citizens of the United Kingdom are other than the British Self. 'The governing story of Islam is the imposition of its doctrines through conquest and submission. Accordingly, it is today attempting to fashion its utopia through conquest and submission.'[89] And thereby, British Muslim citizens are a threat to the British state. The argument has not moved greatly from *Londonistan*. But the totality of the collapse of British/Western values is more profound in the United Kingdom than elsewhere: as she argued in *The Spectator*, 'Britain – first into the Enlightenment, and now first out'.[90] And that is why the securitizing move is so particular and so urgent: the Muslim Other has to be confronted; as only in that confrontation can the British Self be rescued from itself.

[87] Melanie Philips, 'The Fight for the West', *Daily Mail*, 16 October 2006, at www.melaniephillips.com [accessed January 2010].

[88] Melanie Philips, *World Turned Upside Down*, New York: Encounter, 2010, pp. 148–9.

[89] *Ibid*, p. 258.

[90] Melanie Philips, 'Welcome to the Age of Irrationality', *The Spectator*, 28 April 2010, at www.spectator.co.uk [accessed May 2010].

Conclusion

In many forms of social interaction, new relations of identity are under construction, in which processes of securitization are the key determinant. Being British, or a moderate Muslim, or a Radical Islamist, are all recognizable categories with meanings filled by elite and media constructions, by everyday interactions and practices, and by norm entrepreneurs in various social and cultural fields. And these new securitized identities are then transmitted to the performances of everyday life through the ontological security structures such as those of the British, or British Muslim. These identities and performances connect into the ways in which people see one another. In July 2010, YouGov revealed that 'a third of respondents quoted that the attacks [of 7/7] made them more negative towards British Muslims, and a large 43% of respondents think that since the attacks British Muslims have become "less integrated" into British society'.[91] This then translates into behaviour that is seen to be either acceptable and appropriate, or not. At the same time, 42% of the populations gave the highest response on a five-point scale to say that they 'strongly agreed' that the burqa should be banned; overall, 67% agreed with the proposition.[92]

Through these processes then, who is British, and what Britishness is, are redefined. Despite the claims to essential truths and objectivity, these elements remain in motion; and these processes, with different empirical content, can surely be identified in a range of other countries in Western Europe, North America and Oceania.

[91] Alex Hourdakis, '7/7: Five Years On', *YouGov*, 7 July 2010, at http://today.yougov.co.uk [accessed July 2010].
[92] Zara Atkinson, 'Burqa Ban', *YouGov/Channel 5 News*, Fieldwork, 14–16 July 2010, at http://today.yougov.co.uk [accessed July 2010].

Conclusion

Understanding securitization as a process, rather than as an event, allows an analysis of the ways in which securitization affects the identity of the securitizer, as well as that of the securitized. Although a speech act (or a series) by a government leader is crucially important, not least in legitimizing a securitizing move, it is not sufficient just to focus on that level. Securitization means real changes in the lives and life chances of people in their everyday being. This book has sought to show how that is so. In this Conclusion, I will revisit what I mean by a post-Copenhagen securitization theory; I will discuss how a securitization process changes identity structures; I will re-examine the important contributions to understanding these social processes provided by the theory of ontological security; and I will conclude with some comments about the case of Britishness and the Muslim Others.

I have argued that as part of seeing securitization as a process, it is necessary to relax four of the pillars of the Copenhagen School, to produce what I have described as a post-Copenhagen securitization theory. These addressed the range of communicative acts, rather than just the speech act; the importance of social agency in securitizing; the involvement of the audience; and the way in which the introduction of emergency measures needs to be seen broadly, to be beyond the actions of the state, and to be in everyday life.

The first element was to go beyond the focus on the speech act, and to argue that images, silences and intertextuality are all implicated in the process of securitization. In the empirical analysis, we have seen how this is so. For example, the image of burka-clad women, raising two fingers in an aggressive gesture, has frequently been used in newspapers around a whole variety of stories, visually underlining the process of securitizing the Muslim Other. Silence has also been important. While in an atmosphere of zero risk-taking, it seems to many reasonable that the police should act with decisive force should there be intelligence of potential danger – as in the raid at Forest Gate – an entirely different level of risk, and thereby of framing, comes into play in relation to white far-right militants. The stockpiling of explosives may under those circumstances not be seen as preparation for terrorism, as in the case of Robert Cottage. It is 'common sense' that no risk should be taken around the new terrorism; it is similarly 'common sense' that far-right extremists should, in the main, not be seen as part of that new terrorist threat. But of course, this 'common sense' is socially constructed, and is eminently fragile. Should there be an act of extreme violence by someone or a group on the far right – such as the killings by David Copeland, the 'Nail Bomber' – there would be a crisis in which such silences would be interrogated, critiqued and changed. The other element is intertextuality. Morten Morland's cartoon entitled 'Mind the Gap' won the award from the Political Cartoon Society for the best cartoon of 2005. And no wonder. Three empty carriage seats on an Underground train separate a man, dressed in clothes associated with Pakistani dress, from a collection of worried, Caucasian faces … 'Mind the Gap' doubles as the instruction to take care when leaving the Tube train in case of a gap between it and the platform; and as a warning to take care of the emerging, post 7/7, 'gap' between 'Britons' and British Muslims.

The second element emphasized the need to examine the securitizing potential of a range of social actors with influence over society. As I have already written, this is not a point of theoretical disagreement with the writings of the Copenhagen School, who would accept the possibility; however, for Copenhagen, it is the case that the key securitizing move is most likely to be made by the state. In my view, this is quite a traditional perspective. If, as Giddens among others would hold, we now exist in a time of late modernity, that must have implications for the ways in which social authority operates. As Giddens puts it, 'in late modernity, where reflexive attempts to colonize the future are more or less universal, many types of individual action and organizational involvement might shape life-political issues'.[1] Chouliaraki and Fairclough argue that 'struggles over the construction of identities are salient features of late modern social life'.[2] Those

[1] Anthony Giddens, *Modernity and Self-Identity*, Cambridge: Polity, 1991, p. 228.
[2] Lilie Chouliaraki and Norman Fairclough, *Discourse in Late Modernity*, Edinburgh University Press, 1999, p. 83.

struggles sometimes play out in the form of the securitization of particular identities, and that process cannot be limited simply to the
governmental level. As seen in this analysis, the ability to securitize
also lies in certain forms of agency, in religious bodies, the media,
academia, cultural life; in places where norm entrepreneurs can use
their position of social authority to further the cause of securitization. This is to suggest that in processes of securitization, those who
form the social elite can play a variety of roles in front of the audience, some working to develop a particular securitization, such as
the cases of Michael Nazir-Ali, Melanie Philips, Martin Amis and
Anthony Glees. Of course, it is entirely possible that this work should
be alongside that of elite figures in government, as has been shown
in the previous chapter to have occurred on occasion, but it is also
possible that there should be resistance to that securitization within
the governmental elite. However, looking at a wider basis among the
elite for processes of securitization enables an analyst to examine
the multiple ways in which discourses can change and solidify, how
new intertextual readings can develop, and can enforce new silences.
'Speaking securitization' is thereby an act carried out by a variety of
social agents in positions of authority in a range of different fields.

However, it is also important not to reify the division between elite
and audience, and the third aspect of the post-Copenhagen revision
of securitization theory is to consider the ways in which audiences
are not only affected by, but also participate in, securitizing moves.
If securitizations can be focused on identities and not just states, as
would be consistent with a reading of the theory connected with late
modernity, then those securitizations will lead to a reformation of
social identities within and across states. That is very much the case
with the empirical study here. Britishness has been reconstituted as a
means and result of securitizing Islam –into both the Radical Other
and the Orientalized Other categories. That, of course, has practical
implications for everyday life in the United Kingdom and beyond,
speaking to who is accepted as possessing unquestioned citizenship,
and who is constructed as needing to prove their worth. Of course,
these reconfigurations of identity do not 'float freely'; they are based
on a genealogy of othering, providing available resources for contemporary securitizations.

The fourth element is to think about a greater involvement of the
audience in these securitizations than the rather placid formation

given in the previous paragraph. It is the case that for securitization to have affect it needs to move from beyond the level of elite discourse into the materiality of everyday life. It matters when individuals lose their jobs, suffer random violence, or have their potential violence interpreted in a relatively benign way, as was the case with Paul Chambers, Yasir Abdelmouttalib and Robert Cottage, as discussed in the Introduction to this book. Many within the non-elite audience participate in the process of securitization or in the resistance to it. Indeed, in this sense 'audience' is far too neutral a term. How should I react to the way that person has been described? Should I laugh at, or retell, that joke? In what ways is it appropriate and acceptable for me to interact with that individual? All these aspects, and more, are affected by the process of securitizing and resecuritizing identities in everybody's everyday lives.

To this relaxation of four of the pillars of the Copenhagen School's theory of securitization, I explicitly added three other elements, relating to the nature of identity relations, and to the importance of space and of time. Rather than focusing on identity as always in opposites – as being structured through enmity – I argued for a whole variety of different forms of identity interaction. However, in terms of processes of securitization, two forms are of particular importance. The first – the Radical Other – is that to be expected in a process of securitization. The Self constructs an Other that is so radical in its form and challenge that its behaviour, and even its existence, is seen to be existentially threatening to the Self. However, the second form of othering developed through processes of securitization is also highly important. Orientalized Othering takes a particular identity and ascribes to it lesser elements of the Self; it is an identity that is related but is inferior to the Self – separate, weaker, capable of being patronized, needing to depend on the Self for its very legitimacy and indeed its existence. It is the interactions, though, that are important – for the process of rendering particular identities into either or both Radical and Orientalized Others changes the nature of the Self. Here, the development of 'radical jihadi' and 'British Muslim' identities have interacted with the nature of 'Britishness', to change the nature of each identity structure. This is because the means of identity construction at this level is through the development of linked and differentiated signs, which work to encapsulate that which each identity stands for. When we talk about the securitization of identities, it is this practice of outlining linked and differentiated signs that does the work of the securitization, as has been seen in the many examples given throughout this book. These linked and differentiated signs work through the use of spatial and temporal norms and metaphors. In terms of spatiality, given that there are no immutable boundaries, the work of the securitizing move is to collapse inside/outside boundaries, to change spatial imaginings, so that areas previously considered neutral, or even ignored, can be rendered threatening, and in this way can communicate the new identity realities. Martin Amis spoke to this when he said: 'What can we do to raise the price of them doing this? There's a definite urge – don't you have it? – to say, "The Muslim community will have to suffer until it gets its house in order" … Strip-searching people who look like they're from the Middle East or from Pakistan.'[3] Here, 'Middle East' and 'Pakistan' create the image of fear, of danger, of targets worthy of emergency measures. But the temporal dimension has also been important, in creating a lineage for particular views; not in reflecting a genealogy but in constructing a trans-generational connection and solidarity, regardless of social and identity changes over time. Examples can be found in *Celsius 7/7*, in which Michael Gove names the violent other as 'Islamism', and marks it as a totalitarian ideology like fascism and communism; he describes it therefore as a twentieth-century phenomenon, and elides the struggle with it with the other great struggles of that century, suggesting that '9/11' was the start of a global war just as much as the killing of the Archduke was of the First World War, the invasion of Poland was of the Second, and the Berlin Blockade was of the Cold War. And yet we also learn of Islam's repeated historical determination to return to fundamentalism: through Ibn Hanbal in the ninth century, Ibn Tamiyyah in the late thirteenth/early fourteenth centuries, and Muhammad Ibn Abd Al-Wahhab in the nineteenth century. On the one hand, 'Islamism' is imagined to be akin to familiar (and defeated) historical threats. On the other, it is imagined with a cross-temporal essentialism, which even relates to particular individuals, given that Tariq Ramadan is

---

[3] Martin Amis quoted in Ginny Dougary, 'The Voice of Experience', *Times Online*, 9 September 2006, at www.ginnydougary.co.uk. See Amis's explanation in a letter to Yasmin Alibhai-Brown, reproduced in Jonathan Brown, 'Amis Launches Scathing Response to Accusations of Islamophobia', *The Independent*, 12 October 2007, at www.independent.co.uk [both accessed June 2010].

introduced to readers as the grandson of the Muslim Brotherhood, rather than as someone with a contribution of his own to make.[4]

Securitizations, of course, do not occur from nothing. They emerge from particular incidents that are socially constructed as crises. I do not mean by this to deny the materiality of violence by any means; but rather, to point to the significance of the way in which that materiality is interpreted. It is the currency given to those events in discourse, managed through norm entrepreneurs and social agents, that creates processes of securitization. Therefore although there were significant tensions between some groups of those who may have been described as 'British Muslims' and 'mainstream' institutions in the 1990s, with real crises – such as the Salman Rushdie affair – it was the way in which the attacks on the United States in September 2001 were constructed that was important in allowing the securitization processes that have occurred in the United Kingdom during the first decade of the twenty-first century. Nineteen bombers, hijacking four planes in the United States and killing significant numbers of Americans and those working in the United States, became understood as a threat by an organized group, with a global ideology, to the United Kingdom itself. And that became a material reality on 7 July 2005.

Not only do securitizations not come from nothing, but they also connect in different and unpredictable ways to the genealogy of securitizations among particular communities. The silent securitization throughout this text has been that of the 'British' or the 'Irish' at many points over past generations, but perhaps many will be put in mind specifically of the securitization or 'Irish' communities during IRA campaigns. Hillyard's description of the treatment of the 'Irish' as suspect communities was a point of connection with some 'British Muslims' who sought to understand the portrayal of their community a generation later.[5]

To these reconstructions of securitization theory, I have added an understanding of ontological security derived through the work of Anthony Giddens, and focused not on the level of the state as in much work in contemporary international relations, but rather on the way

---

[4] Michael Gove, *Celsius 7/7*, London: Weidenfeld & Nicolson, 2006.
[5] Paddy Hillyard, *Suspect Community*, London: Pluto, 1993; see also Marie Smyth and Marie-Therese Fay (eds.), *Personal Accounts of Northern Ireland's Troubles: Public Chaos, Private Loss*, London: Pluto, 2000.

in which the social constructs the common sense of the individual. This is not a discussion about physical survival, although that sense of the security of the self may, under certain circumstances, dictate that the individual must put his or her physical safety at risk – in certain circumstances, it may actually require the individual to knowingly sacrifice his/her life.

National identity, and here 'Britishness', offers to individuals resources that they can draw on in the construction of their ontological security structures, but in so doing might undermine the ontological security of others. There are four dimensions of ontological security that underpin this. The first is that self-identity is based on a sense of biographical coherence, which is comprehended by the individual, and is communicable to others. The second is that this self-identity, and the actions that it leads to, is produced in a cocoon of trust structures, particularly in the role of social tokens and in confidence in professional experts, which requires constant regrounding. The third element is that the ontologically secure individual is able to act in conformity with his/her sense of self-integrity; which means that the ontologically secure agent has a firm sense of the appropriate and the acceptable. And the fourth dimension is that, no matter how ontologically secure the agent may be, there is always a fragility and a robustness to that position. That is, although a person may have the confidence that comes from being ontologically secure, there is always the dread of falling into ontological insecurity. I will look at each of these elements in a little detail.

First, to be ontologically secure an individual must have a sense of biographical coherence, a sense that the individual can comprehend and communicate. For many citizens in the United Kingdom, part of that sense comes from elements of the national identity, as is the case in many countries of the world, and it is everyday voices that speak to that most powerfully. Sometimes it is most apparent with the elderly, who hark back to a very different sense of Britishness from that which abounds now. Ann Johnson wrote:

Being British means everything to me. After almost forty years in Brussels, I still have tears in my eyes for an identity that has now become practically virtual. Being born British is reflected in an almost Victorian education. School uniform, being caned (as in bamboo cane) or having a ruler slash your finger tips by a furious headmistress when only six years old. As a child, books by Enid Blyton, Bronte sisters or the silly Beano, the Famous Five (my method of escaping and no television). The Archers, strawberries and clotted cream. The hymns that we sung meaninglessly and repeatedly but today brings tears to my eyes. Being born British was my passport to success. Being British meant the liberators of WW2.[6]

But it has meaning to a range of populations in the country. In an email exchange between Muslim women, facilitated by the BBC, Samina Anwar wrote:

Muslims that are born and raised in Britain consider themselves British. Most of them are proud, confident and have a positive definition of their identity as young British Muslim citizens of UK and carry the 'Red passport', proudly. They might not go to pubs or eat fish and chips – they might go home and eat curries with Chapatti, but these are British people. Due to their sense of belonging as British, these young Muslims have taken up the challenge of changing peoples' mindsets, perhaps looking down on Muslims or having the attitude that 'Muslim means terrorist'.[7]

To a range of peoples, then, the national identity interacts with their own biography; it mutually constitutes that story. And as Tariq Modood argued in a Fabian Society debate about Britishness, this has direct security consequences: 'The reaffirming of a plural, changing inclusive British identity which can be as emotionally and politically meaningful to British Muslims as the appeal of jihadi sentiments is critical to isolating and defeating extremism.'[8] National identity explains in part to individuals who they are, and how they should behave, and offers resources to the collective when it believes that it is under threat.

The second element is that self-identity is produced within a cocoon of trust structures, most notably around social tokens and the role of experts.[9] During the 1930s and 1940s, 'ordinary' individuals were

---

[6] Ann Johnson, contribution to the 'Being British' message board, at www.webritish.co.uk [accessed July 2010].

[7] Samina Anwar, in 'Muslim Voices: Women's Views', *BBC News Online*, 7 December 2005, at http://news.bbc.co.uk [accessed July 2010].

[8] Tariq Modood, 'Britishness Voices', *Fabian Society*, at www.fabians.org.uk [accessed July 2010].

[9] See for example the discussion in Michael I. Reed, 'Expert Power and Control in Late Modernity: An Empirical Review and Theoretical Synthesis', *Organization Studies* 17, July 1996: 573–97.

tasked with filling in diaries under the Mass Observation research programme, the most famous of which was Housewife 49, Nella Last. As the war came to a close, she reflected in her diary on what it would mean for subsequent generations, perfectly echoing that sense of the trust structure: 'We older ones have had our day, have made or marred our lives, but we did have chances. Any courage we possess was rooted in security of some kind – home, Church or faith in the clever ones who seemed omnipotent.'[10] The search for social tokens is evident in descriptions about Britishness; the need for these tokens is why it is that there is such a debate about the content of the identity. Another everyday voice, Andrew Wilson, contributed the thought that:

'Living for last three years in Paris I now see more clearly the great British traits: tolerance, understatement, intelligence, the willingness to listen to others (sadly lacking in some other places), a respect for the law without being subservient to it, a love of our countryside and our monuments, and above all the joy of conversation and a good joke shared (preferably over a warm pint) ... The steel of the nation has been wrought from the fire of its history.[11]

It is a description of behaviours that are taken to mean something essential and unique. In this context, then, evidence that there is a declining deference to those in expert positions is important.[12] There is a need for all those who are maintaining robust ontological security structures to constantly reground that sense of the reliability of trust structures; the failure of some will lead to a sense of insecurity, and to a search for others.

Third, the ontologically secure individual seeks to behave in accordance with the sense of what is acceptable and appropriate in his or her ontological security structure. There is a need for self-integrity, which could lead individuals to engage in high levels of risk, because they believe that it is 'the right thing to do'. Thus, doing the 'British

---

[10] Trustees of the Mass Observation Archives, *Nella Last's Peace: The Post War Diaries of Housewife 49*, London: Profile Books, 2008, pp. 51–2.

[11] Andrew Wilson, contribution to the 'Being British' message board at www. webritish.co.uk [accessed July 2010].

[12] See for example 'Declining Deference to "Experts"', in *Trust in Public Institutions*, Mori/Audit Commission, London: Mori, 2003, at www.ipsos-mori.com [accessed July 2010], pp. 21–2.

thing' is a phrase and concept that many frequently fall back on. For example, in describing the political appeal of Boris Johnson, Lizzie Vines, a Devon farmer, explained: 'It's a very British thing to do, to pretend to be stupid when you're not'. Damian Green spoke against banning the burkha, saying, 'telling people what they can and can't wear, if they're just walking down the street, is a rather un-British thing to do'.[13] On the UK Parliament Youth Forum, Mossad declared that 'showing national pride is essentially not a British thing to do anyway'.[14] Actions and behaviours are regularly described as being what 'we' British do, and these include making pancakes, buying your own house, buying a property in Spain, getting emotional … all described as either the British, or in the latter case, un-British thing to do.[15] But then there are more sinister aspects. 'Tryst' comments on the BNP website that Muslims:

incite riots and violence among their culture and then have the audacity to blame the violence on us. Believe me, they have not seen real British violence yet and I don't think they would want to. If a Brit makes a Muslim angry, he will take retribution on the one who made him angry. Make a Brit angry and he won't be satisfied until all Muslims have felt his anger.[16]

The fourth aspect of ontological security theory relates to the power of dread – the dread of becoming ontologically insecure. Dread for

[13] Damian Green, quoted in 'Damian Green Says Burka Ban Would Be "un-British"', *BBC News Online*, 18 July 2010, at www.bbc.co.uk [accessed July 2010].

[14] Mossad, on the *UK Parliament Youth Website*, discussing 'Should England Get Its Own Parliament?', 8 October 2009, at www.ukypforums.org.uk [accessed June 2010].

[15] JohnC, messageboard, at 'British Life and Culture', *Project Britain*, 14 February 2010, at http://blogs.projectbritain.com; oldshep52 messageboard, at 'Are Second Home Owners Killing Our Villages?', *BBC Country File Magazine*, 5 August 2009, at www.bbccountryfilemagazine.com; 'Investing in Spanish Property – a New Strategy', *Shelter Offshore*, 17 October 2007, at www.shelteroffshore.com; on Kate Winslet's emotional response to winning an Oscar, comment by 'its_just_a_thought' a twenty-six-year-old teacher from Derbyshire, on the *After Ellen* lesbian website, under 'Kate Winslet Betrays the British' heading, 14 January 2009, at www.afterellen.com [all accessed July 2010].

[16] 'Tryst' on the BNP website in response to a report entitled 'Mass Immigration Has Turned Britain into "Hub of Worldwide Violent Islamism"', *BNP*, 5 July 2010, at www.bnp. org.uk [accessed July 2010].

the British is often related to social failure – thus 'the British dread of being thought to lack a sense of humour' or 'the British dread of making a scene in public'.[17] But in contemporary times, it is the dread of the Islamicization of life and the country that has been so power-ful. In 2006, the *Daily Telegraph* reported that '[a] growing number of people fear that the country faces "a Muslim problem" and more than half of the respondents to the YouGov survey said that Islam posed a threat to Western liberal democracy'.[18] This is perhaps unsur-prising, given that in the 2008 study of the media entitled *Images of Islam in the UK* the authors found that, 'in sum, we found that the bulk of coverage of British Muslims – around two thirds – focuses on Muslims as a threat (in relation to terrorism), a problem (in terms of differences in values) or both (Muslim extremism in general)'.[19] On *The Sun*'s message board, Chealseaz wrote that 'they may be called british citizens but they are not british … if they regard themselves as british, they should be made aware that treason is still a hang-able offence in this country'.[20] On the 2010 general election website messageboard, 'Jon' expressed his fury at one of the contributors, 'David', with the comment that 'my buddies risking their lifes [*sic*] in Afganistan [*sic*] and you wonder why people like me are full of hate for Islam????????????????? David it is you who is sick! You turn your back on your people by not letting them speak the truth about Islam and the true threat of Britain being an Islamic state???'[21] For these contributors to polls and to message boards, the key dread was that

---

[17] Libby Purves, 'For Once, I'm Giving Bremner the Bird', *Sunday Times*, 27 February 2007, at www.timesonline.co.uk; Graeme Clark, an 'administrator', contribution to 'Review of Close My Eyes', *The Spinning Image*, undated, at www.thespinningimage.co.uk [both accessed July 2010].

[18] Philip Johnston, 'Islam Poses a Threat to the West, Say 53pc in Poll', *Daily Telegraph*, 25 August 2006, at www.telegraph.co.uk [accessed December 2009].

[19] Kerry Moore *et al.*, 'Images of Islam in the UK: The Representation of British Muslims in the National Print News Media 2000–2008', *Cardiff School of Journalism, Media and Cultural Studies*, 7 July 2008, p. 3, at www.cardiff.ac.uk [accessed July 2010].

[20] Chealseaz, a female from Bristol, *The Sun* messageboard, 5 July 2010, at www.mysun.co.uk [accessed July 2010].

[21] Jon – comment on the 'Comment on Islam and the Islamification of Britain Discussion and Poll' thread on the UK General Election messageboard, 24 April 2010, at www.general-election-2010.co.uk [accessed June 2010].

Islam was threatening their sense of Britain and Britishness; and that it therefore was natural for Islam to be securitized.

The availability of a national identity – here Britishness – varies, of course, across the country, and with demographic features. It is not a constant factor, with other identities – perhaps national (English, Welsh, Scottish, Irish, Pakistani), or regional, or religious – all playing parts. We know that Britishness plays differently with different communities. In a study of children, it was clear that 'members of visible ethnic minority groups do not identify with being British to the same extent as members of the White English majority group'.[22] What is being said here does not affect all in the same way. But it is a way of understanding how it is that the national dimension of identity, in all its intersubjectively constructed complexity, and as a subject for deliberate political construction, impacts upon the way in which people live their lives.

What, then can be concluded about the social nature of the securitization of Islam in the United Kingdom in the first decade of the twenty-first century? Three, final concluding issues emerge: first, that the interplay of identities – British, Radical Other, Orientalized Other – might work to increase the very threat that the securitization of Islam is supposed to address; second, that the failure is to specify exactly what the threat is, and to resist temptations to scale up from that into wider identity structures; and third, that there is a cyclical nature to this form of securitization, evident in all societies across time, including in the United Kingdom.

The first set of concluding thoughts concerns the danger that the interplay of identities increases the threat. None of the analysis in this book is to deny that there is a 'real' threat; that there are real people, in real places, planning to kill others, supposedly in the name of Islam. That is not, and cannot be, in dispute. What this is to say, though, is that there are two particular dimensions to this phenomenon that deserve closer scrutiny as part of that phenomenon. The first is the role that Britain and Britishness has played in the co-construction of

---

[22] Martyn Barrett, 'Children's Views of Britain and Britishness in 2001: Some Initial Findings from the Developmental Psychology Section Centenary Project', keynote address presented to the Annual Conference of the Developmental Psychology Section of the British Psychological Society, University of Sussex, 5–8 September 2002, at http://epubs.surrey.ac.uk [accessed July 2010].

the threat. Partly this is, of course, because it has proved discursively possible for al-Qaeda and its sympathizers to portray western and British intervention in Iraq, in Afghanistan and in supporting particular governments in what they would deem to be the Islamic world as profoundly anti-Islamic. And that discourse has proved sufficiently powerful to enter into wider understandings of the world, to become part of the ontological security structures for individuals who see an act of killing through their own suicide as appropriate and acceptable, as part of the self-integrity of their belief system. These are not ontological security structures that can be 'logically' argued against, in the sense that they are based on different discursive norms. Now it may be argued that, in spite of this, British policy was still correct; even though all knew that it would bring massive destruction to the United Kingdom, the declaration of war on Nazi Germany was seen by the vast majority of the country to be the acceptable and appropriate action. Where British state policy towards the 'Islamic world' is not seen in those terms – as acceptable and appropriate – by its own citizens, then there is an inevitable disjuncture between 'Britain' and ontological security structures for individuals, whether they by British Muslims or not.

Yet in addition to this, it is entirely possible that the securitization of Islam in Britain may in itself contribute to the threat that it is seeking to address. Dame Anne Owers, Chief Inspector of Prisons, worried that Muslim offenders were treated not as individuals while in custody, but rather as potential Radical Others. She wrote that without change towards treating Muslim prisoners as individuals, 'there is a real risk of a self-fulfilling prophecy: that the prison experience will create or entrench alienation and disaffection, so that prisons release into the community young men who are more likely to offend, or even embrace extremism'.[23] That is, in the process of constructing an image of Self, Radical Other and Orientalized Other, behaviours may mean that the British may well be constructing constraints on individuals' opportunities, while offering other identities which might seem more acceptable and appropriate. In 2006, Muhammad Abdul Bari, the secretary-general of the Muslim Council of Britain, criticized police

---

[23] Dame Anne Owers, quoted in 'Prison Staff Treat Muslims as "Potential Terrorists"', *New Statesman*, 8 June 2010, at www.newstatesman.com [accessed July 2010].

behaviour and media coverage towards Muslims. He said: 'If that demonisation continues, then Britain will have to deal with two million Muslim terrorists – 700,000 of them in London ... If you attack a whole community, it becomes despondent and aggressive.'[24] This contributed to a sense that all British Muslims were potentially part of the Radical Other: surely not the objective of his exercise. But nevertheless, it reflected the sense that if British Muslims were not to enjoy a full sense of Britishness, some would as a consequence choose that Radical Other identity, rather than the Orientalized Other version on offer. When a secret memorandum by the Quilliam Foundation written to Charles Farr, in the Home Office, was leaked in August 2010, it was found to list a whole series of organizations and institutions as sympathetic to 'Islamists'. The Report stated:

The ideology of non-violent Islamists is broadly the same as that of violent Islamists; they disagree only on tactics ... These are a selection of the various groups and institutions active in the UK which are broadly sympathetic to Islamism. While only a small proportion will agree with al-Qaida's tactics, many will agree with their overall goal of creating a single 'Islamic state' which would bring together all Muslims around the world under a single government and then impose on them a single interpretation of sharia as state law.[25]

The purpose of such a move was clear; to police the boundaries of identity. For organizations to try to construct an 'Islamist' identity – one that was avowedly neither a Radical Other nor an Orientalized one – was not acceptable; and Quilliam's response was to brand any different thinking as, automatically, Radical. Thus, there would be a denial of legitimate political space to those who wish to speak about the role of Islam in contemporary society. This, of course, is not to say that all who wish to speak about the role of Islam in contemporary British society have contributions to make that will be seen as legitim-

---

[24] Muhammad Abdul Bari, quoted in David Harrison, 'Media "Contributing to Rise of Islamophobia"', *Daily Telegraph*, 10 September 2006, at www.telegraph.co.uk [accessed June 2010].

[25] 'Preventing Terrorism: Where Next for Britain?', Quilliam Foundation, cited in Vikram Dodd, 'List Sent to Terror Chief Aligns Peaceful Muslim Groups with Terrorist Ideology', *The Guardian*, 4 August 2010, at www.guardian.co.uk [accessed August 2010].

ate. But it is to call for debate on the issues, rather than the discipline of rigidly imposed identities.

The second set of concluding thoughts considers whether the core problem has been – leading to the importance of the material reality of the impact on the lives of people – a failure of discursive precision. Had the 'enemy' been quickly and effectively named, then perhaps there would have been less possibility to scale up from the guilty few to the 'associated' millions. The 'naming' began quite clearly. In the aftermath of the '9/11' attacks, Tony Blair had said at the Labour Party Conference:

We know those responsible. In Afghanistan are scores of training camps for the export of terror. Chief among the sponsors and organizers is Osama Bin Laden. He is supported, shielded and given succour by the Taliban regime ... Be in no doubt: Bin Laden and his people organized this atrocity. The Taliban aid and abet him. He will not desist from further acts of terror. They will not stop helping him.[26]

The perpetrators were clear: Bin Laden and 'his people', and the Taliban – a very discrete, and foreign, target set. But by 2003, the 'naming' had become more complex. In a delicate discussion of Iraq and terrorism, Blair had said at that year's Labour Conference: 'Suppose the terrorists repeated September 11th or worse. Suppose they got hold of a chemical or biological or nuclear dirty bomb; and if they could, they would. What then? ... I know terrorism can't be defeated unless America and Europe work together.'[27] Now, the enemy had become *the* terrorists. And this remained through to the 2005 speech, given in the aftermath of the '7/7' attacks: 'Today, of course, we face a new challenge: global terrorism.' So now the enemy was *global* terrorism. He went on to draw a distinction between 'Islamic' and 'terrorism': 'Let us state one thing: these terrorists do not, never have and never will represent the decent, humane and principled faith of Islam. Muslims, like all of us, abhor terrorism; like all of us, are its victims. It is, as ever, only fringe fanatics we

---

[26] Tony Blair, 'Speech at the Labour Party Conference, *The Guardian*, 2 October 2001', at www.guardian.co.uk [accessed July 2010].

[27] 'Speech by the Prime Minister, Tony Blair, to the 2003 Labour Party Conference', *The Guardian*, 30 September 2003, at www.guardian.co.uk [accessed June 2010].

face.' And yet, there was a conditional nature to the support for British Muslims: 'But we need to make it clear: when people come to our country they have and should have the full rights we believe in. There should be no second-class citizens in Britain. But citizenship comes with a duty: to give loyalty to our nation, its values and our way of life.'[28] In these ways, the failure to be clear about the nature of the enemy, and then the configuration of a choice specific to British Muslims (are you a Radical Other or an Orientalized one?) has come to frame the debate. And of course, others have filled the 'naming' void, with 'Islamic terrorism', 'Islamist terrorism', 'Muslim-fascism' being some of the mildest.[29]

The third set of comments concerns two genealogical dimensions. The first is the obvious point that the securitization of Islam is not a unique event, as there have been a variety of identity securitizations throughout the world, as well as in Britain. Indeed, as discussed earlier, Linda Colley argues that the othering of particular identities (here, Roman Catholic) was at the core of the creation of the British state. Over time, particular identities were constructed as other-than-British; notably the Irish, as with the example of the 'rint' described in an earlier chapter; or the Dutch, discussed at length in Chapter 1. Jews, Germans and indeed, all those that Aravamudan describes in 'Tropicopolitans' – 'a rhyming (but ironic and parodic) contrast to Linda Colley's *Britons*' which seeks to focus on all those that suffered from the 'Xenophobia, colonialism, orientalism and racism' of the British islands, which 'had just as large a role to play in the constitution of national identity as the admittedly important category of religion'.[30] One can imagine the rendering of a text that seemed

---

28 These quotes are from 'Tony Blair's Conference Speech 2005', *The Guardian*, 27 September 2010, at www.guardian.co.uk [accessed June 2010].

29 Nick Cohen, 'Memo to EU: We Call It Islamic Terrorism Because It Is Terror Inspired by Islam', *The Observer*, 14 May 2006, at www.guardian.co.uk; Lord Guthrie, 'This Is No Way to Counter Islamic Terror', *The Guardian*, 14 May 2006, at www.guardian.co.uk; Sebestyén v. Gorka, 'The Nation-State v. The Federalists & Fellow Travellers', in Sebestyén v. Gorka *et al.*, *How the East Was Won: What Next for NATO and EU One Year after Enlargement?*, London: The Centre for Research into Post-Communist Economies, September 2005, at www.crce.org.uk [all accessed June 2010].

30 Srinivas Aravamudan, *Tropicopolitans: Colonialism and Agency, 1688–1804*, Durham, NC: Duke University Press, 1999, p. 10.

commonsensical in the past in its reference to a particular other, that looks out of place now, unless the naming of that other is switched with 'British Muslim'. Indeed, such work has been done, for example in Alex Massie's piece in *The Spectator*, in which Scottish texts from the 1920s about Irish/Catholics/immigrants were reworded for contemporary contrast.[31] There is nothing new about this process of the securitization of identities – small comfort for those whose everyday lives are transformed by that process and its effects. The second genealogical point is perhaps to be expected; not only have the range of identities above been securitized in the British story, but of course so in the past have Muslims. Edward Said in his famous *Orientalism* focuses on this dimension; so at times does Linda Colley.[32] Muslims were constructed as Radical Others in the struggle against slavery; in the struggle for Khartoum; and in the struggle for freedom of speech in the Rushdie Affair.[33] One can argue with the pejorative use of the term 'struggle' here; this is not to give a normative judgement, but rather a description of what dominated British discourse against that Radical Other. Yet none of this is to argue that there are not important new dimensions; as Jacobsen has argued, 'the contemporary imaginary of Islam is underpinned by a number of processes including international migration, a mass media, new

---

[31] Alex Massie, 'The Muslim Menace to Our British Nationality. For Real!', *The Spectator*, 26 June 2009, at www.spectator.co.uk [accessed June 2010].

[32] Edward Said, *Orientalism*, 3rd edn, London: Penguin, 2003; Linda Colley, 'Britain and Islam, 1600–1800: Different Perspectives on Difference', *Yale Review* 88(4), 2008: 1–20.

[33] On slavery see Diane Robinson-Dunn, *The Harem, Slavery and British Imperial Culture: Anglo-Muslim Relations in the Late-Nineteenth Century*, Manchester University Press, 2006. Robinson-Dunn shows how the connection of slavery with Islam in the mid nineteenth century underlined the 'good versus evil' struggle, and allowed the British to align themselves with modernity by presenting Muslims as backward. On Sudan and the defeat of General Gordon see Paul Auchterlonie, 'From the Eastern Question to the Death of General Gordon: Representations of the Middle East in the Victorian Periodical Press, 1876–1885', *British Journal of Middle Eastern Studies* 28(1), May 2001: 5–24. Gordon was defeated by the Mahdi, known in Britain as the 'mad Mahdi'. For Tariq Modood, 'no minority in the history of British race relations has been as friendless as Muslims in spring 1989'. Tariq Modood, 'British Asian Muslims and the Rushdie Affair', *Political Quarterly* 61(2): 143–60, quote at p. 143.

communications technologies, the *da'wa* activities of transnational Islamic movements, and the increasingly global dimension of political conflicts'.[34] To that I would add, in the context of the United Kingdom, and on the basis of the analysis of this book, the securitization of Islam.

[34] Christine Jacobsen, 'The Quest for Authenticity', in Jocelyne Cesari and Seán McLoughlin, *European Muslims and the Secular State*, Aldershot: Ashgate, 2005, p. 162.

Select bibliography

Abizadeh, Arash. 'Does Collective Identity Presuppose an Other? On the Alleged Incoherence of Global Solidarity', *American Political Sciences Review* 99(1), February 2005.

Adonis, Andrew and Stephen Pollard. *A Class Act: The Myth of Britain's Classless Society*. London: Hamish Hamilton, 1997.

Aitken, Ian. *Film and Reform: John Grierson and the Documentary Film Movement*. London: Routledge, 1992.

Amis, Martin. *The Second Plane: September 11, 2001–2007*. London: Jonathan Cape, 2008.

Anderson, Benedict. *Imagined Communities: Reflections on the Origin and Spread of Nationalism*, 2nd edn. London, Verso, 1991.

Aradau, Claudia. 'Security and the Democratic Scene: Desecuritization and Emancipation', *Journal of International Relations and Development* 7(40), 2004: 388–413.

Aravamudan, Srinivas. *Tropicopolitans: Colonialism and Agency, 1688–1804*. Durham, NC: Duke University Press, 1999.

Auchterlonie, Paul. 'From the Eastern Question to the Death of General Gordon: Representations of the Middle East in the Victorian Periodical Press, 1876–1885', *British Journal of Middle Eastern Studies* 28(1), May 2001: 5–24.

Balzacq, Thierry. 'The Three Faces of Securitization: Political Agency, Audience and Context', *European Journal of International Relations* 11(2), 2005: 171–201.

Barnouw, Erik. *Documentary: A History of the Non-Fiction Film*, 2nd edn. Oxford University Press, 1993.

Blair, Tony. 'Doctrine of the International Community', Chicago, 24 April 1999, at www.number10.gov.uk/output/Page1297.asp.

'Prime Minister's Press Conference', 5 August 2005, at www.number-10.gov.uk/output/Page8041.asp.

Booth, Ken (ed.). *Critical Security Studies and World Politics*. Boulder, CO: Lynne Rienner, 2004.

Theory of World Security. Cambridge University Press, 2007, p. 194.

Boucaut, Rose. 'Understanding Workplace Bullying: A Practical Application of Giddens' Structuration Theory', *International Education Journal* 2(4), 2001.

Bradley, A. G. *When Squires and Farmers Thrived*. London: Methuen, 1927.

Brickhill, Paul. *The Dam Busters*. London: Pan Books, 1999; first published 1951.

The Great Escape. London: Cassell, 2000, first published 1951.

Reach for the Sky. London: Cassell, 2000; first published 1954.

Brown, Katherine E. 'Contesting the Securitisation of British Muslims: Citizenship and Resistance', *Interventions* 12(2), July 2010: 171–82.

Brown, William S. 'Ontological Security, Existential Anxiety and Workplace Privacy', *Journal of Business Ethics* 23(1), January, 2000.

Butler, Judith. *Bodies That Matter: On the Discursive Limits Of 'Sex'*. London: Routledge, 1993.

Buzan, Barry. *People, States and Fear*, 2nd edn. Boulder, CO: Lynne Rienner, 1991.

Buzan, Barry and Ole Waever. 'Macrosecuritisation and Security Constellations: Reconsidering Scale in Securitisation Theory', *Review of International Studies* 35(2), 2009, 253–76.

Regions and Powers: The Structure of International Security. Cambridge University Press, 2003.

Buzan, Barry, Ole Wæver and Jaap de Wilde. *Security: A New Framework for Analysis*. Boulder, CO: Lynne Rienner, 1998.

c.a.s.e collective. 'Critical Approaches to Security in Europe', *Security Dialogue* 37(4), 2006: 443–87.

Calder, Angus. *The Myth of the Blitz*. London: Pimlico, 1992.

Callabero-Anthony, Mely and Ralf Emmers. 'Understanding the Dynamics of Securitizing Non-Traditional Security', in Callabero-Anthony *et al.* (eds.), *Non-Traditional Security in Asia: Dilemmas in Securitisation*. Aldershot: Ashgate, 2006.

Campbell, David. *Writing Security*, 2nd edn. Minneapolis: University of Minnesota Press, 1998.

Carter, Ashton, John Deutch and Philip Zelikow. 'Catastrophic Terrorism', *Foreign Affairs* 77, November/December 1998: 80–94.

Childs, David. *Britain Since 1945*. London: Routledge, 1997

Chouliaraki, Lilie and Norman Fairclough. *Discourse in Late Modernity*. Edinburgh University Press, 1999.

Cohen, Jonathan and Miriam Metzger. 'Social Affiliation and the Achievement of Ontological Security through Interpersonal and Mass

Communication', *Critical Studies in Mass Communication* 15, 1998: 41–60.

Colley, Linda. 'Britain and Islam, 1600–1800: Different Perspectives on Difference', *Yale Review* 88(4), 2008: 1–20.

'Britishness in the 21st Century', *Millennial Lectures*, 8 December 1999 at www.number10.gov.uk/output/page3049.asp

Britons: Forging the Nation 1707–1837. Yale University Press, 2005; first published 1992.

Taking Stock of Taking Liberties: A Personal View by Linda Colley. London: British Library, 2008.

Colls, Robert and Philip Dodd. 'Representing the Nation: British Documentary Film, 1930–45', *Screen* 26(1), 1985.

Connolly, William E. *Identity/Difference: Democratic Negotiations of Political Paradox.* Ithaca: Cornell University Press, 1991.

Croft, Stuart. 'British Jihadis and the British War on Terror', *Defence Studies* 7(3), 2007: 317–37.

'Conclusion', in Paul Williams (ed.), *Security Studies.* London: Routledge, 2008.

Culture, Crisis and America's War on Terror. Cambridge University Press, 2006.

Croft, Stuart and Cerwyn Moore. 'Understanding Terrorist Threats in Britain', *International Affairs* 86(4), July 2010: 821–35.

Crossley, M. L. '"Let Me Explain": Narrative Employment and One Patient's Experience of Oral Cancer', *Social Science and Medicine* 56(3), 439–48, February 2003.

Dabydeen, David. *Molly and the Muslim Stick.* Oxford: Macmillan Caribbean, 2008.

Danermark, B. D. and K. Möller 'Deafblindness, Ontological Security, and Social Recognition', *International Journal of Audiology* 47, Suppl. 2:S119–23, November 2008.

Davidson, Joyce. *Phobic Geographies: The Phenomenology and Spatiality of Identity.* Aldershot: Ashgate, 2003.

Davies, J. Q. 'Melodramatic Possessions: The Flying Dutchman, South Africa, and the Imperial Stage, ca. 1830', *Opera Quarterly* 21(3), 2005, 496–514.

Dupuis, Ann and David C. Thorns. 'Home, Home Ownership and the Search for Ontological Security', *Sociological Review* 46(1), February 1998: 24–47.

Eagleton, Terry. *After Theory.* London: Penguin, 2003.

Ideology: An Introduction. London: Verso, 2007.

Ferguson, Niall. *Empire: The Rise and Fall of the British World Order and the Lessons for Global Power.* New York: Basic Books, 2003.

Floyd, Rita. 'Human Security and the Copenhagen School's Securitization Approach', *Human Security Journal 5*, Winter 2007.

Fraser, Derek. *The Evolution of the British Welfare State*, 3rd rev. edn. Basingstoke: Palgrave, 2002.

Gibson, Guy. *Enemy Coast Ahead*. Manchester: Goodall Publications, 1998; first published 1946.

Giddens, Anthony. *The Consequences of Modernity*. Palo Alto, CA: Stanford University Press, 1990.

  The Constitution of Society: Outline of the Theory of Structuration. Cambridge: Polity, 1984.

  Modernity and Self-Identity. Cambridge: Polity, 1991.

Githens-Mazer, Jonathan and Robert Lambert. 'Islamophobia and Anti-Muslim Hate Crime: A London Case Study', European Muslim Research Centre, January 2010, at http://centres.exeter.ac.uk.

Glees, Anthony and Chris Pope. *When Students Turn to Terror: Terrorist and Extremist Activity on British Campuses*. London: Social Affairs Unit, 2005.

Goffart, Walter. 'The Genesis of John Speed's Maps of Battles in England and Ireland', *The Seventeenth Century* 19(2), October 2004: 170.

Golani, Motti. *Israel in Search of a War: Sinai Campaign, 1955–56*. Eastbourne: Sussex Academic Press, 1998.

Gove, Michael. *Celsius 7/7*. London: Weidenfeld & Nicolson, 2006.

Greenfield, Steve and Guy Osborn. 'Oh to Be in England? Mythology and Identity in English Cricket', *Social Identities* 2(2), June 1996: 271–92.

Hague, Gill and Claudia Wilson. 'The Silenced Pain: Domestic Violence 1945–1970', *Journal of Gender Studies* 9(2), 2000: 157–69.

Hansen, Lene. 'The Clash of Cartoons? The Clash of Civilizations? Media and Identity in the Danish 2006 Cartoon Case'. Paper presented at the International Studies Association 48th Annual Convention, Hilton Chicago, 28 February 2007.

  'The Little Mermaid's Silent Security Dilemma and the Absence of Gender in the Copenhagen School', *Millennium* 29(2), 2000: 289–306.

  Security as Practice: Discourse Analysis and the Bosnian War. London: Routledge, 2006.

Hay, Colin. 'Crisis and the Structural Transformation of the State: Interrogating the Process of Change', *British Journal of Politics and International Relations* 1(3), October 1999.

Held, David and John B. Thompson. *Social Theory of Modern Societies: Anthony Giddens and His Critics*. Cambridge University Press, 1990.

Hillyard, Paddy. *Suspect Community*. London: Pluto, 1993.

Hobsbawm, Eric and Terence Ranger (eds.). *The Invention of Tradition*: Cambridge and New York: Cambridge University Press, 1983.

Hoffman, Bruce. *Inside Terrorism*. London: St Andrew's University Press, 1998.

Hughes, Robert. *The Fatal Shore*. London: Vintage, 2003.

Huysmans, Jef. 'Defining Social Constructivism in Security Studies: The Normative Dilemma of Writing Security', *Alternatives* 27, 2002.

   'Revisiting Copenhagen', *European Journal of International Relations* 4(4), 1998: 479–504.

   'Security! What Do You Mean? From Concept to Thick Signifier', *European Journal of International Relations* 4(2), 1998: 226–55.

Jacobsen, Christine. 'The Quest for Authenticity', in Jocelyne Cesari and Seán McLoughlin, *European Muslims and the Secular State*. Aldershot: Ashgate, 2005.

Jeal, Tim. *Baden-Powell*. New Haven, CT: Yale University Press, 2001.

Jurgensmeyer, Mark. *Terror in the Mind of God: The Global Rise of Religious Violence*. London: University of California Press, 2001.

Kenyon, John. *The Popish Plot*. London: William Heinemann, 1972.

Kiely, Richard, Frank Bechhofer, Robert Stewart and David McCrone. 'The Markers and Rules of Scottish National Identity', *Sociological Review* 49(1), February 2001: 33–55.

King, Anthony. *The European Ritual: Football in the New Europe*. Aldershot: Ashgate, 2003.

Kinnvall, Catarina. 'Globalization and Religious Nationalism: Self, Identity, and the Search for Ontological Security', *Political Psychology* 25(5), 2004.

   Globalization and Religious Nationalism in India. New York: Routledge, 2006.

Knoppers, Laura Lunger. 'Sing Old Noll the Brewer: Royalist Satire and Social Inversion', *The Seventeenth Century* 15(1), April 2000: 45.

Knox, Ellis O. 'Reviewed Work(s): American Negro Slave Revolts by Herbert Aptheker', *Journal of Negro Education* 14(2), Spring, 1945: 206–9.

Knudsen, Olav F. 'Post-Copenhagen Security Studies', *Security Dialogue* 32, 2001: 355–68.

Kochan, Miriam. 'Women's Experience of Internment', in David Cesarani and Tony Kushner (eds.), *The Internment of Aliens in Twentieth Century Britain*. London: Frank Cass, 1993.

Krause, Keith and Michael Williams (eds.), *Critical Security Studies: Concepts and Strategies*. London: Routledge, 1997.

Krolikowski, Alanna. 'State Personhood in Ontological Security Theories of International Relations and Chinese Nationalism: A Skeptical View', *Chinese Journal of International Politics* 2(1), 2008: 109–33.

Kynaston, David. *Austerity Britain 1945–51 (Tales of A New Jerusalem)*. London: Bloomsbury, 2007.

Laing, R. D. *The Divided Self*. London: Penguin, 1990; originally published by Tavistock Publications, 1960.

Laquer, Walter. *The New Terrorism: Fanaticism and the Arms of Mass Destruction*. New York: Oxford University Press, 1999.

Larsen, Henrik. 'British and Danish European Policies in the 1990s: A Discourse Approach', *European Journal of International Relations 5*, 1999.

Lesser, Ian O. 'Countering the New Terrorism: Implications for Strategy', in Ian O. Lesser *et al.*, *Countering the New Terrorism*. Santa Monica, CA: RAND, 1999.

Levine, Joshua. *Forgotten Voices of the Blitz and the Battle for Britain*. London: Ebury Press, 2007.

Madley, Benjamin. 'From Terror to Genocide: Britain's Tasmanian Penal Colony and Australia's History Wars', *Journal of British Studies*, 47(1), January 2008: 77–106.

Marr, Andrew. *A History of Modern Britain*. London: Macmillan, 2007.

McCallum, Neil. *Journey with a Pistol: A Diary of War*. London: Victor Gollancz, 1959.

McSweeney, Bill. 'Identity and Security', *Review of International Studies* 22, 1996: 81–93.

Security, Identity and Interests. Cambridge University Press, 1999.

Mearsheimer, John J. 'The False Logic of International Institutions', *International Security* 19(3), Winter 1994/5: 5–49.

Mills, C. Wright. *The Power Elite*. Oxford University Press, 2000; first published 1956.

Mitzen, Jennifer. 'Anchoring Europe's Civilizing Identity: Habits, Capabilities and Ontological Security', *Journal of European Public Policy* 13(2), 2006.

'Ontological Security in World Politics: State Identity and the Security Dilemma', *European Journal of International Relations* 12(3), 2006: 341–70.

Modood, Tariq. 'British Asian Muslims and the Rushdie Affair', *Political Quarterly* 61(2): 143–60.

Still Not Easy Being British: Struggles for a Multicultural Citizenship. Staffordshire: Trentham Books, 2010.

Montague Woodhouse, Christopher. *Post War Britain*. London: Bodley Head, 1996.

Nazir-Ali, Michael. 'Breaking Faith with Britain', *Standpoint*, June 2008.

Conviction and Conflict: Islam, Christianity and World Order. London: Continuum, 2006.

'Only God Can Save Us from Ourselves', *Standpoint*, July/August 2009.

'We Must Not Leave Afghanistan Yet', *Standpoint*, January/February 2010.

Noble, Greg. 'The Discomfort of Strangers: Racism, Incivility and Ontological Security in a Relaxed and Comfortable Nation', *Journal of Intercultural Studies* 26(1/2), February 2005: 107–20.

Ó Tuathail, Gearóid. *Critical Geopolitics: The Politics of Writing Global Space*. London: Routledge, 1996.

'The Postmodern Geopolitical Condition: States, Statecraft, and Security at the Millennium', *Annals of the Association of American Geographers* 90(1), March 2000: 167.

Padgett, Deborah K. 'There's No Place Like (a) Home: Ontological Security among Persons with Serious Mental Illness in the United States', *Social Science & Medicine* 64(9), May 2007: 1925–36.

Pakulski, Jan. 'Foundations of a Post-Class Analysis', in Erik Olin Wright, *Approaches to Class Analysis*. Cambridge University Press, 2005.

Pakulski, Jan and Waters, Malcolm. *The Death of Class*. London: Sage, 1995.

Pennant, Cass and Andy Nicholls. *Thirty Years of Hurt: A History of England's Hooligan Army*. London: Pennant Books, 2006.

Petley, Julian. 'Fact Plus Fiction Equals Friction', *Media, Culture & Society* 18, January 1996: 11–25.

Philips, Melanie. *Londonistan*. New York: Encounter Books, 2006.

'Suicide of the West', *National Review*, 18 August 2006.

World Turned Upside Down. New York: Encounter, 2010.

Reed, Michael I. 'Expert Power and Control in Late Modernity: An Empirical Review and Theoretical Synthesis', *Organization Studies* 17, July 1996: 573–97.

Reynolds, Henry. 'Genocide in Tasmania', in A. Dirk Moses (ed.), *Genocide and Settler Society*. Oxford: Berghahn Books, 2005, p. 127.

Robinson-Dunn, Diane. *The Harem, Slavery and British Imperial Culture: Anglo-Muslim Relations in the Late-Nineteenth Century Manchester*. Manchester University Press, 2006.

Roe, Paul. 'The "Value" of Positive Security', *Review of International Studies* 34, 2008: 777–94.

Rumelili, B. 'Constructing Identity and Relating to Difference: Understanding the EU's Mode of Differentiation', *Review of International Studies* 30(1), 2004: 27–47.

Said, Edward. *Orientalism*, 3rd edn. London: Penguin, 2003.

Savage, Jon. *Teenage*. London: Chatto and Windus, 2007.

Savage, Mike. 'Changing Social Class Identities in Post-War Britain: Perspectives from Mass-Observation', *Sociological Research Online* 12(3), 2007.

Schrecker, Ellen. *Many Are the Crimes: McCarthyism in America*. New York: Little, Brown, 1998.

Silber, Mitchell D. and Arvin Bhatt. *Radicalization in the West: The Homegrown Threat*. New York City Police Department, 2007.

Silverstone, Roger. 'Television, Ontological Security and the Transitional Object', *Media, Culture and Society* 15, 1993: 573.

Silverton, Peter. *Filthy English: The How, Why, When and What of Everyday Swearing*. London: Portobello Books, 2009.

Smith, Anne-Marie. *Laclau and Mouffe: The Radical Democratic Imaginary*. London: Routledge, 1998.

Smith, Hazel. 'Bad, Mad, Sad or Rational Actor? Why the "Securitisation" Paradigm Makes for Poor Policy Analysis of North Korea', *International Affairs* 76(3), 2000: 593–617.

Smith, Steve. 'The Increasing Insecurity of Security Studies: Conceptualizing Security in the Last Twenty Years', in Stuart Croft and Terry Terriff (eds.), *Critical Reflections on Security and Change*. London: Frank Cass, 2000.

Smyth, Marie and Marie-Therese Fay (eds.). *Personal Accounts of Northern Ireland's Troubles: Public Chaos, Private Loss*. London: Pluto, 2000.

Snyder, W. P. *The Politics of British Defense Policy, 1945–1962*. Athens, OH: Ohio University Press, 1964.

Steele, Brent J. ' "Ideas that Were Really Never in Our Possession": Torture, Honor and US Identity', *International Relations* 22(2), 2008.

  Ontological Security in International Relations. New York: Routledge, 2008.

  'Ontological Security and the Power of Self-Identity: British Neutrality and the American Civil War', *Review of International Studies* 31(3), 2005: 519–40.

  'Ontological Security, Shame and 'Humanitarian' Action'. Paper presented to the 2004 ISA Conference, Montreal, March 2004, at www.allacademic.com

Swann, Paul. *The British Documentary Film Movement, 1926–1946*, Cambridge University Press, 1989.

Taureck, Rita. 'Securitisation Theory – The Story So Far (Part one): Theoretical Inheritance and What it Means to Be a Post-Structural Realist'. Paper presented at the annual meeting of the International Studies Association, Town & Country Resort and Convention Center, San Diego, California, USA, 22 March 2006, at www.allacademic.com.

Thrift, Nigel. 'Space', *Theory, Culture and Society* 23(2/3), 2006: 140–1.

Turner, Brian. 'The Erosion of Citizenship', *British Journal of Sociology* 52(2), June 2001: 189–209.

Waever, Ole. 'European Security Identities', *Journal of Common Market Studies* 34(1), 1996: 103–32.

'Securitization and Desecuritization', in Ronnie D. Lipshutz (ed.), *On Security*. Lipshutz. New York: Columbia University Press, 1995.

'Securitizing Sectors? Reply to Eriksson', *Cooperation and Conflict* 34(3), 1999.

'The Sociology of a Not So International Discipline: American and European Developments in International Relations,' *International Organization* 52(4), 1998.

Wæver, Ole, Barry Buzan, Morten Kelstrup and Pierre Lemaitre. *Identity, Migration and the New Security Agenda in Europe*. London: Pinter, 1993.

Wendt, Alexander, 'State as a Person', *Review of International Studies* 30, 2004: 289–316.

Wilkinson, Claire. 'The Copenhagen School on Tour in Kyrgyzstan: Is Securitization theory Useable outside Europe?', *Security Dialogue* 38(1), 2007: 5–25.

Williams, Michael C. 'Words, Images, Enemies: Securitization and International Politics', *International Studies Quarterly*, 47, 2003: 511–31.

Williams, Rowan. 'Archbishop's Lecture – Civil and Religious Law in England: a Religious Perspective', *The Archbishop of Canterbury*, 7 February 2008 at www.archbishopofcanterbury.org/1575.

Zarakol, Ayse. 'Ontological (In)security and State Denial of Historical Crimes: Turkey and Japan', *International Relations* 24(1), 2010: 3–23.

Ziegler, Philip. *London and War 1939–1945*. London: Pimlico, 2002.

Index